Argentarius:
Letters from a bank director to his son

The Essence of Money

Contents:
Argentarius Letter Collections (1921 - 1923)
Part I: On Money
Part II: Valuta
Part III: The Central Bank
Part IV: Monetary Crisis

Public domain source: Lansburgh, Alfred, The Essence of Money, Berlin: Bank-Verlag, 1923

Digital transcription: Prof. Dr. Jan Greitens, Michael Anton Fischer

Translation: Michael Anton Fischer

Publisher: Jakubiak & Fischer GmbH, Moosstr. 4, 83404 Ainring, Germany

Copyright 2021 Jakubiak & Fischer GmbH, all rights reserved.

Portions of this book may be reused for media articles, personal websites, or in commercial posts and social media, provided they are credited to this edition, and a reference to the website http://lansburgh.de is included. Copying the contents of the book and selling it in another format is not permitted.

Foreword by the Translator

One hundred years have passed, since the first letters in this book were written. Translating them into English late in 2021, I get an eery feeling.
A feeling, as if, when one replaced the 19xx in the letter's titles with a 20xx, the 1921 letters would feel like written today. And the letters written in 1922 and 1923 would seem like prophecy.

In this day and age it is more important than ever to study the works of Argentarius and to act accordingly.

Unlike the author, we have a better weapon to fight the monetary corruption and greed than Alfred Lansburgh could ever hope to in his time.

We have a truly hard and incorruptible money - Bitcoin.

With this money, we can achieve, for the first time in human history, a monetary sign, which accurately represents true money.
A monetary sign which allows you to sell a good or service today and which guarantees you will get back an equal merit in goods or services tomorrow.

I wonder if Alfred Lansburgh would have had agreed with me on this assessment or if he would have raised objections on this claim. Unfortunately we can't ask him.

Please note that Argentarius in his works sometimes uses examples that in my opinion do use the words value and merit synonymously.
This is due to the fact that the word value in German "Wert", conveis the notion of the English word "merit" better than the German word "Verdienst". So I am afraid that, even though he tries to explain himself, thanks to the peculiarities in the German language, his words may not be entirely unambigous.

So, when he talks about a hard money preserving value, what he

in my opinion means is really merit.
When he gives an example, like that one unit of money will buy you a pair of boots today and will buy you a pair of boots tomorrow, he is really saying that the unit of money that buys you the merit necessary to provide one pair of boots today, will buy you that same merit needed to provide you a similar quality pair tomorrow.

This is an important distinction and essential to truly understanding the contents of this book, so I hope I have not overstepped my role as a translator in laying my words into Alfred Lansburgh's mouth.

Throughout the translation, I have tried to stay as close to the original publications from 1923 as possible. I have also restrainend from adding any commentary or unnecessary footnotes.
The word "Wert" has been consistently translated to "value".

Argentarius should speak for himself.

P.S. This publication is a labour of love with virtually no budget. If you find errors, please kindly report them to argentarius@jakubiak-fischer.com

December 2021, Michael Anton Fischer

Part I: On Money

First Letter

Two nations
The crime of ignorance

Berlin, New Year's Eve 1920/21

Midnight. Outside, dear James, the New Year's Eve bells are once again ringing out a great year. A solemn moment for people who let the calendar dictate the hours of their inner upliftment. Disraeli's 'two nations', the two great people into which every so-called cultural state splits, live their existence doubly intensely at this moment. Wealth increases wellbeing through wine, dance and play, up to the point of intoxication; I gaze at it from my study out the festively flashing windows. Poverty, which I do not see because it hides between its bare four walls in distant neighbourhoods, makes the guilty sacrifice to the new year by letting the tears of everyday life flow doubly abundantly.

I myself, as you know, have no sense of celebration. But I still can't completely escape the magic of New Year's Eve. It forces me to gather my thoughts, to reflect spiritually, and many an unclear feeling in me takes on a firm, sharply defined shape.

I see myself standing, as it were, on the narrow ridge that separates the two great peoples in our fatherland, the dancing ones here, the weeping ones there. And as I look down into this divided life and activity, it is as if I could clearly see all the levers and wheels of the great mechanism that determines the social relations of countries and continents and which usually remains hidden from the profane eye. My gaze, sharpened by the consecration of the moment, overlooks the economic laws that cause wealth and poverty to arise, grow, stand still or decline. I see how, under certain conditions, the partition between the people of the haves and the have-nots rises or falls. And with frightening clarity I see how disastrously those eternal economic laws have been at work in the year that has just passed: The abrupt partition between the two people of one and the same country has increased enormously. Tears flow threefold on this side, wine on the other. And at the same time as the dividing wall, the age-old resentment of the two people, who will never understand each other, is growing into an enormous hatred that will one day lay the cultural world in ruins if its causes are not eliminated in time.

In this clear realisation, which I draw from the sound of the New Year's Eve bells, I sit down at my desk to talk to you once again, my dear James. I have decided in this hour to take up again the thread I dropped years ago; the instructive letters I sent you before the World War are to be continued. Docendo discimus: He who teaches others learns himself. I want to become clear about some things by forcing myself to make them clear to you. And conversely, it is my fatherly duty to transfer to you, the son, as completely as possible the knowledge I have gathered over decades of professional activity. Many things would be better in the world if every generation took this duty seriously and if it were taken for granted that the sum of the father's knowledge would regularly form the son's foundation of knowledge, to which he would then have to add a new story for his own descendants. In this way an inheritance of knowledge is created which is equally valuable for the individual as for the whole.

Happy is the state which has the certainty that the sum of the experiences of its ancestors is embodied in each member of a particular profession! It finds established traditions everywhere and knows without further ado where to look for its regents, its diplomats, its officers, its judges and its civil servants. He does not need to experiment and shake up the classes. I know very well, my son, that this does not correspond to your liberal views, and make no attempt to convert you. Conversion will come of its own accord when you are in my years. Then you will understand the profound wisdom of the ancient Egyptian and Indian principle of caste, which leaves every human being where he is rooted, where he finds the conditions of existence corresponding to his constitution and where he is of the best use to the whole with his balanced person.

You are the son of a bank director and a future bank manager yourself. It would reflect badly on me if you were to handle the instrument that I will entrust to you one day, this instrument of such great economic importance, in a bungling manner. Anyone who wants to manage a bank must first and foremost know what a bank is; must know what role the banking system of a country plays within the national economy as a whole must be aware that certain functions of the banks not only have very specific economic effects, but also far-reaching social and political consequences.
But all this can only be recognised by those who have mastered the laws of the capital market, who know exactly under what conditions the productivity of a country is condensed into capital, and how the individual uses of capital have an effect on the productivity of the country. Here the mechanism of the working people as a whole has its real driving force, here the economic fortunes of the state are decided, here lies the social germ which splits one and the same nation into two hostile peoples. There is only one path, my son, that leads to full clarity about this, and at the starting point of this path is money. If there are so few people today, even among my own colleagues, who grasp the deepest essence and workings of the capital market and the banks that direct it, it is solely because knowledge of money is so bitterly lacking today.

Until a few years ago, no one but a few experts dealt with the monetary system, and those who did remained stuck in the purely theoretical and abstract. This is quite understandable: for decades there has been no compelling reason to concern oneself more deeply with the highly concrete money that pulsates vividly through all markets. Just as the best woman is the one who is spoken of the least, so money was spoken of so seldom before the war, because it was doing its duty in all cultural countries in a well-behaved and respectable manner.

Money thus was a matter of course that did not need to be talked about much. Even the national economists, for whom nothing can be taken for granted, were deceived by the housewife virtue of money. Their newer schools put forward theories that one could only read with a shake of the head, remembering the famous assignations from the French Revolution and the other youthful sins that good money had on its conscience.

The prevailing view before the war was that money was a purely expedient institution of the state, like the police and the passport system, useful but not indispensable. One could manage with money but also without it. Its external form and its intrinsic value are absolutely irrelevant. The state is the sovereign master of money, which it can produce from any material it deems suitable and in any quantity it deems necessary. You too, dear James, at that time considered money to be nothing more than a creature of the state's legal system, or, which in this case is the same thing, of the state's arbitrariness. Despite all my efforts, I was unable to convince you otherwise. You were just as unwilling as the others to see that the state basically has nothing to do with the creation of money, and that when it nevertheless acts creatively, it almost regularly ruins the money.

In the meantime, throughout Europe, and not least in Germany, the general ignorance of money matters has taken terrible revenge. Starting from money, social upheavals have taken place that will one day perhaps prove even more momentous than the political changes brought about by the world war. Great causes, small effects: Your unbelief has also been shaken. The seed of my teaching falls on more receptive ground today than it did two years ago. In one of your last letters you yourself asked me to open a little window for you through which you could gain an insight into the hidden mechanism of the monetary system. Well, I will try to open the window wide enough for you to see the enormous building of monetary transactions from the foundation to the gable. The way shall be the old familiar one: In a series of letters I will lead you step by step through the areas of money, credit, capital and banking until you recognise the great connections between them and thus gain the starting point from which you can find your way into the interior of the individual sub-problems through your own reflection. And the letters should follow one another quickly, because I am no less in a hurry to teach you than you are to learn.

Why?

Because I am tired, dear James, because I want to resign soon. I am a man of the old school and do not fit into the new age. Work, a sense of duty and discipline - you know that I cannot function without these three elements. Of course, I have often had to make small concessions; dear heaven, I am a bank director! But the economy, which I am to help develop, must be reasonably healthy as such. The great universal code, which, properly understood and applied, makes all special laws superfluous - I mean the two-tablet law of Mount Sinai - must also be respected in economic life. This is not the case today. We live in the age of organised theft; a theft so refined that the injured party hardly notices how he is being robbed, and the thief does not even need to dirty his fingers in order to take someone else's property. The process that makes property outlawed appears to the simple-minded eye as an elementary test of fate, removed from human influence, which one has to accept godly. Only a few suspect that the supposed natural event is in reality nothing other than a crude arbitrary act of man, which one would have to call sacrilegious if Christ's word did not apply here: 'Lord, forgive them, for they know not what they do. ' They really don't know because they don't know what money is. It sounds like a profanation, but it is. Ignorance of money here actually becomes epidemic immorality.

What disgusts me most is that in the midst of this coven the banking industry is involuntarily dancing in the round of the profiteers. It seems to be a kind of natural law that the great social crises, in which the proletariat rebels, are the fattest days for capital; never have huge fortunes been created more quickly than in the great French Revolution. But the banks, in my opinion, are there to counteract the illegal redistribution of property, not to assist in it. I see with horror how today the banks are making the 'new rich' even richer by putting their resources at their disposal, according to the saying: 'To him that hath shall be given'; and how they are making the impoverished completely destitute by depriving them of the last saving straw, credit. I see how the banks put on fat in the need of the times, like eels in a swamp overflowing with corpses.

I see many of my colleagues, instead of doing practical rescue work, indulging in a disgusting kind of busy idleness, participating in the useless chatter of utopians who believe they can build a brand new economy according to well thought-out plans, but in doing so only betray that they do not know the economic ABC. It may be that these are all inevitable side-effects of our time, and that in this respect the years after the great wars and revolutions are necessarily similar. In any case, it disgusts me. I long for those harmless days when it was one of the greatest crimes if a bank allowed a loss it had suffered to disappear from its balance sheet or influenced the decisions of a general meeting for its own benefit. Quel bruit pour une omelette! How important the small stuff was!

Today, economic crimes of immeasurable scope go unrecognised and unpunished, accompanied by a melodic stream of soporific nonsense.
So it won't be long before I put the steering wheel in your hands, dear James. Your special knowledge of banking in the technical sense is still rather small, but it is sufficient for the management of a large bank as things stand. To whom God gives an office, he also gives understanding. You will see later how true this word is. To the bank director, who is almost always a giver, all sources of technical, commercial and financial knowledge are readily opened. Every industrialist, every wholesaler, every international business intermediary, every finance minister of a state in need of money, in short, everyone who needs your bank's money, becomes, without knowing it, your teacher. The sixty supervisory board positions that I will gradually cede to you will mean a great source of income for you in spiritual terms almost more than in material terms. And your officials are there for the detailed knowledge.

So, my dear son, you are to understand the mechanism before which you will stand in the not too distant future. However, I can only provide you with the basis, the logical bone structure, so to speak, which you must clothe with the flesh of your own thinking; not a mnemonic for the practical resolution of the arithmetical examples occurring in your future profession. Nevertheless, this intellectual inheritance, which you will take on during my lifetime, will perhaps be the most valuable part of my entire legacy. And that is saying something for a bank director who lived through two fat revolutionary years.

With love

Your old dad.

Second Letter

Economic transactions are barter transactions
Barter transactions require credit
'Credit' and 'Money.'

Berlin, 2ⁿᵈ January 1921

How is it, my dear James, that so many, among whom there are also intelligent, independently thinking people, find it so difficult to fathom the nature of money? I believe it is because they have lived in the midst of money since childhood, have grown too close to it and therefore do not find the necessary distance from it. Money performs a certain function in daily life, namely the function of buying and paying, with such self-evidence that it is difficult to get away from the idea that money and the function are one and the same. And the use of language reinforces this idea. If we call a certain pachyderm with a long trunk an 'elephant', there can be no doubt that an elephant is nothing other than this certain pachyderm with the long trunk. And if we call all the things with which we buy and pay in everyday life 'money', money is of course nothing other than the thing which serves in each case as a general means of purchase and payment. Whether it is gold coins or paper notes, salt ingots or cowrie shells, it does not matter. As long as one can buy and pay with it in one's own country for everything he wants to buy it is called 'money' in everyday languages.

But behind this well-known puncture there is a hidden meaning, a law. Just as there are certain laws of nature behind the process of the falling stone, the rolling wheel. You can't get to the bottom of these laws as long as you call a proboscidean an elephant and the elephant a proboscidean, i.e. as long as you keep going in circles conceptually. But if you realise what is common to all processes and punctures of a certain kind, what is typical of them, you will very quickly discover their deeper meaning and the laws they obey.

So, dear James, do not think about the money that mediates the traffic, but think about the meaning of the economic traffic between people as such. Then you will first make an observation that many people before you have already made: namely, that this traffic is basically only a barter traffic. As complicated as our economic life looks, in the end it simply boils down to the fact that countless objects are produced daily for consumption and exchanged for this purpose between producers, traders and consumers.

Whoever sells a good or offers a service is always interested in receiving other goods or other services in return. Put yourself to the test. Look around you and see what your neighbours' wealth is made up of, that is, what they have exchanged and collected for their decades of work. What do you see then? You see houses, furniture, works of art. You also see machines, wagons, ships. Finally, you see objects of daily use, namely stocks of clothing, linen, meat, bread. All these things are the real equivalent of the goods your neighbours have sold and the work they have done.
With many people, however, you will also see assets of an incorporeal nature that seem to be of a very special kind, namely shares, bonds, mortgages and similar documents. In reality, however, these assets do not differ in anything from the concrete objects.

Every share, every bond, every mortgage represents highly corporeal houses, machines, wagons or stocks, which are located somewhere, and which form the equivalent of the goods sold or work done by the shareholder or bondholder.

The only difference is that these houses, machines, etc. are not in the direct possession of the shareholder or bondholder. Instead, they are owned or managed by a third party, who has a corresponding claim on them, which is evidenced in the shares, bonds and other documents. The linguistic usage calls such a claim 'capital' and the annual payment which the administrator must pay for the surrender of the houses, machines, etc., 'interest'. This interest, which for reasons of convenience is usually expressed in money, is in reality only goods of a certain value which the beneficiary wishes to receive, and it often happens that the interest is not fixed in money but in kind, in the countryside for example in potatoes, grain or firewood.

It makes no difference, dear James, whether you find your neighbour's houses, machines and stocks, or shares and bonds. In the one case, the owner himself administers the objects which he has gradually exchanged for his goods and services; in the other, a third party administers them for him. Whatever countries and whatever circles of people you extend your investigation to, as soon as you get to the bottom of it you will always find that goods and services are only given away with the intention of exchanging other goods and other services for them. The economy of our day is therefore based, just like that of the earliest times, on barter. It only appears somewhat complicated because there is such a confusing chaos of owners, administrators, lenders and borrowers who throw the goods exchanged and to be exchanged to each other like shuttlecocks. In other words, because the element of credit is so widespread in our time, we must dwell a little on this element, my boy, for we are dealing here with the most important of all economic factors and - to tell you now - a close relative of money.

I have just said that credit complicates modern intercourse, and that it is therefore not always recognised as the intercourse of exchange that it really is. You might now ask me: why do you not describe to me the transactions in a country in which credit, this intricate troublemaker, is unknown, and in which, therefore, the fact of the exchange of commodity for commodity is revealed to the naked eye? Answer: Because there is no such country and never has been. Credit is as old as human economic intercourse and cannot be thought away from it. Not even in a kraal of man-eaters, let alone in the prehistoric but generally well-organised herd economy of our arch-father Abraham, can or could one get along without credit. There is only one condition under which the economy can dispense with this most important of all aids, or, rather, transform it in such a way that it is no longer perceived as credit. This condition is - but I do not want to anticipate.

I know, my dear, that you are an unbelieving Thomas, and therefore I suspect that you do not yet really believe in the indispensability of credit. Is that true? If this is indeed the case, I would like to ask you to imagine the traffic in a very primitive Negro-state in Inner Africa. The inhabitants of this state have to live from something, don't you see? A part of the population hunts for meat; a second part raises cattle for milk; a third part grows maize; the able-bodied rest, if they are not part of the chief's bodyguards, shakes coconuts, cuts bamboo and palm leaves to build huts or fetches water from the nearby oasis. An even more primitive economic management is hardly conceivable.

Now imagine a shepherd undergoing the following everyday traffic act: A herdsman who has nothing but his herd of zebu cattle needs various items, namely some palm leaves to mend his cattle shed, some maize for daily bread and water for his cows. How does this purchase come about? The nearest way, that of outright exchange, is not viable in this case, for every head of cattle that the cattleman can give in exchange is worth a hundred times more than the palm leaves, the maize and the water. The sellers do not have as many palm leaves, maize and water as there are cattle, and if they did, what would the cattle breeder do with these quantities? At least the water would be spoilt after a few days. Therefore, if the parties want to come to an agreement, the only way out is for one of them to defer payment to the other. Either the palm-treader, the water-carrier, the maize-grower deliver their small product to the cattle-breeder at first without consideration, in which case the latter undertakes to meet his needs from them continuously, and later, when the deliveries of palm leaves, water and maize have reached a corresponding value, to pay off the whole debt at once by handing over cattle; or else the cattle-breeder delivers to the palm-seeker, the water-bearer and the maize-farmer one head of cattle each, in return for which they undertake to supply him with their products as required, and this until the value of the products has reached the price of one head of cattle. In both cases, one party grants credit to the other.

Credit in daily traffic between savages? When it hardly seems conceivable, even in a highly developed constitutional state, that in market traffic, which is made up of innumerable small buyers and sellers, every individual could grant credit to every individual? The objection is very obvious, dear James, I readily admit that. But please tell me yourself how else you imagine the exchange of goods in a primitive country. The fact is that here, just as in the cultured state, only very rarely will two exchanging parties be in possession of absolutely equivalent goods. It is also a fact that even in the rare case of equality of value, the goods to be exchanged will not be available at one and the same moment. If, for example, a pig ready for slaughter is to be exchanged for a ton of rye, the pig can be given away in winter, but the rye only in summer, after the harvest. In almost every exchange that takes place, there will thus remain a residue that must be deferred, i.e. one party will have to grant credit to the other. Where such credit is refused on principle, economic intercourse cannot arise, regardless of whether we are dealing with a highly developed cultural state or a primitive Hottentot kraal.

I can literally see you shrugging your shoulders in annoyance in order to say: 'Tactically, however, there is a lively market traffic all over the world, although nowhere do the buying or exchanging parties think of granting each other credit. Mistake, my dear, a serious mistake! You have not looked at market traffic thoroughly enough. In reality, the principle of deferring the equivalent value to the buyer of a good or service has developed throughout the world. You yourself, my son, make use of credit ten times a day, without knowing it, of course, and without your suppliers being aware of it.

For traffic has found a means of divesting credit of the danger of loss which would otherwise prevent its general application, and this in the simplest way: Every seller has a pledge made by every buyer. Because this happens in all acts of exchange, and because it has therefore become second nature to us to pay and be paid with a pledge, we all see in the pledge a definite consideration and are no longer aware that this consideration has in reality been deferred, credited. We do not see the credit that is inherent in every market transaction, because it is a risk-free, covered credit that we give and take, and because the cover always consists in one and the same sub-pledge.

It has become a custom - among the Hottentots as well as among us - to use a standard deposit. It is not left to the buying parties to agree on any pledge, but a certain, generally valued, sufficiently available, easily divisible and composable, but above all stable in value commodity has been chosen as the customary pledge. This standard pledge, dear James, is called money. The introduction of money into circulation is the only condition I mentioned earlier under which the economy cannot do without credit in the exchange of goods, but can secure it in such a way that it no longer appears outwardly as credit.

I remember once arguing with a colleague, one of those few bank directors who know something about money, about whether money should really be regarded as a 'pledge'. My colleague agreed with me that money in itself was not a definite consideration for a good sold or a service rendered, but merely an instrument that secured the credited claim to the consideration. He thought, however, that the money which secured this claim was not to be called a 'pledge' but rather an 'instruction'. For it provides its holder with the right to take goods of a certain value from the market - to 'buy' - and it thus assigns these goods to him. Therefore, the money does not need to consist of a valuable good, such as gold or silver. This was only necessary if it really went from hand to hand as a full-value pledge, but not if it was an order for goods. For an order it is completely sufficient if it is issued by an authority, such as the state government or a large central bank. What it was made of was absolutely irrelevant; paper served exactly the same purpose as gold or silver.

You see from this dispute, dear James, how important it can be under certain circumstances whether one regards money as a pledge which covers the credit connected with every transaction by its material value; or whether one regards it as an order in which some authority certifies the credit and attests to the lender the right to obtain goods of corresponding value. For, depending on whether one regards money as a full-fledged pledge or as an order of the authorities, one will regard metal money or paper money as actual money. But I do not want to dwell on this question today, because there are even more important questions of principle than that of what money must consist of. You will see this clearly when we are a few letters further along. For the time being, therefore, you need not worry your head about whether you really have to see in money a pledge for credit granted.

On the other hand, you must absolutely adhere to the following guiding principles:
In economic transactions, one service is always and without exception exchanged for the other. However, only one performance takes place in the present. The other only takes place in the future. Until this future point in time, a credit relationship exists, namely a claim of one party (the seller) to the still outstanding consideration of the other party (the buyer). This claim is secured by a transaction instrument called 'money'. The money provisionally takes the place of the outstanding consideration - whether as a pledge or as an instruction. It is therefore usually regarded as the consideration itself. How the money is constituted and who spent it is basically irrelevant. There is only one thing that matters, and that is that the money completely fulfils its task of securing a claim to goods. If it does, it is good, full-value money, even if it is made of cheap paper. If it does not fulfil its task, so that the bearer loses all or part of his acquired right to goods, then it is inferior money, even if it is made of metal and has been issued by the highest authority in the state on the basis of the laws in force. So much for today.

With love

Your old dad.

Third Letter

*Money a right
Is there 'too little money'?
The State and Money*

Berlin, January 5th 1921

There is one sentence, my dear James, that you cannot hammer firmly enough into your mind. The sentence that constitutes the quintessence of my previous letter is: 'Money is the embodiment of a claim to goods that has arisen because someone has performed something but has not yet received the consideration.' Or, more briefly: 'Money embodies the claim to equivalent consideration arising from a service.' This sentence is the be-all and end-all of the entire theory of money. From it, everything that has to be said about money actually follows by itself. If only all nations would memorise this harmless sentence and never violate its meaning, there would be no monetary misery and no currency question in the whole world.

As soon as the claim to consideration, which every market exchange of goods entails, is secured by money, an external change takes place with it. You recognise this immediately if you imagine a concrete case. Think of a worker who has done work for 200 marks, that is, who has acquired a claim to goods worth 200 marks. He has this claim exclusively against his employers until payday. (Up to the payday, every worker grants his employer 'credit'). However, at the moment when the employer pays the worker the 200 marks, the claim against him ceases to exist. The two are 'even'. But this does not mean that the claim itself is extinguished; on the contrary, it remains, embodied in money, in the unchanged amount of 200 marks.

Only now the claim is no longer directed against an individual, the employer, but against the totality, the market. The worker can now collect the consideration promised him for his work wherever and in whatever form he wants. He can buy a pair of boots from the cobbler, food and cigars from the merchant, beer from the innkeeper. Only when he has done this and spent his 200 marks is his claim to property extinguished. Only then is the purpose of the exchange fulfilled, which the worker has undertaken with his employer: he has exchanged boots, food, cigars and beer for his work performance. The receipt of the money was only an intermediate stage, which was necessary because the employer did not himself have the goods which the worker wished to receive, because it therefore required a guarantee that the worker would actually receive the goods earned by his hands somewhere.

Hold this quite firmly, my son: As long as someone has not received anything in return for a service, not even in the interim form of money, he has only a claim on a certain person, namely a claim on the recipient of his service. Our worker, for example, initially has a claim in the amount of 200 marks solely on his employer. But as soon as the same person has received money for his performance, he has a claim on the general public. Our worker now has a claim on the market, which must supply him with boots, food, beer, or whatever else the worker may choose, up to the value of 200 marks. In the first case, i.e. as long as the person rendering the service still has a claim on an individual person or a credit balance with that person, the relationship between the two parties is called a credit relationship. In the second case, i.e. when the renderer has received money, one no longer speaks of credit, although nothing has actually changed in the matter itself, but of purchasing power. One says that the recipient of money can exercise as much purchasing power on the market as is expressed in the amount of money received. Strictly speaking, however, there is still a credit relationship. The recipient of money still has his claim, only that he no longer has this claim against an individual person, but against the totality that constitutes the 'market'.

We have now reached the point, dear James, where we know what money is in essence and what its most important function is. To recapitulate briefly: Money represents an attested right to receive consideration which has been preceded by corresponding services, and its main function is to transfer this consideration from the 'market' to the person entitled to receive it. But this still leaves us very far from our goal. We are still faced with a whole series of unresolved questions. There are three questions in particular. First, how much money, how much purchasing power must exist in a country? Secondly, how much market commodity does one receive for the individual monetary token, i.e. what is the value of the money? And thirdly: How is money created? Basically, all these questions answer themselves as soon as one sees in money only what it is, namely a reference right, and always remembers that in it a deferred consideration is embodied. But since human logic likes to make side leaps, and every deviation from the straight path here infallibly leads to error, I must help you a little in finding the answers that are actually self-evident.

Firstly, how much money must circulate in a country? The most peculiar views on this are widespread among economists. Most of them believe that the quantity of money must stand in a quite definite relation to the production of goods, and that therefore with increasing production more money must be put into circulation; if this does not happen, then a 'lack of money' arises. This view, like every other view that sees money as an article to be increased or decreased according to plan, is fundamentally wrong. It is just as nonsensical as the view that one need only increase the entries in the land registers and house cadasters in the country in order to eliminate the housing shortage. One is certainly able to increase or decrease tangible objects, i.e. houses and flats. But one cannot double or halve an abstract right. And money is nothing other than an attested right. It is - one cannot repeat this often enough - the right to something in return, which someone acquires by giving away his own labour. For the worker who has given up his labour at the agreed price of 200 marks, the money he receives in return means nothing other than the right to procure the agreed counter-value by buying boots, food, beer, etc. His 200 marks correspond exactly to the quantity of goods to which he has acquired a right through his work. With every purchase he makes, his money stock, i.e. his right to goods, is reduced. For in the amount of his purchase he receives the corresponding definite consideration for his labour, for which he must of course give up the provisional consideration, namely the right to receive goods embodied in money; just as in the theatre you forfeit your coat-check token, your right to withdraw a coat and a hat, the moment you receive the things.

Every person who has made an act of exchange, but has not yet received the equivalent value to which he is entitled, possesses money, that is, a certified right to collect the equivalent value in kind. And every money token that exists in the country means that someone has not yet received a counter-value to which he is entitled. Therefore, there can never actually be 'too much' and 'too little' money. There is always just as much money circulating in a country as there are acts of exchange that have been carried out but not yet fully completed, but still remain in abeyance, so to speak. For money is precisely the certificate that an act of exchange has only been half completed, because the person entitled to receive the consideration does not yet have it in his hands; it is at the same time the legal document which legitimises its holder to receive the consideration. Since the money supply in the country must therefore always be exactly as large as the sum of all counter-performances not yet claimed, I cannot with the best will in the world see how the money supply can be increased or decreased by the state. Every arbitrarily created new monetary token signifies a legal title to the payment of a consideration, although no performance has ever taken place to justify it. It certifies an act of exchange which has been left in abeyance and which in reality has not been carried out at all, and is therefore to a certain extent a forgery. Conversely, any arbitrary reduction in the circulation of money, any destruction of money tokens, means a cancellation of vested rights to consideration and thus an act of violence.

I would almost bet you, dear James, that I know the objection you want to make here. 'When the state creates new money, it thereby makes possible a large number of new acts of exchange. Thousands who could not buy before can do so now. A demand arises on the market, which forces producers to manufacture more goods, which thus raises national production. The increased quantity of money is then matched by an increased quantity of goods, so that the demand embodied in the new money can be fully satisfied. 'Am I right? Is that not your train of thought? If not, it is the common argumentation, and since it sounds extraordinarily convincing, I will have to deal with it willy-nilly.

Let us illustrate the matter with a practical example: A state in which a million banknotes are circulating issues another million for some reason. It thus issues entitlement certificates which, just like the money tokens already in circulation, entitle the bearer to purchase goods. Question: For the purchase of which goods? Answer: for the purchase of all kinds of goods; it is entirely at the discretion of the recipients of the new money which goods they want to buy on the market with it. We are therefore faced with the fact that a certain quantity of market goods, which until then had not yet undergone any change, is suddenly confronted with twice as great a demand, because the old and the new money tokens assert the right of subscription embodied in them. In a sense, a competition for the goods arises. Of course, this must have its consequences. It is an old, never disputed fact of experience that when demand is doubled and supply remains the same, the prices of goods rise. The doubling of the monetary tokens therefore leads to the market goods becoming more expensive. How great the price increase is, is a matter of scientific dispute. For the sake of simplicity, let us assume that the doubled demand leads to a doubled price. The result of the increase in money is that every holder of old money has to pay twice as much for his purchases as before.

Here I hear another interjection: 'That's not true! The new demand stimulates the whole production to increased activity through the rising prices. As a result, new quantities of goods appear on the market very soon, which counter the increased demand with an increased supply and push the rising prices down again. ' The interjection is not entirely unjustified. This effect can indeed occur, namely when the factory owners and their workers are stimulated by the price increase to increase their labour output. But this effect need not occur. Realise that rising prices lead to considerably increased profits, that the more abundant profits result in higher wages, and that in this way an ease of earning arises in the whole of production, which very often does not stimulate to increased labour, but to the contrary, to a certain ease and indolence. In such times there is often a call for a seven- or six-hour day in the air. It is therefore very easy for a decrease rather than an increase in the production of goods to occur. But even if production really increases and supply grows, this is always only the gradual and hesitant consequence of the immediate and impetuous rise in prices. The first and certain moment is always the price increase; the price reduction is a later and very questionable eventuality, which, moreover, at best mitigates the price increase somewhat, but never prevents it altogether. We must therefore already come to terms with the fact that the increase of money raises prices, and the only concession I can make to you, if need be, is that we presuppose the increase to be not quite so tempestuous as I have done above. Let us assume, then, in God's name, that a 100 per cent increase in money results in only a 50 per cent increase in prices.

But what does it mean, dear James, if all holders of old money have to pay 50 per cent more for every purchase than they used to? What does it mean if, to remain with our example, the worker no longer receives boots, groceries, cigars and beer for his 200 marks as he used to, but only groceries and cigars, for instance, so that he has to do without boots and beer? This means nothing other than that by increasing his money he has been forcibly deprived of part of the consideration he earned with his work, that he has been expropriated to a certain extent. Naturally, he will try to hold himself harmless by raising his labour tariff and now demanding a wage of 300 marks, that is, by laying claim to as many rights as are necessary to be able to obtain the same quantities of goods as before. Only rarely, however, does he succeed in doing this to the full. And when he succeeds, it is at the expense of other classes of the population, such as civil servants, state pensioners, pensioners. For the fact cannot be eliminated that the one million new money tokens created by the state are seized on quantities of goods into which the one million old money tokens have been divided until then. Some classes of the people must necessarily bear the costs and put up with the fact that their well-earned claim to consideration shrinks by a third or more.

But that should not and must not be, my son! Money is a right and should not become an injustice. That is why the state must never take the liberty of wanting to create or destroy money arbitrarily, for in doing so it creates or destroys vested rights to goods. The omnipotence of the state in the field of money is a special matter. It is an omnipotence that resembles impotence as much as one egg resembles another. For if you go deeper into what I have just explained, you will make a most curious discovery, and I am only sorry that I cannot see your astonished face when you make it. Or is it not a surprising discovery that the state cannot create money at all, no matter how hard it tries? It is indeed so. But what the state can do is to produce new signs of money mechanically. But these money tokens do not fulfil the purpose that money has; they do not provide the people with new rights to goods, they do not make the people one iota more powerful, but they only transfer long existing rights to goods, long existing purchasing power from their rightful owners to other people. They siphon off a certain part of the right to purchase goods, which belongs to the national community and is securitised in the old money, and lend this part to the holders of the newly issued money tokens. By producing such money tokens, the state only gives to the one what it takes from the other. It is not able to create anything new in this way. In a nutshell: the state does not create new money by issuing money tokens, but taxes one part of the population in favour of the other.

That's the way things are, dear James. It is only a deception if, in view of the mountains of note money in which we are threatening to suffocate, you believe that the German Reich has created 70 billion marks of new money in recent years with the help of the Reichsbank. Of course, the notes are there, there is no doubt about that. But they are not new money. The purchasing power inherent in them is not even as great as the purchasing power of the four or five billion marks of coins and notes that circulated in Germany in 1914. And even the little bit of purchasing power that they really represent does not come from the state, has not been injected into them by the creative power of the government, but is the same purchasing power that used to be in the four or five billion old coins and notes and belongs by right to the holders of these few billions. The fact that by far the largest part of the purchasing power has been forcibly transferred from the old money to new products of the banknote press and artificially given a value to them can only be euphemistically called 'monetary policy'. More correctly, it is a brutal act of expropriation. And the only thing the state can do in relation to money. It can only expropriate money, i.e. property rights, never create them.

But the fact that the state is unable to create money when it deems it necessary does absolutely no harm. For money is not an end in itself, but only a means to the end of facilitating traffic, and in every country where the state does not do anything foolish, there is always exactly as much money as is necessary for this purpose. The money system regulates itself automatically, and the state has nothing more to do than to keep the money machine technically in order. There is no room for creative activity here, and it is a fatal error for numerous economists to believe that money is a creature of the state's legal system.

But whose creature is the money in reality? Be patient for a few days, my son, and you will know. For today, my pen refuses to continue its service.

With love

Your very tired dad.

Fourth Letter

Does money have an intrinsic value?
Real money and fictitious money.

Berlin, January 8th 1921

I hope you are now aware of two things, dear James. Firstly, that every monetary token represents a right, a certified right of subscription; secondly, that the quantity of these rights, the quantity of money in circulation, is never too large and never too small, but always corresponds exactly to the need. How great this need is, and what absolute quantity of money circulates in the country as a result, we will see in a few days, namely when we turn to the interesting question of how money is created. Until then, we must leave some things to themselves; for example, the peculiar phenomenon that in every country and at all times it seems as if there is far too little money, regardless of whether there are 1 million or 100 billion banknotes in circulation in the country. I know very well that this universal phenomenon makes you wonder, although you suspect that there is some mistake behind it. But we cannot deal with all the details at once, but must always take one thing at a time. Once the main questions have been clarified, many an error in the details will disappear of its own accord.

The first main question was the quantity of money; my last letter dealt with it in broad outline, and we can now turn to the second main question: What is the value of money?
You should actually be able to deal with this question all by yourself. For as soon as you realise that money is nothing more than an attested right, a right to receive goods, you must realise without further ado that the question itself is meaningless. An abstract 'right' can never have a concrete

'value'. It can certainly transfer the value that any thing has from one person to another, it can regulate the ownership of this value, but it cannot embody the value in itself. You must not let yourself be misled by the fact that there is money of a certain kind which actually has approximately the concrete value which it attests, so that, for example, an English sovereign and a German double crown not only represent a right of subscription worth 20 shillings and 20 marks, but also really have this value by virtue of their physical nature, because they are made of gold. In this case, it is not the money, not the right to purchase goods, that has an intrinsic value, but only the metal on which the right to purchase is certified (by stamping). If you happen to have saved a double crown from the pre-war period into our paper present, you can immediately put it to the test by having the gold piece melted down. Although the gold is no longer a double crown, no longer money, it still has the same value as before, namely 20 gold marks or 4 3/4 dollars. The paper twenty-mark notes, on the other hand, which you still have from the pre-war period, have sunk deep, deep below this value. If money really derived its value from itself, from its quality as money, then the two money tokens, one representing 20 marks like the other, would have to have exactly the same value. In fact, only the double crown has retained its old value of 20 gold marks = 4 3/4 dollars, and this because it has always been something other than money, namely gold, i.e. a commodity of very special stable value.
So we have to frame the question differently, my dear.

We do not have to ask: 'What is the value of money? But: "How great is the claim to goods that money guarantees?"

Put like that, however, the question answers itself. For what is the fundamental sentence that you have to memorise if you want to avoid my paternal wrath and permanent ignorance of the monetary system? It is: "Money embodies the claim to an equivalent service in return for a service rendered." From this it follows without further ado that the claim to goods which money guarantees, or the ideal value which it therefore has for its owner, is exactly as great as the value of the preceding performance.

This may sound to you as if it basically says nothing at all, but is just a game with words. For we know the value of the preceding performance just as little as the value of the following counter-performance. In fact, however, this is a very, very important observation that leads us to a realisation of extraordinary significance. If it is true that the 'value of money' - for the sake of brevity we will stick to this not entirely correct expression - is equal to the 'value of the service' for which its holder received it, then it follows from this no less then that today, almost in the whole of Europe, there is no more money.

I urge you, my dear, not to take this as a joke. As much as it may astonish you, it is indeed literally true that today only in very few countries does real, genuine money exist, that is, a means of payment that fulfils the first and most important task of money, which is to preserve the full value of the service until the service in return is received, to let it resurrect in the service in return, so to speak. The money that you see circulating today, not only in Germany but also in countries with relatively good currencies, such as England, Holland, Switzerland, fulfils many of the tasks that real money fulfils, but it fails in the main. It does not offer its bearer the guarantee that he will really receive the agreed value in return for a commodity which he has delivered or a service which he has rendered. Think, for example, of the worker whom I mentioned several times in my previous letter. Three years ago, when he received 200 marks for his work, he received the value of a pair of boots as well as food, cigars and beer for the needs of about two weeks. Knowing that he could exchange the 200 marks for these goods at any time, he demanded payment for his work to this value and no higher. If he has now waited with the procurement of the things and has kept the money 'saved' in order to only today put himself in possession of all the goods for which he gave his performance three years ago, he sees with surprise that the goods are no longer within his reach. At best he gets a pair of boots for his money. He is deprived of food, cigars and beer. 'Money is no longer of any value,' he says bitterly, and by this he means that money has not fulfilled its purpose of securing for him the full value of his service until the day on which he claims the service in return. A money, however, that does not fulfil this purpose, but shrinks the claim embodied in it, is not real money, but an imperfect imitation. And today the whole of Europe is flooded with such imitations. The imitations are not everywhere as bad as in Germany, Austria or even Russia, where they have caused the claim embodied in them to melt down to a tenth, a fiftieth or a thousandth. But even in England, Switzerland, Holland, etc., where the claim is still half to three quarters of its original amount, the money that has reduced it in this way is not real money but fictitious money.

Genuine money is only such money as preserves undiminished for its bearer the claim to consideration arising from a service. For according to its purpose and essence, money is nothing other than a legal claim. The fact that it also fulfils a number of other functions, e.g. allows the legal claim to pass from hand to hand, is of no importance apart from the main purpose, and as soon as it does not fulfil this purpose, or fulfils it only inadequately, it is no longer money, however well it may still fulfil the other functions.
So let's recap, dear James. Since money is a claim to consideration, its 'value' is exactly as great as this consideration. And since its first and most important task is to ensure that the service in return is in turn as great as the preceding ser-

vice, the 'value' of money is also exactly as great as this service.

'As far as this is true, it is basically a matter of course,' you might interject here. 'Moreover, however, it does not even seem to me to be quite correct. The boots and foodstuffs, for example, to which our worker, who has been mentioned several times, is entitled, may become scarce and expensive as a result of a leather shortage or a bad harvest. In this case, the worker loses part of his entitlement. The money that embodies the entitlement is then only sufficient for food, cigars and beer, but no longer for boots. It thus corresponds to a consideration that is smaller than the original performance, whereas it was supposed to secure the value of the same. So even real money is not capable of fully guaranteeing a claim to goods for the duration. '

I begin with the second objection, which gives me an opportunity to correct myself on an important point. If I have said that the employer pays the worker for his performance in such a way that he guarantees him - by giving him 200 marks - an entitlement to boots, food, cigars and beer, this, I readily admit, is not quite correct. I have only specified the process so sharply for the sake of clarity. In reality, the employer's 200 marks do not constitute a guarantee that the objects which are available for 200 marks at the moment of performance will be available for them for all eternity. Money always secures the claim to consideration only within a certain framework.

By giving 200 marks, the employer leaves to the worker a very definite part of the claims to goods existing in the country at that moment, let us say one millionth of all claims. Today this millionth means a pair of boots and a certain quantity of food, cigars and beer, but tomorrow it may mean more or less. This depends entirely on the greater or lesser productive capacity in the country, which is determined, among other things, by elementary causes. Even real money, which deserves the name 'money', cannot protect the claim to goods against such fluctuations. It cannot, for example, prevent an invention from being made which makes it possible to produce a pair of boots in a tenth of the present labour time, so that the worker, instead of the one pair of boots to which his performance entitles him, may one day obtain two or three. This moment of uncertainty, however, takes a back seat to the guarantee which money really affords, and which consists in the fact that it permanently secures for its holder a fixed portion of all the claims to goods existing in the country. Our worker has no claim to a certain quantity of boots, food, etc., but he has a claim to one millionth of the total claim in the country.

Even if this millionth sometimes corresponds to a larger, sometimes to a smaller quantum of goods, these fluctuations in quantity tend to be so small and even out in the course of time that in practice they are hardly taken into account, even if it is a matter of agreements for 50 or 100 years. But, mind you, only where real, genuine money circulates. For only this money secures its holder the partial claim to which he is entitled, thus guaranteeing the worker, to remain with our example, that he is and remains the owner of one millionth of all claims to goods.

The fictitious money which we now see circulating in almost all countries does not provide this guarantee, but increases the claims to goods so arbitrarily that after a short time our worker no longer possesses one millionth but, depending on the degree of arbitrariness, only one ten-millionth or one hundred-millionth of all claims, i.e. one tenth or one hundredth of the purchasing power to which he is legally entitled.

By the way, so that you don't get in my way again, dear James, I want to interject here that there are also moments which naturally increase the total quantity of all claims to goods over time. The claim of our worker, which today is like 1 to 1 million, may one day sink to the ratio of 1 to 1 1/2 million, even under the rule of real money. But this decline means no harm to him, for new claims, which arise naturally, are always accompanied by productive surpluses. The stock of goods in the economy increases as a result of this additional output to such an extent that the individual share, even if it has become relatively smaller, still accounts for the same or even a larger quantity of goods than originally. I will come back to this point in the chapter 'Origin of Money'.

Now to your objection that the equality of value between money, performance and counter-performance is a matter of course. (You see, I take your objections seriously, even if I only suspect that you are making them). Certainly it is self-evident that money, which is nothing but a right of reference to a consideration, has the same 'value' as the latter. And it is equally self-evident that, as long as the consideration has the same value as the preceding performance, the money is also 'equal in value' to the latter. Unfortunately, this self-evident fact is the only answer I am able to give to the question of the 'value' of money. For money does not have an intrinsic value and, since it is merely a right, it cannot have one.

'Even if the money is made of precious metal?' I hear you ask in your mind, although I have actually already answered this. So once again: No, my boy, not even then. A golden double crown that you throw into the crucible has a certain value not because it is money, but because it is made of gold, i.e. a desirable metal. If the double crown circulates in the country as a means of payment, it is exactly the same: its metal content, not its monetary property, makes it valuable. In the latter case, however, it has, in addition to its intrinsic value, the derived value that every monetary token has in its capacity as a guarantee of a legal claim, i.e. the value that is also inherent in a paper means of payment. But this, as we have seen, is not a real value at all, but only a 'value' in inverted commas, a reflex, so to speak, of the commodity value to which money grants a claim. So we come to the conclusion: money carries no value in itself, but only guarantees the claim to a certain commodity value. And even this commodity value is not a fixed quantity, but fluctuates with the amount of money in circulation. Each money token gives its holder a right to a part of the respective stock of market goods. If there are few monetary tokens, the stock of goods is divided into few parts, so each individual part is valuable. If there are many monetary tokens, each of them grants the right to only a small part of the stock, thus embodying a negligible value. If someone asks you how valuable the single piece of a bowl cake is, you will certainly answer: 'I cannot say that as long as I do not know into how many portions the cake is divided.' It is the same with the single portion of the total stock of goods embodied in a monetary token. Its value depends entirely on how many money tokens the total supply is divided into. The question of the 'value of money' - please always note the inverted commas - is therefore basically only a question of the quantity of money.

And with that, good night!

Your old dad.

Fifth Letter

The 'money' and the 'money signs'
The migration of money
The immortal money

Berlin, January 10th 1921

Let us now, dear James, turn to the question of how money is created. Mind you, the real, genuine money, not the fictitious money that the states today produce on a large scale. The origin of fictitious money is of no interest at all. All that is needed is a broad conscience and a printing press. But as I wrote to you in an earlier letter: real money can never come into being in this way. A piece of paper does not become money when the state designates it as such and forces the population to regard it as money. Real money comes into being as a result of a very specific economic process and always has a performance as a prerequisite. It is not a creature of the state's legal system or of the state's arbitrariness, but a product of traffic. And as trivial as it is to know what a government is thinking when it prints its coloured notes, it is interesting to follow the emergence of real money.

You and I, every single cultural person, witness the birth of money every day. Yet rarely do any of us physically see it come into being. This seems puzzling and yet it is basically quite natural. You only have to visualise the process.
Every baker who sells a loaf of bread, every craftsman who carries out a work, thereby procures for himself a claim to goods. If they assert this claim immediately, i.e. if the baker gets a bag of sugar for his bread and the craftsman gets a few cigars for his work, the transaction leaves no further consequences. We then speak of an exchange. If, however,

the two postpone the assertion of their claim, they thereby become the holders of a right of subscription, which they can exercise at any time and in any manner, and we then speak of monetary transactions. For this right of subscription is nothing other than money. Nevertheless, we do not see that physical money was created on this occasion. Rather, we see that the money which the baker and the craftsman receive, and in which the right of subscription is embodied, already exists and only changes hands. How is this? In the end, should the assertion that money arises from every service that is not immediately compensated with a service in return be false? And if it is false, when does money actually come into existence? For at some point, it is clear, every monetary token in circulation must have come into being.

The matter clears up in a most simple way, dear James, as soon as we speak correctly and keep the terms 'money' and 'money signs' apart. Most mistakes and misunderstandings arise from the fact that people associate different concepts with a certain word, that is, they speak different languages, so to speak, and thus talk past each other. So let us understand each other correctly: The claim to goods that a person possesses, the purchasing power that he consequently exercises, is 'money'. I have repeated to you often enough that money is not something material, but something insubstantial, namely a right. In order to be respected, this right must of course be made outwardly recognisable in some way. It can, for example, be entered in a public book and transferred from one entitled person to another by means of a transfer entry. In this case, the ideal money does not take on a physical form, but only the abstract form of a booking. One then speaks of 'giro money'. In most cases, however, it is preferable to draw up documents on the right and hand them over to the beneficiaries. These documents are then 'money tokens' or 'means of payment'. Unfortunately, linguistic usage has become accustomed to calling these documents the same as the right they certify, namely 'money'. This results in a continuing confusion of terms, and you yourself, my son, have perhaps fallen victim to just such a confusion. For should you really be surprised that you have never yet seen money come into existence, although thousands of rights to draw goods are being created around you every hour, then you would quite simply be confusing 'money' and 'money signs' with each other. As soon as you express yourself correctly, the supposed contradiction collapses. For the fact that every day in innumerable cases new rights of reference, called money, come into being, need not at all have as a consequence that a new document, called a money mark, is issued for each of these rights of reference. On the contrary, it would be very strange if this were the case.

Why? Well, think a little, my dear. You only have to open your eyes and look at daily life. What happens with every purchase and sale? When the baker sells a loaf of bread to the worker, a legal claim to consideration arises for the baker on the basis of this performance. But that is by no means all. Another process goes hand in hand with it. The baker who sells the bread is confronted with the worker who buys it, isn't he? For him, too, the act has an economic significance. Namely, through the purchase, he puts himself in possession of a consideration to which he was entitled when he was last paid his wages. For when the employer paid him 200 marks for his work at that time, this meant that a quite definite legal claim to consideration arose for the worker, which remains valid until the worker himself brings the consideration in the form of boots, food, etc. to himself. The moment this happens, i.e. the worker buys a pair of boots, the corresponding claim has ceased to exist. And so the purchase of the bread from the baker means not only that a new claim has arisen for the baker, but at the same time that an equally great claim has ceased to exist for the worker. And as in this case, so it is with all other acts in commercial transactions. The transaction which constitutes a sale for one party, and gives rise to a new claim to goods, constitutes a purchase for the other party, and causes a claim to be extinguished. That is the reason, dear James, why you have never seen money come into being: Becoming and passing away, birth and death are here opposed and cancel each other out. On the one hand, no new claim needs to be documented, no new monetary sign needs to be created, but on the other hand, no existing claim needs to be annulled, no monetary sign needs to be destroyed. For the purpose of securing the claim of one and extinguishing that of the other can be achieved in a much simpler way, namely by the buyer handing over to the seller the document concerning his previous claim, which expires at the moment of purchase, that is, by handing him the corresponding money tokens.

This is why most people never create means of payment, but only see them circulate from one to the other. This is a technical aid of traffic, which has introduced a kind of 'clearing' for the people's claims to goods. The claims are not cumbersomely authenticated and just as cumbersomely cancelled, but simply exchanged, which is much more convenient.

In this way the claim to goods embodied in money always passes from one person to another. The employer hands it over to the worker, the latter assigns it to the baker, the baker passes it on to the miller, who delivers flour to him, the miller to the farmer in return for his grain, and so the claim circulates through the whole chain of transactions. Whoever has performed something and thereby acquired a right of subscription receives the claim, whoever has received a performance and thereby exercised the corresponding right of subscription loses the claim. The claim as such does not expire, but only changes hands.

This continued existence of the claim to goods, this eternal wandering of the monetary sign in which the claim is embodied, can very easily be misunderstood. Beware, therefore, my son, of seeing in the circulation of money anything other than a technical aid to traffic which wants to make things easy for itself and therefore uses one and the same document again and again instead of continually issuing new documents and cancelling them again. Never forget the real meaning of the process: wherever a monetary token changes hands, one right, a right of reference to goods, has expired and another has come into being. In a state that knows no 'circulating money' but only 'book money', where every citizen has an account in the national ledger instead of coins and notes, this would be more obvious than here.

There, on the account of the baker who sells a loaf of bread, a corresponding subscription right would be newly entered, on the account of the buying worker, on the other hand, a previously entered subscription right would be deleted. It is claimed that in ancient times there were actually states (e.g. Egypt) where this money system prevailed. I myself believe, however, that this is only conceivable for large-scale traffic; medium and small-scale traffic will never have been able to do without the representation of money by physical monetary symbols.

In our research so far, we have only come across money signs that move from hand to hand, not those that appear for the first time in circulation. Consequently, we still do not know how physical monetary signs actually come into being. And the same is true of conceptual money, the ideal legal claim to consideration. We only know of this legal claim that it forms, so to speak, the second half of all acts of purchase and the provisional payment for all services; we therefore only know the what, not the how.

On the other hand, we have learnt something else, something very important: a claim to goods that exists once is a thing that normally does not pass away again, but always just wanders, that always pushes itself anew between performance and counter-performance and is, so to speak, immortal. Just as little as the hour of birth of money have you ever witnessed its hour of death: unless one of your friends once used a banknote as a fidibus in the mood, under the influence of wine, and thus caused a claim to goods to go up in smoke.

And even then the right of subscription represented in money is extinguished only for the individual holder, but not for the totality. Or do you believe that in the whole world some good finds no buyer and spoils only because your friend has burnt his claim to this or another good? No, the right embodied in the burnt money token is indeed immortal. If its rightful holder renounces its exercise, it automatically passes to the holders of the other subscription rights. For each individual subscription right is not for a fixed amount, but for the so-and-so-manyth part of all subscription rights, thus representing a claim to goods that is all the greater the more the number of existing subscription rights decreases.

This in turn leads to a very interesting observation: namely, that the state cannot destroy money, even if it wants to. It can, of course, reduce the number of banknotes in circulation, i.e. withdraw and collect a few million banknotes. But in doing so it only does exactly the same as your friend with his fidibus. He takes away from individuals their rights embodied in the banknotes, but these rights do not disappear but accrue to the holders of the remaining banknotes. Each of these banknotes now accounts for a larger share of the totality of goods. It is common to say: 'The money has become more valuable', and this is correct. The claim to goods, the purchasing power, which are guaranteed by money, have actually increased in proportion to the numerical reduction of the banknotes.

If, then, I have explained to you in an earlier letter that the State cannot, of its own free will, create money, i.e. no property rights, but can only transfer long-existing property rights to other persons, i.e. expropriate them, you see here the counterpart to this: The state cannot destroy existing money, circulating property rights, but can only transfer them to other persons, i.e. restructure the property rights. The only difference is that in the first case the totality of goods is distributed among an increased, in the second case among a reduced number of entitled persons, which in one case means a disadvantage, in the other an advantage for the individual money holders. From which you can see once again that the 'value' of money is never absolute, but is always closely related to the quantity of money and fluctuates with it.

Now that you have seen, dear James, that money in the economy seems to resemble a restless Ahasver, which does not come into being and does not pass away, but wanders eternally, you are certainly doubly eager to find out what actually happens to the genesis and demise of money. For once, that is certain, even an Ahasver must be born and die. I can therefore assume that you are eagerly awaiting my next letter, which is to follow tomorrow.

    With love

        Your dad.

Sixth Letter

Birth of Money
Midwifery of the State
Money and Gold

Berlin, January 11th 1921

It doesn't help, dear James, we have to recapitulate a little again. So: money is a reference right to goods. This reference right arises when someone delivers or performs something, i.e. when, for example, a worker hands over his product to the employer; through the delivery, a right to an equivalent counter-performance arises, i.e. a reference right to goods, and this reference right is called 'money'. If the renderer or supplier has asserted his right to consideration, i.e. if our worker has exchanged a pair of boots, foodstuffs, cigars, etc. for his money, then the economic process of the exchange of performance and consideration has ended, and the reference right that mediated the exchange has expired.

Actually, money should come into being and disappear again many thousands of times a day.

For each of the innumerable services in daily traffic brings a new right to goods, called money, into being, and each of the equally innumerable counter-services destroys this right again. But human intercourse is far too practical to apply such a cumbersome procedure. It would be a hellishly complicated traffic, in which every sale of a roll of yarn would lead to the production of money, and every purchase of a roll of yarn to the destruction of money. Rather, intercourse helps itself in such a way that it objectifies, as it were, the right of reference represented in money, that it makes it an independent instrument of the exchange of goods, which quietly continues to exist even if the subjective right of reference of its respective holder expires. Then it is not necessary to create money anew as soon as the worker receives his weekly wage, and to destroy it again as soon as he buys boots and food for it. The intended purpose can be achieved much more conveniently by always transferring the money, which has now become an independent instrument of circulation, from the hand of the person whose claim expires into the hand of his counterpart who has acquired a corresponding claim. Every seller therefore does not receive newly created money from the buyer, but money that has long been fixed and embodies a claim to goods that has also existed for a long time. In other words, the money is allowed to wander. It is not created and does not perish, but circulates.

That is the rule. This rule must, however, have its exceptions, for after all, money cannot behave differently from all other things, which all have a beginning and an end: On the one hand, every concrete sign of money must necessarily have come into being, as must the abstract right of reference embodied in it. But what are the circumstances under which it comes into being?

We must be careful not to take the current monetary practice in Germany and other countries as a model. The mechanical production of money in these countries has nothing whatever to do with the creation of real, genuine money, which is always organic. The money which our printing presses spit out is imitation money, just as the shares which a dishonest director of a company has printed, and which are not matched by a corresponding increase in the company's assets, are imitation shares. Both money and shares lack the economic cause of origin which alone makes them genuine documents. The fact that the public does not notice the illegitimacy of the issue either in the one case or in the other, but regards the money just like the shares unseen as 'fully valid', does not change the fact that both are counterfeits.

Since money is not a claim to goods per se, but a claim to goods of a very special kind, and since it necessarily presupposes that it has been preceded by an equivalent performance, the paper notes which the note presses bring into existence without economic cause, simply by order of the state, are anything but 'money'

Money, i.e. an economically justified claim to goods, always arises when and only when someone has performed something but has not yet received the consideration. It is identical with the legal claim to the outstanding consideration. The existence of such a legal claim must, of course, be stated by someone, formally certified, and normally no one is better qualified to carry out the certification than the authority of a constitutional state entrusted with this special task. But this is also the only help that the state can and may give in the creation of money. Its ability and its authority are only to authenticate a new claim that has arisen without its intervention and to prescribe the external form in which it is to be clothed (metal, paper or book money, small or large denominations, etc.). It has neither the power nor the ability to create a property claim. To put it drastically, the government is only ever the midwife who receives the new citizen of the world and prepares him for life, never the mother who gives birth to him.

The best way to recognise the circumstances under which real, circulation-born money comes into being is by means of a concrete process from everyday life.

The worker who has a wage claim of 200 marks and demands from his employer the corresponding right to receive goods in the usual form of money is usually satisfied with 'wandering money'. The employer hands over to him means of payment which he himself received when he sold his manufactured goods (e.g. axes) to a merchant; the latter in turn procured the money by selling a stock (e.g. wood), and this from a craftsman to whom it accrued as payment for work delivered (e.g. a table). But even the craftsman's predecessor was not the physical or spiritual creator of the money. He was only a link in a long, long chain of persons among whom the money circulated until one day it came into his hands. Every single one of these persons received the money when they performed something, and gave it away again in order to exchange the consideration for it in the form of some goods. In other words, they received it when they produced and gave it away when they consumed. One can trace the path that money has taken through countless stages of production and consumption, but eventually the path will be lost somewhere in the mist. One will only very rarely find the point where money began its journey, the place where it was born.

Besides this normal course of events, there is also another possibility. The employer, who owes the worker and ten thousand of his colleagues 200 marks each, is not in a position to give the people the money. He owns 'capital', namely factory premises, machines, stocks etc., but no right to goods, no 'money'. He has not sold anything recently, i.e. he has not paid anything, and therefore has no claim to consideration at present which he could assign to the workers.

In this case, the employer has only the choice, under the compulsion of the obligation to pay, to perform something after all, i.e. to sell stocks under unfavourable conditions, or to avail himself of credit (i.e. to borrow foreign rights to purchase goods), or finally to produce the money which he does not possess. The preconditions for the creation of money seem to be given. The workers, through their performance, have created for themselves a claim to consideration, i.e. a right to receive goods, and money, as we have seen, is nothing other than a guaranteed claim, a certified right to receive goods. In order for the workers' legal claim to become 'money', nothing more is necessary than that the claim be officially recognised and guaranteed as legitimate.

The employer therefore goes to the office that the state has set up for this purpose and asks it to issue him with documents on the validity of his workers' claim, which would then represent money and could be used for payment. The body, however, raises objections. It explains to the claimant that it cannot recognise the workers' claim without further ado. It could not certify a right to receive goods on the basis of a simple declaration by two parties. Not out of mistrust, although if she were to be satisfied with such a declaration on principle, she would immediately be overrun with innumerable applications and would have to create many billions of new money. But because it could not certify anything impossible. How should it be in a position to recognise rights to property as legitimate and to legitimise them by means of the state stamp, as long as it has not received proof that the property to which the claim is to be made actually exists? If it is to certify claims to property, it must have the unconditional guarantee that the claims can also be satisfied.

The factory owner replies that the goods are available because the workers have just produced them; the claim that is to be certified to them is precisely the consideration for this. The workers had created goods for more than 2 million marks and were now justifiably demanding the certification of their well-earned right to other goods worth 2 million.
But the state office does not agree with this line of thought. According to them, the question of whether goods worth 2 million Marks were really created by the workers' efforts would only be decided at the moment of sale. It could then

turn out that the goods had only half the value or no value at all and were unsaleable. At the moment - to give a figure - there are 100 million marks in circulation. The holders of these money tokens, which changed every hour, had a certified claim to all the goods currently on the market. There was no other way to get possession of one of these goods - apart from theft - than by handing over a part of the existing 100 million marks in money tokens, the holders of which were in fact the only entitled purchasers of those market goods. If the state office wanted to certify the required millions of new claims, then instead of 100 million marks, 102 million of these stamps would be in circulation and would lay claim to those market goods, which were only intended for 100 million.

This could not even be the case if the new products produced by the workers really and demonstrably had a value of 2 million marks. In this case, however, there would be an increase of 2 million not only on the money side but also on the goods side. But the example would not work. On the contrary, the situation would be as follows:

At present, the total quantity of goods that comes onto the market within a certain period of time, the value of which we would like to put at 10 billion Marks, is matched by a total stock of monetary tokens, i.e. claims on goods, amounting to 100 million Marks. These 100 million change their owners on average 100 times in the same period. When the period has expired and the circulation of money has ended, the 100 million marks of money tokens have consumed 100 times 100 million marks or 10 billion marks of goods. So up to this point the calculation works out perfectly. But if 2 million are added to the money side and 2 million to the goods side, the calculation reads:

10 billion + 2 million goods =
100 million + 2 million money tokens.

Thus, there are now 10,002 million marks of goods for 102 million marks of money, i.e., for every unit of money there are no longer 100 but only about 98 units of goods. In other words, the old money has experienced a reduction in its purchasing power as a result of the certification of the 2 million marks of workers' subscription rights, i.e. as a result of the creation of 2 million marks of new money.

The reason for this, the state office instructs the factory owner, is that the 2 million marks of newly created goods only appear once on the market, satisfy a single claim to goods here and then disappear for good, dissolve into consumption. The 2 million new claims to goods, on the other hand, which we are to authenticate and recognise as fully-fledged money, live eternally, so to speak. They mediate one purchase after another, always enter the market anew with their purchasing power and thus perform their function not only a hundred times, as in the example just given, but a thousand times, a hundred thousand times, innumerable times. By recognising the 2 million marks of new money tokens, we would therefore have the effect that many billions of new claims to goods could be asserted little by little, while the goods on the basis of which we are to certify the claims, as I said, are only sufficient to cover a one-off claim of 2 million marks.

Therefore, says the state office, we can only certify the goods claim under two conditions. Firstly, it must be proven to us that the performance on the basis of which instructions for counter-performance are issued, i.e. new subscription rights, new money tokens, are created, has actually produced goods that are worth 2 million marks and remain worth 2 million marks. Secondly, these goods of stable value must be handed over to us in kind. For if we are to demand of the people that they recognise the new subscription rights and surrender valuable products in exchange, we must give them the certainty that they can exchange the subscription right at any time for a good of full value. We must guarantee her that she will always exchange a full 100 units of goods for 100 units of money and not, as in our example, only 98 units of goods, or even, as is now the case in Germany, a paltry 6 or 8 units of goods.

Therefore, the goods that correspond to the new 2 million mark money tokens are to be handed over to us. We shall then either put our stamp on these goods ourselves and thereby make them into money-marks; in this case we have the guarantee that the goods will appear on the market just as often as the money-marks, that is, a hundred times, a thousand times, innumerable times, satisfy the demand, and not only once; and every money-holder will then know that he cannot suffer any loss, because he has in his hands the value in which the money is denominated in the form of a good of equal value. Or else, in order to prevent the goods from wearing out, we shall take them into custody and replace them for circulation by paper tokens. These will then circulate, as it were, by proxy of the goods, which, however, will remain the property of the holders of those paper money tokens and can be withdrawn from them at any time. At present, by the way - says the state office - only one commodity is considered suitable to provide proof of a full-value service and to justify the certification of a new claim to consideration, namely gold. And this for the purely external reason that the decisive part of foreign countries only pays a fixed minimum price for this metal and thereby guarantees its value.

The factory owner shrugs his shoulders and leaves. For he has no gold. So, in order to satisfy his workers, he must of necessity sell stock goods at a loss, i.e. procure old circulating money tokens, and do without new money. The economic meaning of this process is that only those have a claim to a service in return (in this case the workload of

10,000 workers) who have either already performed something themselves and therefore have money, i.e. a legal claim to the corresponding service in return, or to whom a third party assigns his legal claim by way of credit. It is economic nonsense to demand of the state that it should certify the legal claims which the individual businessman does not know how to acquire through performance, i.e. claims which he does not in reality have, and hand over new money to the man, for instance against a bill of exchange. 'Legal claims' created in this way are in truth illegitimate claims, and the money that represents them is counterfeit money. It is the service that creates money, not the state. The state has no other task than to confirm the emergence of money from performance by its seal.

Is it any wonder, my dear James, that this natural, non-state theory of money, which sees in money neither a pledge nor an order, but a right acquired through services, has never been to the liking of merchants? The merchant always believes he has a God-given claim to even more money, to even more rights to goods, than he has bought through his services. He believes that there is 'too little' money in the country - although everywhere there is as much money, i.e. as many legal claims to goods, as one has known how to acquire - and therefore demands of the state that it hand over new money, new rights to purchase, in exchange for the promise of later repayment. He does not know that the state cannot do this, and unfortunately very often the state itself does not know either. Both the merchant and the state believe that new rights, new rights to goods have arisen as soon as the state or its bank has fresh notes printed that resemble the previous money. In reality, however, no new rights have been created, but parts have been broken out of the legal rights embodied in the old money in circulation and these parts have been lent to the recipients of the new money. One has expropriated the holders of the real money by exactly as much as one has given to the holders of the pseudo-money. There is no longer any question of 'right' here, but only of blatant injustice. Real money, which respects the existing legal rights and represents an increase in the honestly acquired rights to goods, an actual increase in purchasing power, can only ever come into being in the way the apocryphal state agency said in the aforementioned dialogue with the employer: A performance must have taken place in traffic life, out of which a good has arisen that carries in itself the guarantee of the greatest possible stability of value. Only that claim to goods which refers back to this special good is genuine, full-value, legally created money.

With love

Your old dad.

Seventh Letter

*The many goods and the little money
Useful run, idle run and price
Production strength and money supply*

Berlin, January 15th 1921

Money is synonymous with the securitised right that its owner has to a certain part of all market goods. In a sense, it is the key according to which all market goods are distributed among people. A lot of money means the right to a large fraction of the goods, little money means the right to a small part.

This is so clear, my dear James, that a child can understand it. Less clear, however, is the mechanics of the distribution process. For example, it is strange to us that on the one hand we see an enormous stock of goods, but on the other hand only a relatively small stock of money. This is all the more strange to us because the enormous stock of goods is replenished every day, since fresh quantities of goods are constantly flowing onto the market, while the far smaller stock of money always remains more or less the same under normal conditions. How does the distribution work? How does the small money supply cope with the large quantities of goods, and what mechanism ensures that each individual gets his right, namely his right to goods embodied in the money tokens?

Seen from above, this also seems to be quite clear. For even if the money tokens are only relatively small in number, they multiply through their great mobility. Just a moment ago, one saw how they handled the turnover of goods at a certain point in the traffic, and already one sees them at another point, where they are again about to mediate turnover. The same money tokens appear here and there, and wherever they may be, they always distribute new quantities of goods. The quicker they change hands, the more mobile they are, the more efficient they are; just as a small but effective troop achieves more than a large but cumbersome army. For the effectiveness of the money tokens, therefore, it is not so much their number that is decisive, but rather the frequency of their change of place, their so-called 'speed of circulation.'

But what does this actually mean? Does it give us any insight into the meaning of economic processes if we know that the turnover of market goods is as large as the money supply multiplied by its velocity of circulation? Can we draw any reliable conclusion from this fact? Can we conclude, for example, that every increase in the velocity of circulation corresponds without further ado to a corresponding increase in the exchange of goods and in production? If this were the case, we would have a splendid and most simple means of increasing turnover and stimulating the economy: We would only have to let the money roll rather quickly, that is, to let the wage payments to the workers take place daily instead of weekly and the payment of rent and capital interest take place fortnightly instead of quarterly. The egg of Columbus!

But unfortunately, trade and change cannot be revived in such a simple way. It is true that there are naive people who really believe that the 'lack of moneywhich ' they perceive could be eliminated by making the money signs do their work more quickly, and for this reason it has often been suggested that wages, rents and interest payments should be made in shorter periods. In reality, however, no one would gain any advantage from such a measure. Neither the worker nor the employer, neither the tenant nor the landlord, neither the creditor nor the debtor would be enriched by a single penny. If there were any financial effect at all, it could only be an unfavourable one: The amounts of wages, rent and interest would shrink so much that it would no longer be worth while to give them to the bank before paying them out or after receiving them, i.e. to let them have a productive effect. Instead, the sums would idly accumulate in the safes and wallets.

The fact that the mere speed of circulation of money is not important is best seen, by the way, if one visualises the circulation of money on the so-called capital market and on the stock exchange. Nowhere does money circulate faster than here. In times of speculative excitement, a share can change hands ten times or more in one day, triggering corresponding payments. But does this rapid turnover of money have the slightest economic effect? No. This is not to say that the money market and the stock exchange are useless institutions. But the benefit they create has nothing to do with the speed of circulation of money.

As you see, my son, it does not depend on how often and how fast the money circulates, but on whether it circulates 'in useful circulation' or 'in idle circulation'. If the farmer brings grain to market, or the craftsman delivers his work, the movement of money which this process triggers is useful circulation. But if a speculator sells shares, or a house broker arranges the change of ownership of a villa, it is a case of money idling. In a healthy economy, money does not need to circulate excessively fast if it only conveys economic benefits in the largest possible number of transactions.
Whether this happens or not, however, never depends on money. Neither the quantity nor the turnover figure of money determines whether the acts of payment it mediates are useful or harmful or neutral. How could that be possible? Money is nothing more than a securitised right, a right

to receive goods. This right arises from the fact that someone has done something and thereby acquired the right to something in return. Once the right exists, however, it can pass through innumerable hands without necessarily being connected with a service, an enrichment of the economy. The father can assign it to his son, the son can assign it to his friend, the latter can assign it to some lady. These are then three acts of circulation without any economic benefit. There must therefore necessarily be an element outside money which regulates its circulation and ensures that the rights of reference to goods represented in money change hands as frequently as possible in fulfilment of a productive purpose. And indeed such a regulator exists. It fills the whole economy with its effectiveness, and not a day goes by in which each of us does not encounter it several times. This regulator is the price.

It is very easy to see in which way the price performs its regulating function. One need only ask the question: When does the capitalist buy shares? When does he buy a villa? In other words, when does the holder of a right to purchase goods use it unproductively, by appropriating long-existing values, instead of using it productively, i.e., having the values in question produced anew and thereby enriching the economy? The answer then is: He will acquire shares in an existing enterprise (stocks) if these are cheaper in terms of earnings than the shares in an enterprise that is first to be built, and he will buy a finished villa if this is cheaper for him than a newly built one. Of course, the possible comforts of immediate possession of old properties are just as much a factor in weighing up the price as the advantages (modernity, longer life) of new properties. If, taking these factors into account, the price of a share in a new enterprise or the price of a newly built villa is lower than the price of the old objects, the capitalist will be inclined to build or have built, i.e. to use his money 'productively'.

Most people, as we know, are not satiated capitalists, but people who are forced to 'earn their money'; that is, people who have to buy their entitlement to the goods they need to live through services. The environment, however, as we have seen, only has a use for its services if they are offered at a price which - taking into account all the factors involved - is cheaper than the price of the old, 'fossilised' services which are offered in the form of movable and immovable stocks. New and old production are thus in constant competition with each other. I recall a well-known example: How anxiously the American cotton farmer studies the annual statistical reports on world cotton stocks! Why? Because he knows perfectly well that the price he will be offered depends entirely on the price and quantity of cotton from the previous year's harvest. More or less all producers are in the same situation. They must keep their price, i.e. their claim to consideration, below a very definite level. If they do not, large amounts of money circulate in the 'idle run' instead of the 'useful run,' and productivity in the country shrinks.

The price thus attracts money to the market of newly produced goods when it is low, and it repels money from this market when it is high. In the former case it increases, in the latter it reduces the real, effective velocity of circulation of money. Producers must therefore produce 'cheaply'; they must give a large consideration for every claim that has arisen from a service and is handed over to them in the form of money. This means nothing other than: They must produce a lot if they want to increase the effective velocity of circulation of money. What results from this? It follows that it is not the velocity of circulation of money that determines production but, conversely, production that determines the velocity of circulation of money.

Yes, there is more to it than that, and it is a very interesting fact. Since the producer, to the extent that he increases his production, attracts money to himself at an ever faster rate, he himself becomes more and more powerful in consumption. Every time the money passes through his till in accelerated circulation, he thereby comes into possession of new rights to the purchase of goods, which he can assert. If he has at first strengthened the external demand by his pricing and countered it with his supply, he now for his part strengthens the demand by exercising the right to consideration acquired through his performance, i.e. by spending the money he has taken in again. In this way he increases not only his own but the general production. The performances become ever greater and succeed each other ever more rapidly, and they generate claims to consideration, which likewise become ever greater and more frequent. But since a claim to consideration is nothing other than money, it follows that every increase in production itself procures the money necessary for its accomplishment. It procures it even if there is no externally perceptible increase in money tokens, and it does so by attracting and repelling the existing money tokens ever more rapidly, i.e. by increasing their speed of circulation.

In this way, the economy itself, without any outside intervention, without any state intervention, generates new money as soon as it needs it, and in exactly the quantity it needs. Anyone who says that there can ever be 'too much' or 'too little' money to manage the circulation of goods has recognised neither the nature of money nor the nature of the circulation of goods. Money circulation and goods circulation are quite simply identical, even if for reasons of convenience, above all because of easier proof of ownership, the abstract 'rights' to the circulating goods have been made into an independent, concrete economic factor, namely 'money'. To use an image: production and consumption are the piston of the economic machine that slides up and down, and money is the flywheel that is set in motion by the piston, sometimes slowly, sometimes quickly. This movement, called the speed of circulation, is regulated by the speed of the piston's movement. The piston, not the wheel, drives the machine. The wheel is only a technical expedient. It is more advantageous to let the piston act on the gear of the machine through the flywheel than directly. It is more advantageous, but not absolutely necessary. One can also divide the rights to goods among the population without the aid of money; that would then be a barter economy instead of a money economy.

But the barter economy is so cumbersome and, since the goods to be exchanged are almost never of equal value, so much needs to be supplemented by credit, which is warmly disliked in small-scale commerce (cf. my letter of January 2nd), that an exclusive barter economy does not exist anywhere and, in my opinion, has never existed.

Get it?

Your old dad.

Eight Letter

Working and resting money
The interest premium
Production and consumption

Berlin, January 17th 1921

When someone performs something, i.e. does work or gives away a good, he thereby acquires a claim to consideration, which takes the form of 'money'. He can deal with this claim in various ways. He can assert it immediately by spending the money again and in turn procuring a good or a labour service for it, e.g. buying a watch or having a suit made. In this case, the money is returned to its purpose of mediating the turnover of goods; it does its service, it "Works" so to say. But the man can also act differently. He can leave the acquired claim to consideration unused in order to make use of it only on a later occasion, for example, to go on a trip next summer or to buy a rowing boat. In this case, the money lies idle in the cupboard until the summer. It does not mediate any turnover of goods, it does not work, and the purchasing power embodied in it remains unused. The purchasing power 'rests'.

If most people act like our man in the first example, i.e. immediately spend the money they earn again, the money supply in the country circulates very quickly. A lot of turnover takes place and there is a lot of activity. If, however, most people act as in the second example, leaving the money unused for a long time, the money circulates slowly, the turnovers are low, and commercial life pulsates weakly. It is therefore extremely important whether people are in the habit of using their acquired claims for consideration quickly or slowly, i.e. whether they keep the money they have collected for a short or long time.

But this habit is subject to certain laws. It is almost never purely arbitrary whether a community of people acts in one way or another, but depends on the peculiarity of the economy. A population which can count on the fact that a sum of money which it spends today will be collected again tomorrow, will not hesitate long with the expenditure, but will quickly let the money flow back into circulation. A population, on the other hand, which cannot count on a quick return of money, must economise with the money at hand, and will therefore spend it only gradually and hesitatingly. In other words: quick earnings spend, slow earnings save.

But the speed of earning is not a random phenomenon, but is also determined by economic laws. Every receipt of money, i.e. every claim to consideration, must be acquired through performance. Whoever performs much, money returns to him quickly; whoever performs little, it returns to him slowly. But it is not enough for the individual man himself to be intelligent and industrious in order for him to earn money quickly. The other men with whom he has to do in his working life, that is, all the members of the national community, must also be like him, they too must achieve much. For if they do not do this, they have nothing with which to pay for the work of the industrious man; they have nothing in return to reward his performance. The prerequisite for quick earnings and correspondingly quick circulation of money is therefore a general activity in the country, a large production of goods. And it is quite clear that the faster and the more the whole national community produces, the faster and the more each individual can consume.

The speed of circulation of money, i.e. the fact whether the individual monetary tokens remain for a long or short time in one and the same possessing hand, is not only decisive for the greater or lesser demand that prevails on the market and stimulates production, but it is at the same time in turn dependent on the degree of productivity in the country. Thus, basically, only the national productive power determines the speed and size of demand. Production determines consumption, and a rapid circulation of money, with much money 'working' and little money 'resting,' is only the outward sign of lively commercial activity. The impetus for this activity is provided by the mental and physical ability of the population to produce new goods with the least possible expenditure of energy and material, i.e. at a cheap price. And the price must be so cheap that it becomes advantageous for the population to no longer be content with the existing goods, such as houses, railways, ships, machines, etc., but to take up new goods in addition to these old ones. The increasing ability to cheapen production in this way is called 'progress'.

Therefore, 'work' and 'rest' of money depend on the state of national productivity. They are the 'object' not the subject of activity. But although this is 'so' there is a means of making them, at least outwardly and apparently, the subject of activity, thus influencing the economy from money. There is a means of 'enlivening' production by artificially converting 'dormant' money into 'working' money, i.e., by forcing money to perform an activity which it would not voluntarily perform. One can, for example, induce the man of whom we spoke earlier, who wanted to let his money rest for the purpose of a summer trip or the later purchase of a boat, to abandon his intention and put the money back into circulation, to make it work again immediately. The means by which this is effected is interest.
Interest is nothing more than the premium granted to the holders of dormant money in exchange for the interim assignment of the claim to property embodied in money,

which they themselves do not wish to assert for the time being, to third parties who intend to exploit it immediately. The introduction of interest, i.e. the lending fee for dormant claims to goods, into the economy is a most ingenious means by which the owners of money are compelled to exercise immediately the claims to goods which they possess, or to have them exercised, and thus to create a demand on the market which would otherwise be lacking. The coercion consists in appealing to human self-interest and usually proves very effective. For any owner of money who prevents his money from working and leaves it idle in the box is punished for it by losing the interest he would otherwise receive.

Here, however, one must be very careful not to fall victim to a serious error. For, in view of the intimate relationship between interest and money, it looks as if money were the real engine of the economy; an engine so important that one pays a regular and often very high fee for its use. But this is a deception of the eye. One strikes the sack and means the ass. One speaks of money and thinks only of the goods to which it confers a right of reference. This, by the way, can be seen quite clearly. If today I lend a manufacturer or a banker ten million marks in money tokens for one year, but attach to this the condition that he does not exercise the right to draw goods embodied in the money tokens, but leaves the money lying quietly, the manufacturer or the banker will not pay me a penny of interest for it. Why not? Simply because people do not care in the least about money itself, but all the more about the goods to which money grants a right, and which can only be obtained by giving the money away again, by bringing it to the market.

Strictly speaking, it is not even the goods themselves for which the borrower pays a fee, an interest. For if I wanted to dictate to the banker or manufacturer that he may only obtain this or that good for my ten million marks, for instance a house or a collection of coins, he will again not grant me any interest. He will not do this even if I leave the choice of goods to him, but require him to use the goods for consumption, e.g. to burn the wood he has bought or to consume the sugar he has bought. He only pays me the interest if I leave him the money for the purpose he has in mind. And this purpose is not directed towards the possession and consumption of a certain good, but towards the labour, towards the performance which the possession of the good makes possible for him. The textile industrialist, for example, does not pay me interest for my money because he can lay down so-and-so much woollen yarn for it. He has no interest whatsoever in the possession of this yarn, in its storage in his rooms. Rather, he pays me the interest because I enable him to perform a service with my money, namely to refine the chamois into cloth. The yarn, like the money, is only a means to an end. I receive the lending fee for making a service possible, and I receive it from the benefit that the service has for the general public. To be precise, I receive it in return for the fact that the industrialist, in return for his performance, earns more claims to goods than he owes me, by taking in more money than my ten million marks.

He cedes to me a part of the increase in goods by which he has enriched the world with his work, to which I have enabled him with my money.

The individual economist has therefore not yet completely fulfilled his duty if he has achieved a great deal and thereby acquired a claim to a great deal in return. In order to be a useful member of society, he must also assert the claim; he must draw the consideration or, if he cannot use it himself immediately, leave the drawing to a third party. If he does not do this, but keeps the claim in the form of money for years in order to exercise the right to receive goods only late or not at all, he cheats the economy as a whole and violates the meaning of monetary transactions, which is an exchange of performance and counter-performance. If the environment has taken his performance from him, it has a right to have its counter-performance taken from it. Otherwise it will look in vain for buyers for it on the market, and productivity will decline for lack of corresponding demand. 'He who works shall also eat. 'Those who produce should consume. Otherwise the economy will fall into disorder.

The economic instrument with which this danger of a stagnation in the economy is avoided is the interest rate, which places a premium on the immediate procurement of counter-performance, namely - how wisely the economy is set up - on the productive procurement of counter-performance, i.e. on the immediate procurement of goods which permit the use of labour and thereby increase the stock of goods in the country. On the other hand, interest also ensures that no more goods are produced than the consumption capacity justifies. If, for example, all money-holders were to refrain from receiving the consideration to which they are entitled in the form of consumable and expendable goods, but were, in order to earn interest, to cede in principle the whole consideration to the producers, production would very soon exceed the possibility of consumption. The producers would look in vain for buyers for their goods. That is why the interest rate, the premium for the surrender of the right to draw goods, rises as soon as productivity lags behind consumption, and it falls as soon as the reverse occurs. It then falls until the interest premium appears insufficient to the money holders, so that they prefer to consume themselves or at least no longer to increase production by granting rights to purchase goods.
So, as you can see, interest is a very important economic factor, dear James. It determines the pace and direction of production and aligns production and consumption. It attracts goods when it is high and repels them when it is low;

in this way it fills and empties the reservoirs from which national production draws the necessary motive forces. But these reservoirs are the money market and the banks.

With love

Your old dad.

Ninth Letter

*The condition of the money market
The property rights and the third hand*

Berlin, *20 January 1921*

We have become accustomed, dear James, to taking the money market for granted. We regard it as the indispensable meeting place where those who are in possession of temporarily expendable money seek and find people who have a use for this money and pay interest on it. Reduced to its actual economic sense, this means: The money market seems indispensable to us because anyone who has a subscription right to goods but does not yet want to exercise the subscription right has the opportunity here to assign it to third parties against a lending fee.

Here there are people who have a use for productive goods such as workshops, machines and manufactures, or for labour and raw materials from which workshops, machines and manufactures are made, and who, in return for his enabling them to obtain these things with his money, gladly grant him a share in their profit from production in the form of interest. What, we argue, should he do who possesses many rights to draw goods (has a lot of money), but is unable to use them himself, if there were no money market on which he could lend the rights, and no capital market on which the rights could be sold? (The difference between the money market and the capital market is usually ignored. It consists in the fact that on the money market money, i.e. rights to purchase goods, are lent for a certain period of time, whereas on the capital market the same money, the same rights to purchase goods, are definitely ceded, exchanged for so-called fixed assets, i.e. sold).

Nevertheless, the money market itself is dispensable. In a country where the social conditions of the population are fairly uniform, a money market is not needed, and if it exists nevertheless, it does not play a major role here. What is the need for a money market, for example, in an agrarian country where almost every inhabitant has his piece of land which feeds him today and which will feed his children in thirty years' time? He exchanges his products for money, i.e. for goods purchase rights, and then obtains the goods he needs in exchange. If he takes in a lot of money, he buys a lot of goods, otherwise he buys little. He has no reason not to exercise a part of the reference rights embodied in money, to systematically renounce the purchase of goods and to 'save the ' money. This can be different if, in the course of time, so much stranded property is concentrated in one hand that the owner takes in more money than he wants to or can spend on goods without wasting it. But then he easily finds a neighbour who takes the money from him and pays interest. He now possesses a capital, represented in a loan to the neighbour, i.e. in a mortgage. In such a country it is not necessary for the exchange of money on loan, the exchange of rights to draw goods, to be organised on a market basis.

Even in an industrially advanced country it can be the custom for every tradesman to exercise the right to purchase goods which he acquires with his products, that is to say, that he buys consumer goods for his money and uses any surpluses which exceed his needs to expand his business, or creates an existence for his children with it by setting up businesses for them. This patriarchal use of the reference rights represented in money only comes to an end when a very great inequality of property has become the rule. In countries where the population is divided into 'two nations', namely into a rich upper class which owns most of the land and all means of production, and an uprooted proletariat which has nothing or little except the labour of its hands, in such countries the use of money by the owner himself necessarily ceases.

The proletarian, who has no means of support in the form of his own property, and who must always fear that he will be left without earnings and means of subsistence in the event of old age or reduced capacity to work, and who also leaves no source of income to his relatives, must willy-nilly leave a part of his income unspent. For him it is: 'Save in time, and you shall have in time of need!' He must reserve rights to goods for his old age and his family if he does not want to act very frivolously. If he does not do it himself, the state must do it for him by way of social legislation. Both amount to the same thing. Property rights are withdrawn from immediate consumption by their owners, collected for later decades and lent to third parties until the time of their use. These are quite enormous sums, which are expressed in the statistics of the state insurance institutions, the savings banks, the small life insurance companies, etc.. Their movement requires an organisation, and this organisation is the money market.

A very similar change occurs in the opposite stratum of the population, among the big capitalists. Here, however, the causes are partly of a different nature. However, even in these circles, who are on the sunny side of life, there is an endeavour to build up reserves for the future; for in a country set up for industry and big capitalism, the business cycles change quickly, and a fall into the depths is quite within the realm of possibility for the individual. In the main, however, the renunciation of immediate and independent assertion of the rights to purchase goods is quite simply due to the fact that many more such rights accumulate in one and the same hand than can reasonably be utilised, much more money than can be spent for daily needs even with luxurious habits of life. To put the money into one's own business, however, as the farmer likes to do, is repugnant to the modern capitalist. He does not like to put all his eggs in one basket and, if he expands his enterprise very much, prefers to work with other people's money rather than with his own. The capitalist, too, and he in particular, needs a market in which he can dispose of his surplus rights to purchase goods for a shorter or longer period of time.

Thus we see that the money market is not at all a natural product, not an elementary economic phenomenon, but that it only becomes a need under very specific conditions. Today, however, this is the case in all cultural countries, because they have undergone a decidedly large-scale capitalist development in recent decades. Money must have a special market today, because on the one hand an ever greater surplus is seeking use, and on the other hand the need for a reserve for the future is becoming ever more urgent; both moments have the effect that the 'third hand' can no longer be dispensed with in the use of money.

In fact, each country not only has a money market, but also numerous small markets, each of which has an inflow and outflow to the large central market. The small markets are the banks. They are where the money of the 'two nations ' accumulates, primarily the surplus money of the capitalist circles flows to them. It is their task to look for the third hand which exploits the property rights embodied in the money so expediently that, over and above the interest to be paid to the owner, a high surplus is achieved for the national community. The use to which the productive goods are put and the direction in which they develop the economy of the country depend on their credit principles. For whether the banks themselves find the third hand which is to administer the goods and convert them into profitable capital, or whether they avail themselves of the cooperation of the great central market, the choice among those entitled to administer the goods is always left to them. This is the reason for the enormous responsibility of the banks and at the same time their position of power, which often makes them a state within the state.

Since the banks, by means of their credit sovereignty, show the way for economic development, they would actually have it in their hands to mitigate the alarming tendency which divides the population into two hostile social camps and thereby endangers the existence of the state. They would have it in their hands to direct the property rights given to them for distribution to such circles as do not cooperate in strengthening the proletariat. They could promote the industrial middle class and the handicrafts and thereby set limits to the rapid growth of big business. Unfortunately, however, the banks in most countries do not act in this way, but in precisely the opposite way. They feed the unspent surpluses of capital back to capital and thus strengthen the money-concentrating tendency which, while making the money market ever more indispensable and powerful, gradually undermines the roots of the state completely.

In part, selfish reasons play a role here. But to be fair, a considerable share of the blame lies with the state and its legislation. Since the banks administer entrusted property and are responsible for the integrity of the funds entrusted to them, not only for reasons of private law, but also because of their public position as masters of economic development in the country, they must focus on the aspect of security. The most suitable administrator of the money therefore always appears to them to be the one who offers the greatest guarantee of punctual repayment, and this is naturally the big capitalist. The little man does not offer such a guarantee, since the state laws, in the pursuit of humanity, protect the unreliable debtor to a large extent from persecution by the creditor. When the debt tower still existed, the craftsman and petty trader was a relatively safe debtor to whom credit was readily available. The threat of imprisonment made him cautious and a reliable steward of other people's money. Today, he is no longer threatened with debtors' prison, but he himself bears the damage, for he is now no longer creditworthy. This social act of legislation is like so many others: It slays those whom it seeks to protect and is therefore in reality antisocial to the highest degree.

This must not be completely disregarded when accusing the banks of pursuing a big-capitalist credit policy and acting according to the principle: 'To him who has, to him will be given. 'But one thing is certain: the current way of overfeeding capital, of capitalist inbreeding, so to speak, cannot be allowed to continue for much longer if the 'collapse of the West' is not to occur from within.
And there is another point on which the banks have to relearn; that is interest policy. Interest is that highly important factor in economic life which decides whether the rights to purchase goods embodied in money must be exercised in a productive or in a consumptive sense. The interest rate is the tipping point in the balance of the economy and indicates precisely whether the burden of production or of consumption must be relieved. If this index is abused, if production continues to be increased in defiance of it with the help of money centralised in the banks, although its shell has long since sunk, an economic crisis breaks out which could be avoided with the right policy. The real understanding of the symptoms of the business cycles is still too much replaced by schematism and routine in the bank offices today.

During the next few days, I must devote myself to the balance sheet of my bank, dear James. So don't be surprised if a little more than the usual time elapses between this letter and the next one.

    Sincerely

        Your dad

Tenth Letter

The principle of the central bank
The 'gold mania'
Money supply and one-third coverage
Central bank and conversion fund

Berlin, January 26th 1921

As old as money, dear James, is the complaint of people that there is 'too little money'. This is a misunderstanding that I dare not hope will ever completely disappear from the world. It will probably only ever be a very few people who realise that 'too little money' is an absurdity. Money is the scale according to which the available goods are distributed among the population, and one can only increase the individual portions of goods by increasing the quantity of goods, but not by lengthening the scale. Whoever complains that he has too little money, in reality complains only that he has not sold enough goods or services and has therefore only been able to procure a small portion of the available quantity of goods. This can be a question of personal inability or a question of social injustice, but never a question of the amount of money.

But since the masses do not realise this, they demand that the state produce more currency tokens, and the state recognises this demand as fundamentally justified by setting up central banks which are to issue currency tokens 'as needed'. In doing so, of course, it sets certain limits to the creative activity of the banks. But if his recognition of the public demand for money already makes us smile wistfully, because it is based on an error, the 'limits' he sets for the demand seem completely humorous. For the state herewith grafts a second error onto its first.

How the two errors came about is transparent enough. In the course of the centuries, the state, wizened by damage, has come to the realisation that not every money really fully guarantees the claim to goods represented in it, i.e. that it is 'stable in value'. Rather, he recognised that only money that either consists of precious metal (gold) or can be exchanged for this precious metal at any time has the property of stable value. However, the reason for this fact has remained hidden from him. He sees in it only the outflow of a human whim of a prejudice. He attributes the stable value of gold money or gold-backed money to the fact that people consider only money for which they can receive the full equivalent value in the noble world metal at any time to be of genuine value. Even if this is only a fad, which probably stems from the traditional overestimation of precious metals, it should nevertheless be taken into account and, if possible, only such money should be issued that can be exchanged for metal at any time at the request of its holder.

But this is a mistake. The actual superiority of gold money - in the eastern part of the world of silver money - has a far deeper cause than the whim or obstinacy of the great masses. The relative stability of value of gold money is rather due to the fact that the production of such money is beyond the arbitrary power of the state. Gold money can only come into being when gold is produced and brought to the market, i.e. when something is done. The requirement that performance and only performance gives rise to money is ideally fulfilled in the case of gold money (or money fully backed by gold). Such money can never produce more than is justified and needed by human intercourse, which exchanges performance for performance. And since the quantity of money, or the relation between this quantity and the services, decides on the purchasing power, on the 'value' of the money, gold money, in which the quantity or the relation cannot undergo any arbitrary shift, is stable in value.

Exactly as stable in value, however, would be any other money that arises exclusively from performance, that is, that is produced by circulation itself and is not forced upon circulation from outside according to any principles whatsoever.

As I said, the state does not recognise this. It believes in a fixed idea of the people, in a kind of 'gold mania,' and now tries to take this prejudice into account through a certain monetary policy. It therefore authorises the central banks to fulfil the people's demand for 'more money' on the condition that the notes issued are covered to a certain extent by gold. The quantity of notes could be as high as desired, provided that there was always enough gold available to satisfy those note holders who, in their 'gold mania', wished to obtain metal for once. Since experience shows that in normal times on average only every tenth or fifth, at most every third noteholder demands gold in exchange for his notes, it is sufficient if the metal stock amounts to one third of the total amount of notes issued. If this condition was fulfilled, the banks could calmly put into circulation any quantity of notes that corresponded to the 'need for circulation'; the latter could best be seen from the number of commercial bills of exchange submitted to the banks for discounting.
All existing central banks have emerged from this train of thought.

The principle is the same everywhere, even if at one bank the presence of 40 per cent gold instead of 33 per cent is made a condition, at another bank again some numerical moderate maximum limit is set for the notes to be issued; a maximum limit which is almost regularly raised as soon as the 'need for circulation' seems to demand it. The privilege of all central banks is thus based on the twofold error that the 'value' of money has nothing to do with the amount of money in circulation in the country, and that only gold, or the possibility of exchanging it for gold, gives money its stability of value. Whereas in reality it is just the other way round: Gold as such has no influence on the 'value of money,' whereas the money supply has the sole influence.

That is why, my dear fellow, all central banks without exception have failed as soon as they wanted to put it to the test and make a considerably increased quantity of notes available for circulation - for instance in war or in a crisis. Their notes then immediately lost a part of their purchasing power, and the note-holders besieged the banks to exchange the notes for gold, because only this international money, which could not be increased arbitrarily, retained its value. (It retained its value not because it was gold, but because it was the only money that could not be arbitrarily increased and was, above all, an international money).

It soon became apparent that the gold one-third cover was not sufficient to satisfy all claims, and therefore the exchange was stopped and the redemption of notes in gold was suspended. This means breaking a solemn promise made to the people and has only ever been resorted to after other, milder means had failed. Before that, they either tried a little trickery by handing out old, worn-out and no longer fully important pieces to the note holders instead of full-value gold coins, thus depriving them of part of their gold claim, not to harm them but to deter them. Or they tried the shame pole: they declared every noteholder who made gold claims on the central bank at this critical moment to be a traitor to the fatherland. In fact, however, all these means were already a veiled breach of law and the first step on the way to an outright, open suspension of gold payments.

In some countries, governments have gradually realised that the whole principle of central banking is based on a faulty knowledge of the monetary system. But England alone of all the European states has mustered the energy to break with the principle. There, in 1844, the famous Peels Act stipulated that no new notes were to be put into circulation apart from those then in circulation. Henceforth new notes were to be issued only against gold; for each note its full amount in gold was to be deposited with the bank. In other words: It was no longer the state or the banks privileged by it, but the circulation, as it is in the nature of things, that should create new money; the state or the bank should henceforth confine themselves to stating the fact that gold had been created by the handing over of gold, i.e. by a service, by means of an embossed stamp or by means of a gold certificate (banknote).

Because England in this way eliminated the bank as the creator of money and created a money for itself that was born out of living circulation, the country had the best money in the world until the great war, the only money that was really stable in value. But when, during the war, the creation of money was once again made a matter for the state and its printing press, and new signs of money were imposed on circulation that did not originate from the state itself, the full value of the claim to goods represented in money was, of course, a thing of the past.

From this it follows, dear James, that a bad, money-spitting bank of issue is harmful, but a good one is superfluous. For the mechanical task of certifying the money created in circulation can be performed by any mint. It also seems as if this realisation is beginning to germinate here and there, less in Europe than in South America. There, some states, when they started to rehabilitate their monetary systems, deliberately refrained from founding central banks and instead set up 'conversion coffers', i.e. coffers that merely authenticated the creation of new money by issuing certificates for deposited gold that circulated in circulation like gold itself. Vox populi, which always cries for 'more money', is not satisfied with this, however, and since there are domestic political moments when one has to follow the 'street', it is questionable how long, for example in Argentina, reason will prevail in monetary matters.

And we in Europe? We have paid such an expensive lesson in recent years that we should actually gradually come up to the level of Argentinean realisation. But my hopes are not very high in this respect. We talk too much and think too little.

    With love

        Your old dad.

Eleventh Letter

Cashless payment transactions
'Giro money'
Invisible inflation

Berlin, January 28th 1921

The terrible effect, dear James, which an arbitrary increase in money has on the 'value of money', i.e. on the size of the claim to goods embodied in money, is usually only recognised rather late. The effect must already be quite profound, the deterioration of money must have reached an ominous degree, before the state or the central banks admit that the devaluation of money is a consequence of their own wrong monetary policy. But once they have recognised this and publicly admitted the connection between the devaluation of money and so-called 'inflation', something happens that could be called amusing if it did not have such serious consequences. The state or the central bank then try to mitigate inflation in a very specific way, in a way that clearly shows that one can suspect the connection between monetary debasement and inflation and still have very amateurish views about money.

The central bank - let us leave the state out of it for once - argues as follows: There is no doubt that it was a mistake to issue such large quantities of banknotes and thereby weaken the value of money. It would therefore be necessary to attempt to withdraw a part of the banknotes, but in such a way that no holder of a banknote suffers a loss as a result. Cashless payment transactions are best suited for this purpose. The holders of the withdrawn banknotes are credited with the equivalent value in an account and are induced to make their payments no longer in cash, i.e. with banknotes, but by means of a transfer from their own account to the account of the other bank customers. In this way, all parties win: the traffic gets rid of part of the excessive circulation of notes, which has a favourable effect on the value of money; the bank shows correspondingly fewer notes in its statements, which silences the criticism; and the bank customers who have exchanged their notes for an account enjoy the advantages of the transfer traffic compared to the cash traffic. Everyone has an advantage, no one has a loss. Probatum est.

That is why, my dear son, you will always hear the praise of cashless payments sung when inflation and monetary distress have reached a high level. With pleas and threats, with enlightening writings and with the well-known imperatives ('Pay cashless!!!' 'Promote remittances' 'Fight inflation!'), the public is urged to hand in their banknotes and have an account opened for them, either with the central bank itself or with another bank which in turn has non-cash dealings with the central bank. In fact, the propaganda is usually successful. The private credit balances at the banks, the bank credit balances at the central bank experience a considerable increase, which clearly shows how much banknotes would have had to be issued if the public did not now often pay by cheque and transfer instead of banknotes.

Only one thing remains missing, and that is - success. The fact that so many billions of notes can be withdrawn or do not need to be spent, because the traffic now uses the account for its payments, does not have the slightest effect on the value of money and on prices. And one wonders with concern what mistake has been made again. For since it is certain that only the excessive number of banknotes is to blame for the deterioration of money and the identical inflation, the reduction in the number of notes must lead to an improvement in money and a reduction in prices. As a rule, however, no good reason is found, but in the end the view is reached that not enough has been done in the field of cashless transactions. There must be much more non-cash payment, the banknote must gradually disappear completely from large-scale traffic. And the propaganda starts again: 'Pay cashless!'

As I said, this would be very amusing if it did not show in such a frightening way at what a low level the knowledge of money and its laws still stands, even when one has finally understood the connection between inflation and monetary distress. For, to put it briefly, my dear fellow: the whole idea of wanting to fight inflation by promoting cashless circulation is hare-brained nonsense. Cashless transport may be a very useful institution under certain circumstances (by no means always!). But it cannot counter inflation for one very simple reason, namely because it is - itself - a part of inflation.

Money, it cannot be said often enough and loudly enough, is not only identical with the monetary signs that one encounters in traffic. In its essence, money is nothing material at all, but something abstract: a right to purchase goods. Whether this right is embodied in gold bars, in coins, in cash notes, in bank notes, or finally in current account balances, is completely irrelevant. The only thing that matters is that there are only so many rights to draw goods as the traffic with its daily services and counter-services generates from itself. Every note and every current account balance that comes into being in this natural way is good, sound money. And every note, every sight deposit arbitrarily created by the state or a bank is surplus, bad money. Whether the arbitrarily issued banknotes are left to circulate quietly or whether they are withdrawn and replaced by book credits, so-called 'giro money', is of no importance. Or have the wrongfully issued rights to goods been eliminated because they no longer pass from hand to hand in physical notes but in incorporeal giro money? Will even one single iota of purchasing power in the country be exercised less if payment is made in non-cash instead of cash? And that is what matters: Less purchasing power must be exercised if one wants to reduce the price of goods or, which is the same thing, increase the 'value of money'.

If one wants to prove the illogicality of an idea, it is always good to pursue the idea to its last consequences. Let us therefore imagine that the appeal made to the public by the governments and the central banks would have the extraordinary success that all payments, except the very smallest, would no longer be made in cash but in giro transactions. All banknotes exceeding 50 centimes or 2 marks would be withdrawn, thereby restricting the circulation of money by nine tenths or even more. What would be the consequence? Would a single demand therefore cease to exist? Would the current accounts, which the central bank now grants anew to civil servants and state suppliers, have a different effect on the volume of traffic and on the prices of all goods than notes did before?

And let us imagine, to go to the end, that a draconian law forbids all cash payments without exception, thus forcing small-scale traffic to pay with postal cheques, just as large-scale traffic now pays with bank cheques: What would be the consequence? The banknotes that would have to be submitted to establish a postal cheque account or a bank account could now, however, be stamped without exception. Visible money would disappear, and with it visible inflation. But we would have exchanged nothing but invisible money and invisible inflation. Traffic would buy, deliver and pay in exactly the same way as before, except that the individual payment would no longer be made by handing over a monetary token but by a book entry. Technically everything would have changed, factually absolutely nothing.

So be careful when assessing cashless payments!

There is much abuse of it and many errors are associated with the propaganda for it. Money is money, even if it appears incorporeally. Yes, it comes even closer to the actual concept of money in the form of the bank deposit, in the form of 'Giralgeld', than in the physical form of the coin or the note. For it is only now, when it stands as a claim in a book and is 'credited' as a transfer sometimes to this, sometimes to that, that the true character of money as an abstract right, a right to receive goods, emerges clearly; whereas hitherto there has always been a confusion between this right and its physical representative, between the money itself and the money tokens.

With love

Your old dad.

Twelfth Letter

Effects of monetary degradation
Inflation and morality
Spillovers of currency and economic life

Berlin, January 31st 1921

It is a well-known phenomenon, dear James, that in a house where a seriously ill person is lying, usually only one person does not realise the full seriousness of the illness, namely the sick person himself. He thinks he is quite well as soon as he has a little appetite. Like this sick person, so it is with the people who are ill with money, who suffer from the decay of their currency: Because they eat, drink and do business as before, they believe that things cannot be so bad for them; the decline in the value of money is admittedly unpleasant and has many evil consequences, but after all there are more serious diseases for a people. If one looks at the matter in the light of day, the whole question of currency is basically only a harmless example of multiplication. One simply has to multiply all one's expenditures by 10 or 100 or 1000, according to the devaluation of money or the increase in prices. Objectively, this means nothing, because every expenditure of one is an income of the other, and therefore the income also increases by 10, 100 or 1000 times. One only has to get used to adding a zero to all numbers in traffic life.

One can hear this harmless view expressed many times. And indeed: Does it do a nation much harm if it calculates with the large multiplication table instead of the small one, and if all its turnovers increase tenfold? After all, there is ten times as much money in the country as there used to be to cope with the turnover. The inflation of all figures is the result of this enormous increase in money.

This harmlessness, my son, cannot be countered strongly enough, for the ignorance that expresses itself in it borders on the criminal. It is bad enough when a nation slides down the slippery slope of inflation in clueless recklessness. But if it then blithely ignores the consequences of this slide or tries to see the best side of them instead of taking hold of the reins of the state and putting the brakes on in time, then the people are hastening towards their doom. For, to put it in meagre words, the decline of its currency is probably the greatest misfortune that can befall a nation. Even a lost war does not bring it such serious immediate damage as the ruin of its monetary system.

The people who see in the whole question only a trivial arithmetical experiment overlook some accompanying moments of the decline of the currency. Above all, they overlook one significant circumstance: the devaluation of money, i.e. the multiplication of expenditure, affects the whole. The counterpart to this, the increase in income, however, benefits only a fraction of the population, and this fraction, of course, to such an extent that the relationship between income and expenditure improves extraordinarily. And it is mainly capital, in so far as it possesses material assets, which profits in this way. On the other side, however, which only learns about the moment of the increase in expenditure from the devaluation of money, are, apart from the pensioners, who are particularly severely damaged, mainly the mentally and physically working classes, the civil servants and the state pensioners.

How it is that some perceive inflation as a never-recurring stroke of luck, while others perceive the same inflation as a catastrophe, cannot be explained in a few words. The mechanism that brings this about is rather complicated. But if one wants to sketch the process roughly, one can probably say: Everyone who possesses claims expressed in money, such as interest, pension, salary, wage, pension and the like, is harmed to the extent of the deterioration of money. Anyone who owns certain real assets, such as real estate, livestock, furniture, stocks, etc., is normally neither harmed nor benefited, because the real assets rise in price by approximately the same amount as the money in which the price is expressed loses purchasing power. (Forcible harm, such as that done to homeowners by the state's housing policy, is not considered here.) Finally, everyone who owns advertising values, i.e. factories and machines, and produces real values with them, as well as everyone who sells these products, profits from inflation; and this because the selling prices of his products, i.e. his income, adapt themselves faster to the falling value of money, i.e. rise faster than his expenses for wages, rent, interest, taxes, etc., and because this favourable relation appears not once, but many times, with each act of sale anew. In short, the first class is expropriated by inflation in favour of the third class.

Now one could take the view that compassion is not a matter of economics and that one should not view the process through the lens of sentimentality. One rises high, the other sinks low, that's just human fate. What matters is not the individual, but the whole. But this is precisely where the catch is: although these processes seem to affect only certain classes of people, it is the totality that suffers the most serious damage.

First of all, from a moral point of view: In the whole nation, even if it is straightforwardness and honesty itself, every sense of right and fairness is gradually disappearing. Namely, because all classes, even the inflationary profiteers, believe themselves cheated by the state. And indeed, we know that money is a right, namely a right to obtain goods of a very definite value. And what is law must, as is well known, remain law in a state of order. No right, however, must stand more securely and last longer than the right of possession, which is embodied in money, for in trusting in its existence, states and peoples conclude sacred treaties which are valid for 100 years and more. This right, this right of all rights, has been grossly violated by the state, which has decimated the value of money through inflation. Every worker, every civil servant, every pensioner feels cheated out of his or her rights by the state, which is supposed to protect them. But also the beneficiaries of the deterioration of money, who, so to speak, feed off the fat of the general public, feel that their rights are threatened by the state, because the state demands from them the taxes that it needs in order to alleviate, at least to some extent, the misery for which they themselves are responsible. Since only a few of the beneficiaries know the real connection between their income and the misfortune of others, and most of them attribute it to their own efficiency, which is only the effect of inflation, they regard it as an act of violence and a disenfranchisement when the state wants to tax away part of their profits. Hence the general 'tax evasion' in which the legal confusion of the inflationary profiteers is expressed. The confusion of rights of the victims of inflation is expressed in disobedience, violation of the law, refusal to work, theft, and finally revolution and murder. This leads to a struggle of all against all, which shakes the state and often enough causes it to disintegrate.

For when we see today that the injustice inflicted by inflation on the workers, the civil servants, the employees, etc., has been made good to a greater or lesser extent by wage and salary increases, - how has this been achieved? Only through struggles, through unceasing, bitter, ruthless struggles. Compensation between the beneficiaries and the victims of inflation never takes place voluntarily; compensation must be fought for step by step through strikes, threats, inflammatory speeches, whipping up the popular passions. Today the worker fights against the employer, tomorrow the peasant against the townspeople, the day after tomorrow the townspeople against the 'usurious' merchant, the tenant against the landlord, and so on.

The whole country is breaking up into innumerable trouble spots, and each of these trouble spots means a fire hazard for the state. This is the social and political side of the deterioration of money.

As you know, dear James, I have an archive in my library room to which I add newspaper reports about important or interesting events. Anyone who takes a look at this archive, specifically at the heading 'Money, Currency,' looks at me with astonishment. For under this heading he will find reports about strikes, coups, railway robberies, robbery, defraudation, suicide, usury, death by starvation and many other things that do not seem to belong here at all. Yet it all belongs there. For the effects of monetary misery break through at the seemingly most remote points of the economic body.

For example, I read something about a housing shortage. Where to put it? Under 'money'. Because the state's rent policy, which prevents the building of new houses, is the necessary consequence of the expropriation of half the people through the devaluation of money. I read something about a 16 billion deficit of the railways. Where to? Under 'money'. For the deficit stems partly from the fact that the railways have to pay their civil servants, who have been damaged by inflation, high wages, and that on the other hand the larger, expropriated part of the population cannot pay the corresponding fares and goods tariffs.

I read something about coal shortages: not under 'spa,' but under 'money'! I read something about child poverty. Not

'Versailles,' but 'money'! I read something about waste efforts of the Rhineland. Not 'Over there', but 'money'!

Corruption, forced economy, racketeering, moral brutalisation - everything comes under the heading of 'money'. So, I look at the effects of a currency that has fallen into disrepair. There is hardly an area of the national economy, even of politics, that can escape these effects.
Bad money is, I repeat, about the greatest misfortune that can befall a nation. The outcome of the World War, which was so unfortunate for Germany, is certainly a catastrophe such as a nation experiences only once every few hundred years. And yet I don't know which is more disastrous for Germany at the moment, the tragedy of war or the comedy of money. Admittedly, the disastrous political and economic consequences of the war will remain for a long, long time; the devaluation of money and its effects, on the other hand, will pass or at least in a few decades will no longer be felt in all their severity; the grandson of the man who was expropriated today grows up as a proletarian and thinks it has to be that way.

But today, monetary misery is Germany's most terrible scourge, although it is perhaps some consolation that other countries also feel this scourge.

So, my dear James, now you know what 'money' is! It is by no means all you need to know before you are ready for the post of bank director, that is, a bank director as I imagine it. It is merely the entrance gate to banking, to the money market, to the stock exchange, to entrepreneurship, which I have opened for you in the series of letters that I have ended herewith; and even only half-opened, because we have so far only spoken about the money in the country itself, about the so-called 'internal value' of money, not about the 'external value,' the currency. God willing, we will soon make up for this omission.

So I declare the first lesson over and lay down my pen.

   In old love

      Your dad.

Part II: Valuta

First Letter

The economic multiplication table
External value and internal value of money Abnormalities

Berlin, September 1st 1921

Two wonderfully beautiful summer months lie behind us, dear James. I do not remember in all my life such a long string of blue and gold radiant days. Unconcerned about the worried look of the farmer and equally indifferent to the satisfied smirk of the fruit grower, the sun has blazed down, obedient to some law of nature that we do not know. We took refuge in the shade, we fought the embers with water where we could. But we have not been able to force the fireball to dampen its rays, we have not been able to command the winds to draw a protective curtain of clouds in front of the burning light. We have been able to subordinate ourselves humbly to the higher power, to adapt ourselves wisely to the facts: that is all we have been able to do.

Most people also realise this and make no attempt to grind themselves up in a useless struggle with nature. They do not rebel against the laws which they have recognised as eternal and unchangeable. But why do they act so sensibly only in the field of the forces of nature, and not also in the economic field? Why do they believe they can dictate the direction of development by arbitrary interventions and measures of force as they see fit? Why do they deliberately overlook the fact that the economy, too, has its eternal laws, to which there is no other wisdom than subordination and adaptation? Is our economic science really still in such infancy that it believes it can act imperatively and dictate to the state: 'Do this and do not do that, so that this or that undesirable consequence of certain causes disappears'? Instead of starting from millennia-old knowledge and saying: 'The laws of economics infallibly cause this cause to produce that effect. Pay attention to this causal connection, respect it, act according to it, avoid the cause if you don't want the effect, but don't miss wanting to change the connection and bend it in a direction that suits you. 'Economic development, too, has its one-time rule and does not ignore those who violate the principle that 'two times two is four'.

In the letters which I wrote to you at the beginning of this year, I tried to make clear to you how grossly almost all European governments have violated the iron law of economics, according to which the goods coupons which we call 'money' can arise solely from the traffic which produces and distributes the goods. I have shown you how the superstition that it is the state which creates money, and that it is up to the state to decide on the kind and quantity of money, has taken its most disastrous revenge, in that the value of money has sunk deeply, in many cases to the bottomless pit, through this presumption on the part of the state to want to play creator: that a large part of the population has thereby been deprived of possessions, that is to say, has been dispossessed or robbed, depending on the opinion: that almost all our social struggles, with their attendant symptoms of political incitement, public immorality, general unscrupulousness in acquisition, epidemic robbery and murder, are a consequence of this disregard for economic laws: Indeed, even the German Revolution of 1918 was largely due to this disregard, because the arbitrary manipulation with the yellow coin, even more than the war, brought about the division of the people into the group of the exploiters and that of the exploited, and thereby created the mental disposition for the collapse.
Above all, however, I have shown you to what a grotesque degree the governments everywhere have deceived themselves when they believed that by flooding the countries

with vast quantities of bank and state notes they had sovereignly created 'new money' and 'new purchasing power'; how in fact they have done nothing other than dilute the purchasing power of the old money in order to transfer the greater part of it from its rightful owners to themselves and then further to certain privileged strata of the population.

But in stating all these facts, dear James, we have by no means exhausted the problem of money. Since a modern industrial and commercial state is not an isolated area, not a self-contained entity, but a part of the great economic union of nations, its monetary system is not an internal affair with only internal economic effects, but it also has external effects. Any arbitrary intervention in the monetary system must, in addition to the disastrous consequences within the country, necessarily have a far-reaching influence on all mercantile and financial relations between the domestic country and all foreign countries. For if goods at home increase their price tenfold or a thousandfold and halve it again another time, this cannot remain without some effect on the world market which the goods seek out or from which they flow into the country, and likewise not without effect on the price of foreign money in which the foreign goods and any debts abroad must be paid. Thus a whole chain of problems is linked to the main problem of national money and its value in the country itself.

We only have to look around us and immediately the strangest and most contradictory phenomena force themselves upon us. For example, when we look at the exchange rate slip, which tells us the exchange rates and thus at the same time the value that foreign countries attach to our own money. It goes without saying that this foreign value must fall if our money has lost value in the country itself. For if foreign countries were still to value and pay the German mark at its old gold value, German money would migrate abroad, where it would be overvalued, buy up enormous masses of goods there and flood Germany with its products. This would force down the German price level or, in other words, raise the value of the mark in Germany. But no sooner would this happen than the reverse process would take place: the outflowing masses of marks would flow back to Germany, pour into the markets here to buy and drive prices up again, but the value of money correspondingly down, whereupon the game would begin anew. This is, of course, an impossibility. Just as the price of a security, a bill of exchange or a precious metal in one country cannot deviate considerably from the price in a neighbouring country, so the money of a state outside its borders cannot be valued considerably higher or lower than in the state itself. Its price, like water in communicating pipes, will have to occupy approximately the same level at home and abroad.

That is a matter of course, isn't it? But when we then try to verify this self-evident fact, we are taken aback. Something is not right. For what do we see in reality, my dear? We see that there are in fact quite considerable differences in valuation. Sometimes the mark is paid more abroad, sometimes less than its value at home. In the summer of 1920, for example, the mark temporarily had much more purchasing power abroad than in Germany. In Germany, one mark could only buy about the tenth or twelfth part of what one had received for it before the war; abroad, on the other hand, since the mark was valued at about 1/33 dollars or 1/7 shillings at that time, one still received about a seventh or eighth of the former quantity of goods. And today it is just the other way round: at home the mark has about one thirteenth or fourteenth of its former purchasing power, while abroad it has scarcely one twentieth; a fact which is completely contrary to the natural order of things, to which only a complete or at least approximate correspondence between the internal value and the external value of money corresponds, but which must have its reasons. For what it is, is reasonable and the consequence of some cause.

But no sooner have we noticed this abnormality than new problems present themselves. If the external value of German money is so much lower than its internal value, this means that German domestic prices are lower than the corresponding prices abroad. As a result, German goods must flow out onto the world market in enormous quantities. And indeed we see that this is the case today; the whole world complains about German dumping competition and seeks to protect itself against it. But how is it then that the external value of the mark has not now risen at least to the level of the internal value? The strong German export of goods must be paid for by the hole and create a correspondingly strong demand for German means of payment abroad, i.e. raise the mark rate at least to the level of the domestic mark value. Why does this not happen? Why does the divergence between the internal and external value of the mark still persist?

You will of course answer me, dear James, what almost everyone would answer in your place: namely, that the diminished value of the mark abroad is not a problem at all, but a matter of course, because Germany is unbelievably burdened with payment obligations and in June, July and August of this year alone had to pay 1 billion gold marks or 19 to 20 billion paper marks as 'reparations' to the Entente. Of course, I am not completely unaware of this fact, and I also know its effects on the market rate. But how is it, my dear fellow, that last year, when we had to pay just as large or even larger sums to foreign countries for grain, cotton, copper and similar necessities, the same effect did not occur as now? If you look at the trade statistics, you will find that Germany alone has imported more than it has exported in the form of regularly approved and correctly cleared merchandisen for about 40 billion marks. Add to this the numerous billions of smuggled goods or goods pushed over through the 'hole in the West'. We have had to pay all this and much more, and yet in the summer of 1920 the mark was valued higher abroad than at home! So again, something must be wrong here.

But above all: If the reparation tribute imposed on Germany really and absolutely has the consequence that the mark is exposed to a constant strong supply on the world market and is thereby depressed below its internal value, then we would have to reckon under certain circumstances for thirty years and more with two different market values, a higher domestic and a lower foreign one! For, as is well known, reparations are to extend over several decades. We would therefore not be able to think about rebuilding a healthy, stable German currency for thirty years or more. In fact, however, there is already a strong current in favour of starting the currency reform as soon as possible, and quite clever people believe that we can fortify the German monetary system very quickly if we seriously want to - in spite of our foreign debt and in spite of the reparations. How do we get over this new contradiction?

And furthermore: Let's assume that for some reason reparations would suddenly cease; world history has by no means stood still since the Peace of Versailles, but is constantly creating new, bizarre constellations and all kinds of unforeseen possibilities. So how would it be if we no longer had to pay tomorrow? Would the correspondence between the internal and external value of the mark then be restored in one fell swoop? Or would other disturbing factors then stand in the way of the balance? And are there conditions under which the disturbances do not occur and others under which they do?

And again: If it is true that as a result of reparations or other unfavourable circumstances the external value of the mark is permanently depressed below the internal value, must it not then necessarily come to a violent trade war between Germany and foreign countries? A higher internal value of the mark means cheaper prices for German goods, which means mass exports, which are perceived as dumping competition on the world market, and finally means violent defensive measures by foreign countries, which do not want to have their industries ruined by this dumping competition. In other words, a bitter struggle in which import bans and prohibitive tariffs provide the ammunition, but which must nevertheless remain ineffective because the poor external value of the mark, which is synonymous with German indebtedness and payment obligations, keeps pumping German goods abroad like a powerful suction apparatus.

Or will this conflict be resolved in another, more peaceful way?

You see, my son, the problems pile up and become more complicated. And if one does not have a firm foundation under one's feet and a precise knowledge of what 'money' is and what 'value,is ' namely the external value of money, one will infallibly go astray on this sea of problems. No sooner has one wave been dealt with than the next, higher one is approaching, and behind it, the third is already gathering. You have to steer wisely. For me, as your helmsman, this means the duty to work systematically and to begin the alphabet of the value question not with any letter, but from the beginning, with the A. Without elementary instruction, it is not possible to learn the basics. Without elementary instruction it is not possible to navigate in this field, because even a small error in a seemingly insignificant basic question immediately leads us in the wrong direction and does not allow us to find the right path again.

So my next letters will begin with the foundation: How do the nations consort? With what do they pay? What is the so-called. World Money? If we know these basic questions, we can confidently continue on the path that leads to the actual question of value without fear of being distracted. You will then see how simple, how self-evident things basically are. It is the same with this apparently difficult branch of economic science as with the others: Everything is basically quite clear, and the one always follows from the other. It is not the things that are complicated, it is rather our way of approaching them that is complicated. Remember once and for all, my son: difficult is always only that which one cannot do, and complicated are only those problems which one does not overlook.

    With love

        Your old dad.

Second Letter

*The International Exchange
Commodity as World Money
The Placeholder Service of the Bill of Exchange*

Berlin, September 4th 1921

Every commercial intercourse between people, dear James, is a barter intercourse, a continuous reciprocal giving and taking of goods or services in exchange for other goods or services. We already established this back when we dealt with the nature of money, coming to the conclusion that money is ultimately nothing more than a proxy; namely, the proxy of goods and services to which one has a claim because one has performed something oneself, but has not yet received the equivalent; that the giving of money is therefore, as it were, a provisional measure which will sooner or later be replaced by a service or a commodity. Only when this happens is the act of exchange completed, the actual payment for the service or commodity that gave rise to the act of exchange takes place.

It is no different from the traffic between members of one and the same state with the traffic from country to country. Here, too, goods and services are exchanged for goods and services. You will easily recognise this if you consider the details of international traffic. The largest component is the import and export of goods, which is carefully recorded in customs offices and statistical offices. Another part is formed by the transport and intermediary services which the railways, shipping companies and banks render to the nationals of other countries, and which are paid for either by similar services or by a corresponding import of goods. The exchange character of these two main items of the transport balance is clear.

But all other items also have this exchange character, although it is not so clearly recognisable here, because one sees all kinds of documents, in particular government securities and private bonds, shares and similar effects, moving from country to country, which seem to have a different purpose. In fact, however, all these documents are in the service of international exchange in exactly the same way as they are in the service of domestic exchange. I see from my letterheads that I have already explained to you on January 2nd what shares, bonds, mortgages and all other instruments of credit and participation really are: namely, rights to houses, machines, marques, stocks or to the enterprises in whose possession these things are. They are documents which show that certain goods are not the exclusive property of the person who disposes of them, but the joint property or pledge of the owner of the document. Whoever sends such documents sends the abstract right of ownership or pledge of certain concrete goods, which in its economic effects is exactly the same as if he sends these goods in kind. And when an individual or a state authority sends such documents of title or claim abroad in order to pay for cotton, lace or oranges imported a short time before, in reality an outright exchange of good for good has come about.

In addition to such documents, which certify a property or a long-term claim, another type of document passes from country to country, in which a short-term credit relationship is securitised. In economic terms, these documents say nothing more than that a service is to be rendered in the future, say after three or six months, instead of in the present, and that therefore a merchandise which a country has received will not be paid for immediately, but later with another commodity. This is why, in a country's foreign trade, the assets and liabilities do not always balance out exactly, as should actually be the case according to the principle of 'goods against goods', but rather that one side soon outweighs the other. The difference is provisionally balanced by the credit papers, i.e. by the promise of a later payment, and as long as this is the case and the difference still exists, a corresponding quantity of goods or services is de facto unpaid. Sooner or later, however, the definitive payment must be made in the only possible form in the consignment of goods or the provision of services, otherwise the person, company or community liable to pay commits a breach of trust.

If the normal and legal intercourse between the individual countries is always a barter intercourse, it does occasionally happen that abnormal relations take place which fall outside the framework of the law. For example, one country may be forced by another to provide services which are not reciprocated. The best-known example of such processes, in which force replaces law and condemns a country to make unilateral payments, is what antiquity called 'tribute', and what today is more mendaciously called 'war compensation', 'reparation' or something similar. Here the recipient countries want 'money' from the payer country, i.e. ration coupons on goods and services with the help of which they can put themselves in possession of any goods. But even in this case, in which they use brute force, they do not succeed in overturning the economic law according to which traffic from country to country takes place exclusively by means of the exchange of goods. For the country condemned to pay has nothing more than goods or services in order to be able to pay. Even if it apparently pays in money, that is, pays the entire tribute to the countries entitled to receive it in its national money, it in reality gives goods. For you know, in so far as my earlier letters have fulfilled their purpose, that the national money is only an order for national goods or a pledge for these goods, and that it has a value only in so far as the right of subscription to the national goods embodied in it is exercised. In the money that is handed over to them, the tribute-taking countries therefore merely receive a coupon on goods and services of the tributary country, and in order to obtain their 'money' they must present the coupon, i.e. return the national money and obtain goods or services in exchange.

This has never been more evident than just now, when Germany is fulfilling the reparations obligation imposed on her and is complying with the demand of the allied victorious states to pay several billion gold marks annually in American, English and other currency. Germany raises the necessary dollars, pounds sterling, etc., in such a way that it buys from its exporters the foreign exchange they receive as the equivalent of their exports, and from its banks the credit balances they have abroad, and pays them as tribute to the victors. It pays all these foreign exchange and credit balances in German money, in marks, which it procures by way of taxation and borrowing and, unfortunately, also, even mainly, by way of red printing. But that is only the technical course of events. The factual situation is that Germany pays with the goods which her exporters must export in order to obtain the necessary foreign exchange, and with the bonds, shares and other assets exported, for which her banks see themselves in possession of the urgently needed foreign credits. The actual payment is thus made, like every payment from country to country, in goods, and the receiving countries, which have already triumphantly booked the ordered German reparation payments as income, now see with horror that 'receiving money' means nothing other than 'being flooded with goods'. Like Goethe's sorcerer's apprentice, they have not grasped the implications of their order. They now do not know how to eliminate the unforeseen consequences of their clumsy demand for payment and how to protect their industries from the destructive competition of German reparations goods.

Two souls dwell in their breast: one demands 'pay! 'the other laments 'don't pay in goods!' For centuries to come, it will be a disgrace to contemporary European finance that it did not instruct the governments on this point in time and tell them: No person and no nation can pay otherwise than in goods or services. If you condemn Germany to several billion gold marks annually, you condemn the recipients of payment to accept the corresponding quantity of German goods or German labour. You must therefore take goods and labour, since gold cannot be procured in such quantities and, moreover, would be useless, even a misfortune for you - we shall come to this point in detail later, dear James, or else you will have to do without the whole reparation.

Nobody told the governments this in time; but now they realise it themselves, and they are endeavouring to stem the flow of German goods in every possible and impossible way.

All this, dear James, is only to illustrate the fact that payments from country to country, even if they are stipulated in money, are in reality in commodity form. A country, therefore, which is in debt to another, and to which neither the creditor nor a third country is willing to grant a corresponding credit, has no choice but to export goods or render services.

However, this method of payment encounters obstacles, especially if the amounts involved are exceptionally large. For exporting, like kissing, always requires two people: one who exports and one who accepts the exports. The supply of goods and services from the country liable to pay must be matched by a demand from abroad, otherwise the best will to export is of no use to the first country; it cannot then export and consequently cannot pay. In such a case, the foreign country has no choice but to defer the debt, i.e. to grant credit. But it is often not prepared to do this either. There are constellations in which a country can neither get rid of its merchandise because it is too expensive for the other countries, nor can it obtain credit because this seems to be a financial risk for the other countries. What happens then? Will the debtor country still be able to pay, or will it not be able to pay, so that it has to declare bankruptcy?

I will spare you the long pondering over this delicate point, dear James, and tell you straight away that such a dilemma as I have just sketched out here does not exist in reality. I started from an impossible premise. For it never happens that a foreign country does not want to take a debtor country's goods or grant it credit. A debtor country that is serious about its willingness to pay always finds either buyers for its goods or sufficient credit. This may seem strange to you, and I admit that it sounds strange when I say that a foreign country is not free in its decisions, but is faced with a constraint that leaves it only the choice of whether to buy or to give credit. But that is indeed the case. And if you ask me: 'Who can force a foreign country to buy a commodity that is too expensive or to grant a loan that seems too dangerous?' I answer you: 'the exchange rate'.

The exchange rate is the price of foreign means of payment - with which a country can cover its debt and which it receives by exporting goods - expressed in a certain amount of its own means of payment. Since means of payment are nothing other than commodity warrants, the exchange rate indicates how much commodity the debtor country must give up in order to pay its debt. If the exchange rate is favourable, i.e. if the foreign means of payment are cheap, this means that the debtor country does not need to add much of its own goods to cover a certain amount. If, on the other hand, the exchange rate is unfavourable, i.e. the price of the foreign means of payment is high, the debtor country will have to give up correspondingly more goods for the same debt. Seen from the side of the foreign country, this means: in the first case, the foreign country is in the disadvantageous position of receiving few goods for one unit of its money, i.e. of buying expensively; in the second case, on the other hand, it is in the advantageous position of receiving many goods for the same unit, i.e. of buying cheaply. The worse the state of the exchange rates for the debtor country, the better the purchasing opportunities in this country for the entire foreign country.

Now let us assume that my assumption, that the foreign country as a whole does not want to buy goods from the debtor country or grant credit, has really come true in a concrete case. What would be the consequence? The debtor country would be embarrassed. Neither its exporters would be able to provide it with the foreign commodity bills (foreign exchange), nor its banks with the foreign credit balances it needs to cover its debt. The country or the financial institutions commissioned by it would search in vain on the foreign exchange market for the necessary quantity of foreign means of payment and would therefore of necessity pay a high premium to all those who could and would provide them with such means of payment. For example, they would offer 60 or 80 marks for dollar bills, which cannot be obtained at a rate of 40 marks per dollar. In accordance with the law that strong demand increases the price when there is insufficient supply, the foreign means of payment, i.e. the exchange rates, would become extraordinarily more expensive in the debtor country.

What would be the consequence? If you were to face me here, my son, you would now have to describe the further course of events to me yourself, for everything develops quite logically from facts that we already know. But since I unfortunately cannot listen to your lesson at a distance, I must of necessity continue to spin the logical thread myself. So: We have seen that unfavourable exchange rates of the debtor country mean an opportunity for the entire foreign country, namely the opportunity to buy goods cheaply in the debtor country. Let us assume that the price of a certain German machine is 400,000 marks. At a dollar exchange rate of 40 marks, this would amount to exactly 10,000 dollars. If the dollar rate in Berlin deteriorates to 80, the same machine costs the American importer only half, namely 5,000 dollars. And if the price of 10,000 dollars seemed too high for him to buy the machine, he will probably no longer find a price of 5,000 dollars too high. From which the theorem follows: The worsening of the exchange rate, with the domestic price remaining unchanged, increases the propensity to buy abroad and causes an increase in exports.

There are now two possibilities: Either the increase of the dollar exchange rate from 40 to 80 marks (and a corresponding increase of all other exchange rates) is sufficient to awaken the hitherto lacking inclination of foreign countries to buy and to stimulate exports to the necessary extent: Then the debtor country, in this case Germany, will find the necessary amount of foreign exchange to pay its debt. For every exported commodity naturally brings it a sum in foreign means of payment corresponding to its price. The exchange rate has then done its duty. Or, second possibility: despite the strong rise in the exchange rate, exports do not increase sufficiently, either because the price reduction of the goods is not sufficient for the foreign importers, or because the foreign nations have imposed high customs duties on German goods. Then Germany, the payer, still lacks part of the necessary foreign exchange material, the demand for foreign means of payment on the foreign exchange market continues and drives up the exchange rates further. The dollar exchange rate then does not stop at 80 marks, but climbs to 100, 120 or even higher. In this way the exchange rates deteriorate so long, or, what is equivalent, the prices of German goods become cheaper for foreign countries to such an extent that every reluctance of foreign importers and every tariff of foreign negations, no matter how high, is finally overcome, German goods pour over foreign countries in a broad stream, and Germany thereby gains the disposal of the necessary quantity of foreign exchange. If foreign countries want to put an end to this collapse of German goods, which threatens their industries, they have no choice but to relieve Germany of the necessity of buying foreign exchange, that is, to grant it the necessary credits.

In this way, dear James, the inner logic of things, by means of the exchange rate, forces the foreign country either to allow the debtor country to pay off its debt in commodities, or to grant it a respite on this debt. There is no other possibility. For even if we assume that it is conceivable that the whole world would unanimously barricade itself against the goods of the debtor country by prohibiting imports, and that it would just as unanimously refuse any credit, - a precondition which every practitioner will laugh at as fantasy, - the German merchandise would nevertheless penetrate abroad by surreptitious means and in the most outlandish disguises.

The power of the cheap exchange rate is absolutely insurmountable, and as long as a debtor country wants to pay, no power on earth can prevent it from paying in the way that is the only conceivable way in traffic from country to country, namely by handing over goods.
Thus we see that the mediating role played by money in domestic trade is played by the bill of exchange in international trade. But the bill of exchange is as little a definitive means of payment as money.
Like money, it is rather a provisional means, a place-holder, which represents the commodity (in the broadest sense, that is, including all services of some kind) until it, which constitutes the sole object of all traffic, allows it to be replaced by money, which then later replaces it again. The bill of ex-

change, therefore, as distinguished from money, is a provisional measure of the second rank, which stands in the same relation to money as the latter does to commodities.

So much for today.

>With love

>>Your old dad.

Third Letter

The balance of payments
The world commodity 'gold'
Gold and its three properties

Berlin, September 6th 1921

We have seen, dear James, that the exchange rate, which expresses the value of one country's money in units of another country's money, depends entirely on the country's balance of payments: that it improves when the country has more to demand than to pay, and that it deteriorates when the reverse is the case. But we have also seen that the exchange rate not only registers the state of the balance of payments but at the same time corrects it by setting the price level in the creditor and debtor countries in that relation to each other which makes possible the outflow of goods from the debtor countries to the creditor countries and in this way balances the balance of payments.

This leads to several important conclusions. Firstly, the favourability or unfavourability of exchange rates does not depend exclusively on whether a country is very heavily indebted to other countries, or very lightly indebted, or not indebted at all, but much more on whether it is easy or difficult for it in a given case to settle a debt balance by exporting goods, or to make it irrelevant for the moment by drawing on credit. One country can easily cope with a high debit balance, while another has difficulties even settling a small balance: this is a question of export capacity and creditworthiness. Consequently, in one country a small deterioration in the exchange rate is enough to produce the desired effect, while in the other a very considerable deterioration in the exchange rate must occur in order to eliminate a relatively insignificant balance of payments liability.

It follows, secondly, that it will be all the easier for a country to repay a debt abroad, and that it will suffer all the less from exchange rate fluctuations, the more it possesses certain goods which are excellently suited for export purposes. The exchange rates have the task of shaping the value of the individual national currencies and thus the price relationship between the countries in such a way as the state of the balance of payments requires, and they will fulfil this task all the more easily and quickly the more mobile the margins are which move from country to country as intermediaries for the settlement of payments. In the country which has the most mobile goods, i.e. those taken everywhere with the greatest preference - or an unlimited credit - even a very slight improvement or deterioration in the exchange rates establishes equilibrium in the balance of payments.

It follows, thirdly, that the commodities to which it is chiefly incumbent to bring about the adjustment of the balance of payments by their outflow and inflow must hook another quality than that of great mobility. Remember, dear James, in what way the exchange rate eliminates the passive balance of the debtor country. It does this by causing, through its own movement, the average price of the exportable goods of the debtor country to become cheaper for the foreign country. If the dollar quotation in Berlin rises from 40 to 80 M., a batch of German dyes costing 1200 marks no longer costs the American 30 dollars, but only 15 dollars. Although the price in marks has remained unchanged, it has been reduced by half for the American.

But at the same time, my son, you see from this example that this reduction in price only occurs under a very specific condition; namely, only if the goods in question, in this case dyes, retain their old price in marks and do not increase in price. For if dyes no longer cost 1200 marks in Germany, but rise to 1800 marks, the American loses half of the reduction. And if they rise to 2400 marks, there is no price reduction at all.

The goods that balance the equilibrium of payments must therefore not only be very mobile, but at the same time also very stable in price. They must not become more expensive, or at least not considerably more Habe expensive, at the moment when foreign demand for them arises. The ideal commodity would be one which, when foreign demand arises, not only does not increase its own domestic price or the general domestic price level, but on the contrary even reduces it. For in this case the export commodity would become cheaper for the foreign country not only by the amount of the increase in the exchange rate, but also by the amount of the fall in the domestic price level; there would then be no need for a particularly perceptible deterioration in the exchange rate, because the purpose of this deterioration, namely the cheapening of the export commodity, would already be partly fulfilled by the fall in the price of the commodity at home and the exchange rate would thereby be relieved. If, therefore, to return to our example, the price of dyes were to fall from 1200 marks to 900 marks, the dollar exchange rate would no longer have to rise to 80 marks, but only to 60 marks, in order to induce the Americans to buy; for 900 marks at the conversion rate of 60 yield the same dollar price as 1200 marks at the rate of 80, namely 15 dollars.

I can see now, dear James, how your face twists into a smile because you are thinking: 'I would like to get to know the goods that become cheaper at the moment when foreign countries begin to buy them, or even reduce the general price level in the country! I have learned that much already, that when demand begins, the price of a commodity rises and does not fall! There can be no doubt that if the dollar exchange rate in Berlin deteriorates and the Americans begin to buy up German dyes as a result, the price of dyes will rise from 1,200 to 1,800 marks or even higher, but not fall to 900 marks. The premise that with increased demand prices will decrease is an absurdity, is a logical impossibility, and my old dad seems to have fallen victim to a fatal error in thinking here. 'I bet you 10 to 1, my dear, that this is your reasoning when you read these lines.

But your old dad, despite his years, still thinks quite clearly and knows what he says and writes. In principle, of course, you are right: increased demand raises prices, not lowers them, and it must be very strange goods that lead to a price reduction the moment they are sent abroad and therefore become scarce at home. But there are such peculiar goods. And above all, there is one such commodity that you are very familiar with, practically from your own experience and theoretically from my earlier letters: gold.

Gold is the commodity which not only unites in the most perfect manner the two most estimable qualities of every export commodity, namely mobility and price stability, but which, in addition, even has the special characteristic of having a price-depressing effect as soon as it is in great demand and is sent abroad. And you will soon realise where this accumulation of estimable qualities in gold comes from.
First of all, there is the great mobility. You know that most of the civilised states have somehow connected their monetary system with gold, although money, which you have come to know as a legal title that secures its holder the claim to a consideration corresponding to a previous performance, does not in itself need a connection with gold. It has just turned out in practice that money, as soon as it consists of gold or can be exchanged for gold at any time, fulfils

its most important function much better than when this is not the case. The most important function of money, as we know, is to adjust the value of the consideration embodied in it exactly to the value of the preceding consideration, i.e. to ensure that the price level in the country is maintained as perfectly as possible. And there is no better way of achieving this stability than by identifying money, which measures and expresses prices, with gold, which for many reasons is subject to less fluctuation in value than other commodities.

We do not need to go into the reasons for this high esteem of gold in its indelicate connection with money. It is sufficient if you consider the fact that gold is considered equal to national money in all civilised countries, because it can be transformed into such money at any time. For this fact is the real reason for the extremely great, almost unlimited mobility of gold. Since in the most important countries it is at least equal to currency money, it is readily accepted everywhere. A country which has sufficient quantities of this metal possesses a commodity with which it can always and under all circumstances cover a deficit balance on its balance sheet, without having to stimulate the buying appetite of foreign countries by offering a price reduction. For there is always sufficient buying power for gold.

The fact that this purchasing power not only exists in itself, but also occurs under quite definite, unchanging and everywhere known conditions, constitutes the second advantage of the commodity 'gold,' namely its price stability. One can always count on gold being taken at the price which corresponds to the legal ratio in which it can be converted into the highest-value national money, i.e. the dollar at the moment. It will not fall below this price, even if it is offered in the largest lots. The country which possesses sufficient gold can therefore not only easily cover its balance of payments with it, without having to make any concessions with regard to the price of this export commodity, but it can also dispense with the stimulant of exchange rate deterioration. In the case of every other export commodity, the foreign buyer's inclination to buy must be aroused or strengthened by the exchange rate depressing the value of the currency of the debtor country, thus making the prices fixed in this currency appear lower to the foreigner, although they have not been reduced at home. In the case of gold there is no need for such an increase in the propensity to buy, for this is in any case unlimited. If, therefore, a gold-owning country has to make large foreign payments, it does not need to search anxiously for foreign exchange, to raise its rate by its demand and to reduce the value of its own national money accordingly, until at last the foreign country declares itself willing to buy the greatly reduced national commodity, but it can procure the necessary foreign exchange without further ado by sending gold abroad. For this gold it then receives the foreign exchange it needs to cover its debt, without an increase in the exchange rate and a deterioration of the national currency.

'But is there any country which has at its disposal such enormous quantities of gold as are necessary to cover any balance of payments, however large, with it?' This question is so obvious that I would very much resent it, dear James, if you did not want to ask it. Certainly, there are many countries that do not own such large amounts of gold. Germany, for example, is not in a position today to cover the reparation payments of a single year from its gold stocks, although more than a billion gold marks made of pure gold are resting in the Reichsbank. But you must not conclude from this that a gold stock of this amount would under all circumstances be insufficient to settle a debt of 3 1/2 or 4 billion gold marks. Under normal circumstances, a very small fraction of that gold stock is sufficient to enable even greater payments to be made. That this is not the case in Germany today is solely due to the fact that normal conditions do not prevail here, that the German monetary system is thoroughly sick, and that German gold has therefore completely lost the third and most valuable property of gold. And that is the property of gold to generate price pressure in the exporting country when it is exported. Here we have arrived at such an important point that I must ask you to read the following with the greatest attention.

A country in which the gold currency prevails, i.e. whose national money either consists of gold or is redeemable in gold at any time - as was the case in Germany before the war - can pay any amount of debt to foreign countries without the exchange rate rising above the so-called 'upper gold point'. This is the exchange rate at which it is more advantageous to send gold abroad and thus create corresponding foreign credits than to buy foreign currency on the exchange market. In Germany, the normal price of a pound sterling used to be 20.43 marks, because an English sovereign for 43 pennies contained, or contains, more gold than a German twenty-mark piece. The 'upper gold point' deviated from this parity by only about 6 or 7 pennies; i.e. the exchange rate in London could not normally - occasional deviations are irrelevant here - rise above 20.50 marks.

Why not?

Because any import company or bank that would have paid more than 20.50 marks for a sterling bill would have thrown cash out the window. Because for 20.50 marks they could withdraw as much gold from the Reichsbank and send it to London as was necessary to have a sovereign, equal to one pound sterling, minted from the gold. And if one can obtain a pound sterling in gold for 20.50 marks and use it for payment, one is certainly acting foolishly if one spends more than this amount to buy a bill of exchange in London, which at best has the same value as that pound sterling in gold.

Ergo: Where gold currency prevails, the price of foreign bills of exchange can never rise far above parity, i.e. above the gold value of a foreign coin expressed in domestic money. For as soon as the exchange rate shows a tendency to exceed the parity by more than the one-third of a per cent which the freight, the loss of interest and the insurance of a gold bullion exchange roughly account for, i.e. to go beyond the upper gold point, the whole commercial world knows that it is more advantageous for it to export gold than to buy foreign exchange. Immediately the export of gold begins, while the demand for foreign exchange ceases. An increase in the exchange rate above the upper gold point, also called the export gold point, is such an impossibility in a country with a healthy gold currency, as was the case in almost all the old industrialised countries before the war, that if the export gold point is nevertheless exceeded in a country, this is an unmistakable sign that the country is turning away from the gold currency. It cannot be otherwise than that the state bank will no longer promptly redeem the national money in gold on demand.

Gold-currency countries can thus easily pay their foreign debts at any time for several reasons. First, in gold they have a highly mobile commodity that can move out and back again at will, since all countries are happy to accept it in lieu of payment. Secondly, in gold they have a commodity whose price is stable and whose valuation does not fluctuate appreciably either at home or abroad. It does not fluctuate at home, because here it is taken at will for national money or given in exchange for it, and can therefore never be worth more or less than its fixed equivalent in national money. And its valuation by foreign countries does not fluctuate, or fluctuates only insignificantly, because the exchange rates, whose improvement or deterioration amounts to an increase or reduction in the price of all merchandise, are anchored between the upper and the lower gold point (export and import gold point) and can only ever oscillate back and forth in the tiny space between these two points.

For these reasons, the gold-currency countries can make any payment abroad, no matter how high. But you must not believe that the foreign debts of a gold-currency country are covered in the primitive way that the country pays the whole amount of its debt in actual gold. This is, of course, an outright impossibility, for not a single country possesses as much gold as would have to be paid in this case. In reality, foreign debts are covered in a completely different way, in a technically very interesting and highly instructive manner for monetary theory, whereby the gold-currency countries benefit from a very important third property of gold as a commodity. This is the property of gold, which I have already mentioned, of generating a general price pressure when it leaves the gold-currency country.

Since the concept and essence of money are no longer a mystery to you, I can explain the process to you in a few words. In a country where the gold currency prevails, the gold available, whether it is in circulation or in the banks or in a state treasury, forms a component of the national money. But now you remember that the value of the national money and thus the price level in the country are absolutely dependent on the quantity of money. If, therefore, gold flees from the country, the quantity of money decreases, which inevitably has the consequence that the value of this remaining quantity of money, its purchasing power, increases or, what is the same, the price level in the country decreases. Exporting gold therefore means a fall in prices.

In this property of gold to push down the price level when it leaves a gold-currency country, we have to see the lever which switches the economy of the country in such a way that it is now able to make any payment, even a payment of the greatest magnitude, to the foreign country. It is not with the gold that the country pays: the amount paid in gold will always make up only the smallest part of the debt. Instead, payment is made with the goods which, through the outflow of a relatively small part of the country's money, are made so cheap that they stimulate the purchasing power of the foreign country. A small, relatively harmless export of gold thus has exactly the same effect as a catastrophic deterioration of the exchange rate and is sufficient - small causes, great effects - to enable the country to pay the most significant sums imaginable, provided only its production is efficient. It is not the gold issue as such, therefore, that is the healing factor that allows the country to recover from a passive balance of payments, but the gold issue in its capacity as a price regulator. In this capacity, similar to the ripcord on a balloon, it opens a valve in case of need, through which goods can flow abroad in sufficient quantities to cover the country's debt.

But it should be noted that only in countries with a gold currency does an export of gold have the beneficial effect of enabling the balance of payments to be balanced without a sharp deterioration in exchange rates and thus a decline in the national currency. In countries whose monetary system is detached from gold, even an export of gold worth billions has no other effect than the export of any other commodity would have. In these countries, the export-promoting price reduction does not come from gold but from the exchange rate; heavy indebtedness is identical here with monetary misery and its disastrous ethical, social and political consequences. The fear of this misery and its consequences, dear James, and not any kind of currency-theoretical prejudice or a 'gold mania,' is one of the many valid reasons why countries always instinctively strive back to the gold currency, like the animal to the manger, once they have turned their backs on it out of necessity or lack of understanding...

Whew! The pen is falling out of my hand. Read this long letter twice, dear James, because its contents form the actual framework of the whole Valuta question. And with that, good night!

Your extremely tired dad.

Fourth Letter

Gold Currency and Paper Currency
Gold, Bills of Exchange and Balance of Payments
The Short Gold Cover

Berlin, September 10th 1921

In my letters of last winter, dear James, I explained to you why every country does well to accept the gold currency, although in purely monetary theory every other currency serves exactly the same purpose. The main reason was that the identification of the monetary system with gold protects the country from the arbitrariness of its government. Experience has shown that governments are only too easily inclined to violate the basic law according to which real money of stable value can only be created and perish out of circulation, and to use their powers to create money at their own discretion for the benefit of any interests. This mischief is not possible in a country where money consists of gold or is backed by gold and exchangeable for it. But we have now learned of a second, equally important reason which makes the gold currency superior to any other currency: namely, the fact that a gold-currency country can maintain its balance of payments even under the most unfavourable conditions without exposing the exchange rates, i.e. the ratio of the value of its own money to that of the money of other countries, to strong fluctuations and thereby shaking all the mercantile, productive and social foundations in the country.

Admittedly, even in a gold-currency country, the payment of an unusually large debt sum to a foreign country is not without internal disturbances.

If a country - for example, as a result of a lost war - is forced to pay enormous sums to another country without any consideration, this is a national misfortune that cannot be eliminated even by the best currency. For since every payment from country to country must be made in commodities, the operation amounts under all circumstances to the paying country having to renounce certain goods of capital, use or affection value in favour of the receiving country, and thus to impose privations on itself. But even if the gold currency cannot eliminate the embarrassing consequences of a strong obligation to pay, it is nevertheless able to alleviate them considerably.

We have seen that the export of gold, with which a gold-currency country covers a small part of its debt obligation, procures the large remainder of the debt sum in basically the same way as the exchange rate does in a paper-currency country: namely, by depressing prices in the paying country until the foreign country buys goods at the reduced prices or, in order to reduce the unwelcome supply of goods, grants credit. The export of gold creates this price pressure -even in a more visible, more obvious way than the exchange rate and brings the price pressure, which can easily degenerate into a crisis for individual industries, to the attention of the population. It depresses, by reducing the purchasing power in the country, and thus the price pressure. It presses directly on prices by reducing the purchasing power in the country and thus domestic demand, whereas the deterioration of the exchange rate does so only indirectly, in an insidious way, so to speak.

For the bad exchange rate cheapens the commodity by taking away part of the value of the national money in which prices are expressed. The foreign country, which is now in a position to buy the national money cheaply and with its help also to acquire the goods cheaply, although their price has nominally remained unchanged, notices very quickly the price pressure that has occurred and takes advantage of it. The domestic market, on the other hand, is easily deceived by the unchanged nominal price of the goods, believes that everything has remained the same on the domestic market and that only the value of its money has deteriorated for some reason. That this deterioration in the value of money is merely another expression for the actual fall in the price of the commodity is recognised only by a few people who have been educated in monetary theory, but never by the great mass of the population.

But although the export of gold in a gold-currency land shows its price-depressing effect more openly, it is nevertheless a much milder and more expedient means of effecting large foreign payments than the exchange-rate debasement in the paper-currency countries, which has a clandestine effect. For it achieves the purpose of bringing domestic goods to export much more quickly and at a relatively higher price level than the impulse emanating from the exchange rate.

This is because foreign countries are much more willing to buy in a country with a healthy, stable currency than in a country whose currency is subject to strong fluctuations. Since the foreign importer never knows what the exchange rate of the exporting country with paper currency will be at the moment when the ordered goods, which often have to be manufactured first, are shipped, he does not know how high the effective price of the ordered merchandise will be for him, so he must reckon with a considerable risk and include this in his prices. Another considerable risk arises from the fact that he does not even know whether the ordered goods will be delivered at all. For in a country with a rapidly changing monetary value, there are always wage disputes, strikes and social unrest, which make it difficult or impossible for the manufacturer to comply with the agreed terms of delivery.

In such a country, therefore, foreign countries will not buy if the price of the goods is only slightly lower. On the contrary, the fall in prices must be so considerable that it amply indemnifies the buyer against all the risks mentioned and any other risks - it is impossible for me to list them all for you. The deterioration of the exchange rate must therefore continue much further and depress the prices of goods for the foreigner much more deeply than appears necessary from a purely numerical comparison of domestic and foreign prices.

On the other hand, the export of gold in gold-currency countries already achieves its purpose as soon as it has pushed the domestic price a little below the world market price. For here there are no dangerous fluctuations in the exchange rate that have to be taken into account in the price, and the other risks of the foreign buyer are either non-existent or infinitely smaller than in the paper currency countries. Here, therefore, a much lower price pressure is sufficient to increase national exports to the extent required by the balance of payments. However, this also goes hand in hand with a much more prompt, greater and more accommodating willingness to lend on the part of foreign countries. For the faster and more intensively the goods of the debtor country collapse abroad and compete with the home industries here, the sooner the foreign country also decides to grant the necessary credits and to free the debtor country from the burdensome export compulsion, and these credits are not only granted to the gold-currency country more readily, but also to a much greater extent and on much more favourable terms than to the countries with paper currency, because here, too, the risks attached to the exchange rate cease to exist and a gold-currency country is almost always a safer debtor than a paper-currency country, in which it necessarily festers as soon as the exchange rates begin to play catch-ball with the value of the national money and the prices for reasons of the balance of payments.

The superiority of the gold currency over the paper currency, which is at the mercy of incomprehensible governments and almost regularly leads to inflation, is therefore quite immense from the point of view of trade policy, finance and payment. And even if the gold currency can be dispensed with for internal traffic in a rationally governed country where people know what money is, it is nevertheless indispensable for external traffic if the country does not want to be at a serious disadvantage against its competitors on the international market for goods, capital and credit. This is why many countries that cannot afford the luxury of an all-gold currency have switched to a paper currency with a gold edge, i.e. they calculate and pay in paper at home but in gold abroad. I only remind you of Argentina and Brazil: India with its core of silver or silver-covered paper and its edge of gold also belongs here.

I'm not quite sure whether you're not again hitting me in the foot with the question: 'Is the available amount of gold sufficient to enable all countries to adopt the gold currency, even if it's only a marginal gold currency?' The question, if you were really to ask it, would be extraordinarily naive, but that does not prevent scholars from seriously grappling with it and racking their brains about the 'too short gold supply'. Well, to put it succinctly, gold can never be too short for the very simple reason that it is the subject, not the object, of the monetary system, that is, because the need for money depends on it, on gold, and therefore gold need not depend on the need for money.

In the countries of the gold currency, money receives its fine value from gold, with which it is identical. If gold is in strong demand and therefore expensive, the monetary unit containing or representing so and so many grammes of gold will also become expensive and exert a correspondingly great purchasing power.

If, therefore - and you know that I am a friend of illustration - gold should soon be in exceedingly great demand, because all money-sinning countries should say pater peccavi and want to return to money-honesty, the consequence would be that gold would increase in value, let us say to twice its current value, and that one would therefore receive twice as much goods for an English sovereign as at present. In other words, if there is only half as much gold as all the countries would like to have, the prices of goods in the gold-currency countries fall by 50 per cent, so that every country now gets by with half the quantity of gold it originally wanted to have and would have needed under the old price standard. The changing value of gold itself ensures that the demand of the countries adapts to the available quantity of gold and gets by with it, however large or small this quantity may be.

But even if this were not so, the concern that the world might one day face an acute gold shortage would nevertheless be a fantasy. It has often been believed that we are on the brink of this calamity or even in the midst of it. Over and over again in the last three or four decades people have lamented about the 'too short gold cover', so that one would have to assume that the value of gold has doubled or tripled in this period as a result of strong demand with scarce supplies, and that prices have fallen accordingly by half or a third. In fact, however, when I think back to the good old days of my youth, I find that prices in gold-currency countries have become more expensive from decade to decade, so gold has become cheaper. I conclude from this that gold cannot possibly be in short supply; on the contrary, it meets demand far more abundantly today than it did a few decades ago. And indeed, the precious metal statistics tell us that from decade to decade increasing quantities of gold have been industrially processed, which could not have been the case if the countries' need for coins had not been fully covered.

The gold requirements of a gold-currency country are generally overestimated outrageously and, above all, people have fantastic ideas about the quantities of gold required to maintain the balance of payments. In reality, England, which before the war was not only the largest trading state but above all the most important capital market, got by with a centralised gold stock averaging 35 million pounds sterling. (At the outbreak of war, the German Reichsbank held about 1300 million marks in gold, i.e. considerably more). And this gold supply has hardly ever fluctuated by more than ten million pounds a year; with this minimal sum, which may occasionally have been augmented a little by private gold holdings, England has been able to finance the whole world.

The reason must be familiar to you: it is based on the three properties of gold which I described to you in my previous letter; in particular, on the third, that gold, when it leaves a gold-currency country, creates a price pressure here which strengthens the export of goods, so that by far the greatest part of all payments is either made immediately in goods, or, in the expectation of a later export of goods, is provisionally met from credits. The more reliable the gold currency of a country and the greater the confidence of foreign countries in it, the lower the price pressure must be which triggers the necessary exports and credits, and consequently the smaller must be the respective gold export and subsequently the gold stock of the country.

A reliable gold currency - remember that, my boy! - is not recognised by a high gold stock, but by the fact that the balance of payments of the country can be kept in equilibrium with relatively few gold exports, and that the gold that has flowed out returns as soon as the disturbed equilibrium is restored.

Now you will certainly want to know why and by what means the gold flows back to its country of origin when it has fulfilled its task of being the pacemaker for export and credit. A little more patience, my son, and you will know this too. For today I must break off the chat.

With love

Your old dad.

Fifth Letter

General good 'commodity' and special good 'gold' Price, interest and arbitrage

Berlin, September 15th 1921

What is 'world money,' dear James? When economists and financiers use the word, they always mean gold. But is that correct? Are payments from country to country really made in gold? We have seen that this is not usually the case, that it is only very insignificant peaks of payments that are made in gold. And we have also seen that in this kind of peak regulation gold performs its main service not in its capacity as an internationally valued means of payment, i.e. as a kind of world money, but as a component of the currency in the exporting gold-currency country, i.e. as domestic money; namely, by flowing out, it reduces the money supply in the country, thus lowering the price level and creating the preconditions for the country to be able to meet its payment obligation in a way other than through gold rationing.
Gold, then, cannot be called the world's money, but only its pacemaker.

But what do we then have to regard as the world means of payment in which countries settle their debts and claims? You will probably answer me: The bill of exchange.

We do indeed see that the private individual, the bank, the government, in short, everyone who has to make a payment abroad, procures a foreign bill of exchange, a so-called foreign currency, for this purpose and sends it to his creditor, with which he then fulfils his payment obligations. But please consider what a foreign bill of exchange basically is, and why it is generally taken in lieu of payment. You only need to read the text of the bill of exchange, which is roughly the same in all countries. Then you will see that the bill of exchange is a request to a domestic person or company to pay the amount in dollars, pounds, francs etc. to the legitimate holder of the bill on such and such a day. In a bill of exchange, therefore, you own a paper that has no intrinsic value, but only a derived value, namely derived from the dollar, pound or franc amount to which it gives a right. Consequently, it is not the bills of exchange that play the role of 'world money'; rather, the various national types of money in which they are denominated, and into which they must first be exchanged in order to determine whether the bills of exchange are 'good' or 'bad', share this role. The money, however, as we have seen before, is likewise without independent value; it is a reference note for goods, which the country has to deliver to the holder of its peculiar money on demand. Only when this delivery has taken place and the holder of the money received for the bill of exchange knows the quantity and value of the goods delivered, is the payment from one country to the other finally completed. Thus, in the final analysis, the commodity is the 'world money'.

Among the innumerable types of commodities that make up this world money, there is also gold, from which the impetus for the regulation of payments by commodities originated. For gold, too, is nothing other than a commodity as soon as it has left the circulation of money in the paying country and has migrated abroad. Only this commodity has the advantage over the other commodities of greater mobility, because all countries accept it at a fixed price. The fact that this is the case merely because gold is identical with the national currency in many countries does not stamp gold into a special category or strip it of its commodity character. For when it is shipped for payment purposes, it is shipped as a commodity, not as money. No gold exporter can say what use his gold will find in the recipient country. It can, however, be minted into national coins there. But it can just as easily go on to the gold industry and be turned into watch covers and gold goblets. Or it can remain in the form of bars in some bank until it decides where to go. Only in the former case does the commodity gold become money, but even then only through a process of transformation that it undergoes in the recipient country. During its transport from country to country, gold is always a commodity and nothing but a commodity, even if it has already taken on the form of a coin, which the receiving country can leave or take away at its own discretion.

The actual world money, dear James, is therefore the commodity, divided into countless groups of different mobility and led by the most mobile commodity, gold. In addition to being world money, the commodity has the task of balancing the countries' balance of payments. And this is an extraordinarily important task. For in order that the legal order in the world economy may be maintained, and that every man in every state may receive what is due to him, the balance of payments of each individual country must balance at zero. If one country owes another, it must pay or it is bankrupt. Unless its creditors expressly grant it a deferment of payment, i.e. credit. This credit is then equivalent to a deletion of the corresponding debt item in the present and its re-entry on an account sheet in the future. The present balance sheet is thereby relieved, its liability balance reduced. However, the country must pay this reduced liability balance under all circumstances, because some foreign creditors have a claim on the amount of this balance which is due and which they inexorably insist on being paid immediately. For if they did not do so, they would have granted the country a corresponding credit, i.e. they would have agreed to the transfer of the debt item to a future folio and thereby relieved the present balance of payments.

The multiform world money 'commodity', composed of innumerable types, now generally fulfils its task of balancing the claims and debts of the countries so well that it is only necessary in exceptional cases to call in the most movable special commodity 'gold' to assist. Except for insignificant peaks, the enormous claims which the countries have against each other, and which amount to hundreds of billions (gold billions) a year, are balanced out by the movement of other commodities, supported by credit, which defers partial claims for a shorter or longer period, thus postponing their settlement from the movement of commodities of the present to that of the future. I need not remind you again and again that the term 'commodity' must always be understood in the broadest sense, that is, that it includes all services (transports, bank intermediation, insurance services, etc.) which countries render to each other, and also all documented property rights (shares, mortgages and the like), which are nothing other than legal titles to commodities or goods which are in the administration of third persons. Understood in this most comprehensive sense, the general good 'commodity' fulfils its function of debt settlement so well that it is only exceptionally necessary to call in the special good 'gold' with its three special characteristics - mobility, price stability and influence on the price level in the exporting country.

Where this comes from is already known to you in broad outline. It is the effect of the price changes caused in countries of paper currency by the great fluctuations of the exchange rate, and in countries of gold currency by the occasional inflow and outflow of small quantities of gold. Through these price changes, the demand for the commodity is strengthened or weakened, as is necessary to balance the mutual credits and debts through this world means of payment. But with this you have actually only become acquainted with the last two pillars of the balance of payments, to a certain extent the crude artillery that is always brought in when milder means no longer fulfil their purpose. In normal times, however, this is rarely the case. As a rule, the small incentive that certain milder means exert on the propensity to buy and sell is sufficient to keep the balance of payments in equilibrium.

First of all, there is the interest rate, a real devil of an instrument, which produces the most extraordinary effects with fluctuations of a fraction of a percent, that is, with a subtle instrument. We have already become acquainted with it when we dealt with the value of the national money, and we saw then (in my letter of January 17) that it exerts a quite tremendous influence on this value and thus on the price level. Depending on whether the interest rate increases or decreases, it transfers 'resting' money into circulation or puts 'circulating' money into a state of rest, which increases the price in the first case and makes it cheaper in the second. In this way, he coordinates production and consumption in a far more appropriate way than the most precise planned economy with all its economic provinces and self-governing bodies is able to do. This interest, so inconspicuous and yet so powerful, also exerts an enormous influence on the external economic relations of the countries and contributes to a great extent to keeping the balance of payments of the countries in equilibrium.

If a country has to make extraordinarily large payments to foreign countries, and if a significant part of the available purchasing power (i.e. liquid money) has to be reserved for the purchase of foreign exchange, so that the purchasing power remaining for domestic transactions becomes scarce and prices consequently fall until foreign countries intervene and provide the country with the foreign exchange necessary for payment, then interest alleviates this price pressure, which is always felt to be disturbing and easily develops into a crisis. It alleviates it by going up itself. The direct cause of its rise is the aforementioned scarcity of purchasing power, which increases the lending price for available money - nothing else is interest - accordingly. And the effect of its increase is that foreign countries now show a greater willingness than before to grant credit and thereby make part of the foreign exchange purchases superfluous. Many a foreign bank, which at 4 1/2 per cent interest flatly refuses any loan because the money in its own country yields the same return, can be found willing to grant a loan when the interest rate rises to 5 or 5 1/2 per cent. Here the mild means of interest replaces the sharper means of price pressure to the advantage of the national economy.

Of course, here too a distinction must be made between gold-currency countries and paper-currency countries. In the former, credit reacts to the stimulus of the interest rate much more quickly and reliably than in the latter, corresponding to the different degree of exchange rate fluctuations and the exchange rate risk associated with the credit. Where the gold currency prevails and the exchange rate differences can therefore only ever amount to pennies, an increase in interest of 1/4 to 1/2 per cent already tends to be very effective. Where, on the other hand, the security of gold is lacking and, as a result, sudden fluctuations in the exchange rate have to be taken into account, a whole 2, 3 or even 5 per cent in additional interest often has only an insignificant effect. Here, the stimulant of interest must often be so strongly dosed in order to be effective that it practically amounts to an abdication of interest, and one must of necessity leave the settlement of payments to the more brutal means of price pressure - via the exchange rate.

Another, very mild and yet effective auxiliary factor of debt equalisation is arbitrage, for which I unfortunately cannot give you a correspondingly short German word. It is based on the exploitation of the valuation differences of one and the same international trade object in the different countries. It, too, is connected with credit, just like interest, except that its stimulant is not the interest rate, but the exchange rate. The field of its activity is mainly foreign exchange, stock exchange values and coupons. Thus, for example, foreign exchange arbitrage takes advantage of the fact that a country with a heavy momentary debt seeks the bills of exchange of the creditor country at a higher rate than the usual rate, by offering it these bills of exchange, which it is able to procure more cheaply in countries with an active balance of payments, either for sale or on loan. In so far as it does this, it spares the debtor country the recourse to interest and price pressure. Securities arbitrage takes advantage of the fact that in a country with a high level of instantaneous debt, international securities tend to be subject to price pressure, and buys up such securities on the country's stock exchanges in order to sell them again immediately on other exchanges with a certain, usually very slight, price advantage. And the coupon arbitrage acts in the same way, buying such coupons, which are payable in several currencies at a fixed conversion rate, relatively cheaply in the debtor country and selling them or redeeming them in countries whose currency is particularly valuable at the moment. All these operations give rise to foreign credit balances for the debtor country, which it can use to cover its debit balance.

Arbitrage, too, naturally works much more promptly and advantageously in a gold-currency country than where the exchange risk is great. Since their profit is always only modest - in arbitrage it has to come from the quantity - the danger of relatively small exchange rate fluctuations is enough to make it impossible for them to work or to turn it into naked speculation, in which case they no longer calculate by the per thousand but by many percentages and seek to enrich themselves at the expense of the debtor country.

All these means which I have mentioned to you here, dear James, either serve the purpose of converting the merchandise, and indeed commodities of the most diverse kind, from the 50,000 ton ship to the pin and from the million bond to the 5 shilling coupon, into 'world money' and using it to cover the passive balance of the national balance of payments; or they serve the purpose of procuring foreign credits which reduce the liability balance of the present balance sheet and, as it were, 'carry forward' men's eradicated debt amount to a new account. The new account, of course, is already a matter of concern in the next quarter if the credit is short-term, whereas a cura posterior is a question that will only become acute in decades if the debtor country has succeeded in obtaining long-term credit with the help of the means described.

I hope I have expressed myself sufficiently clearly in this letter so that the facts have become clear to you. If, to my regret, you have not understood everything, the fault lies not with you but with me and my insufficient talent for common understanding. For the things themselves are exceedingly simple and transparent.

With love

Your old dad.

Sixth Letter

Is gold expendable?
Balancing the Balance of Payments by Technical Means Gold Currency and Gallows Currency

Berlin, September 17th 1921

The following, dear James, are the results of our epistolary teaching course so far:
Neither gold nor bills of exchange are 'world money'. Rather, both are only means for the purpose of setting in motion the actual world money, which balances the debits and credits in the balance of payments of the countries through its outflow and inflow. This real world money, in which all claims are collected and all debts are paid off, is the commodity.

As a rule, very small stimuli suffice to induce the commodity to migrate from the debtor countries to the creditor countries and thus to perform its service as world money. The best known of these are interest and the exploitation of the smallest price differences through arbitrage. Only when the commodity does not fully react to these harmless stimuli, and credit is not induced by them to perform its important auxiliary service, do other, more powerful stimuli come into operation, namely the exchange rate and, in gold-currency countries, the gold movement.

The exchange rate, whose deterioration is synonymous with a reduction in the price of the merchandise in the paying country, acts directly and with brute force. It acts on the merchandise like an expulsion order and, by depressing its price, throws it into the countries with higher prices in the quantities necessary to balance the balance of payments. The gold movement also acts with irresistible force, but only indirectly and at least more gently. By allowing gold to flow out, it reduces the existing money supply and purchasing power in the gold-currency country, causes the price level to fall accordingly and thereby also opens the export valve for the commodity, which now flows abroad as the real world money.

Hence, my dear, it is that such exceedingly small quantities of gold are sufficient to bring even an extraordinarily passive balance of payments into equilibrium. If gold itself were the world's money, even the largest gold stock of a country would not suffice to pay a national debt of billions. But since in reality it is not the gold but the commodity that pays the debt of billions, and the gold only provides the pacemaker for the commodity, it does not require too great a quantity of gold to keep the balance of payments in equilibrium.

I have seen that even in England, whose enormous trade and extensive credit relations make the country active with gigantic sums, and passive with gigantic sums, before the war a few million pounds sterling of gold cleared out any balance of debts or claims. As soon as interest and arbitrage failed, a few per cent of the debt sum in gold sufficed to set as much commodity in motion as was necessary to cover the total of the debt.

A gold currency can therefore be maintained with a relatively small stock of metal, provided that everything else is in order in the monetary system. For internal circulation there is no need at all for a stock of gold; here it is sufficient to ensure that the quantity of money, which alone determines the value of money and the level of prices, is determined exclusively by circulation and is not altered by any arbitrary act of the state, however well-intentioned. And in external traffic, as we have seen, only small quantities of gold are required, because the main payments from country to country are not made in gold but in commodities.

Would it not now be possible - this question certainly suggests itself to you here - to do without even the small quantities of gold which do the pacing work in international payments? In other words, would it not be possible for a country to give up the gold currency externally as well as internally without endangering its balance of payments in any way? Or is a certain stock of gold, in view of the balance of payments, indispensable for a country interwoven with world trade?

I am not referring to the obvious possibility of a country maintaining a stock of foreign gold bills, gold foreign exchange, instead of a stock of cash gold. Since gold foreign exchange can be converted into gold at any time by discounting at the banks of its country of origin, it is normally to be regarded as equal to gold in every respect. A currency based on gold foreign exchange is - except in times of war - nothing other than a gold currency, and therefore does not mean a renunciation of this principle, but adherence to it.

The question of whether a country can completely dispose of gold without harming its monetary system and its balance of payments is self-answering in view of what was said earlier. For since gold has a clearly defined task in the foreign trade of a country - namely, the task of forcing the world money commodity to balance the balance of payments by influencing the price level in the country - it can only be dispensed with under a very specific condition. If there is a means which triggers the effect brought about by gold just as conveniently and reliably as gold, then the latter is dispensable. If there is no such means, gold is indispensable.

So everything depends on the answer to the question whether it is possible to shrink the circulation of money in the country when the balance of payments is passive and to expand it when it is active. For in a gold-currency country, gold outflows and inflows affect prices and the movement of goods via the money supply. Now there is no doubt that in principle the money supply in a country can be increased and decreased without the intervention of gold. We see that in fact all countries are now operating with a larger, now with a smaller circulation of money. Another question is that of the measure. Whether the increase or decrease can be adjusted to the balance of payments as precisely and as gently as it is done by gold, seems doubtful. And it also seems doubtful whether this adjustment of the money supply to the requirements of the balance of payments takes place automatically, out of circulation. For we know that only traffic may change the money supply in free self-determination, and that any arbitrary intervention from outside will infallibly ruin the monetary system of the country.

Very interesting studies can be linked to this question, which, however, would only distract us from the topic today. I will therefore anticipate the result by saying: There is an excellent means of keeping the money supply in the country at all times in exact accordance with the requirements of the balance of payments. For if the balance of payments is passive, and foreign means of payment (foreign exchange) are therefore in demand, so that they begin to rise in price, this is a sign that the circulation of money is oversaturated, i.e. that the prices of goods are too high and prevent the world money 'commodity' from flowing out. One must therefore carefully lift money out of circulation - whether by a tax or a loan is quite indifferent - and provide it with a state of rest. The price pressure, imperceptible at first, then slowly increasing, which emanates from this reduction of purchasing power, promotes exports and thus wipes out the

passive balance which has manifested itself in the scarcity of foreign exchange. As soon as this purpose has been achieved, i.e. the foreign exchange has been sufficiently supplied and has fallen back to its normal price, this is an unmistakable sign that money in circulation and the balance of payments are now in harmony and that traffic does not demand a further reduction of the national money. If the exchange rates fall below the normal level, this means nothing other than that the hitherto passive balance of payments is beginning to become active and that one must therefore restore the balance by releasing a part of the withdrawn money.
For if this is not done, i.e. if the command of traffic is not respected, the price level is kept unnecessarily under pressure and the country is deprived of more goods than necessary.

The tasks that gold automatically fulfils can therefore also be accomplished in another way, without the intervention of this metal. And a theorist would therefore be quite justified in saying: gold can be dispensed with not only in the internal traffic of a country, but also in its external traffic. A sound currency and a solid position in international payments do not in themselves require that the country in question have the gold currency or even a certain amount of gold. It is neither harmful nor inconvenient if a country keeps its balance of payments in equilibrium by other, so to speak, technical means instead of gold. But - and this is the sore point - one basic condition must be fulfilled: The contraction and re-expansion of the circulation of money must be subordinated solely to the command of the balance of payments, expressed in the exchange rates. Only the level of the exchange rates and nothing else may have the determining influence on the quantity of money in circulation. The state, with its financial, commercial and social needs, aims and purposes, must on principle keep its hands off the monetary system. It must respect in money something that is outside its sphere of power, something that is subject to special elementary laws, a commodity reference right born of traffic, towards which it must observe the strictest neutrality. He must always only watch out, remove inhibitions, secure respect for the command of the exchange rate, but never arrogate to himself creative functions. For as soon as he does this, as soon as he begins to tamper with the law embodied in money according to his own arbitrary will, he not only falsifies this law by changing its content, but he also disturbs the harmony between money and the balance of payments, he disrupts the monetary system of the country in a disastrous way, of which we have the saddest examples before our eyes today.

In abstracto, I can well imagine a country in which the above requirement is fulfilled and the monetary system is strictly separated from the state. I can imagine a wise legislator, a new Solon, who would consecrate the state. How immensely great is the temptation for the state to abuse the money machine for its own purposes, and who at the same time knows the pernicious effects of this abuse, would erect an insurmountable wall between money and state power. For instance, by imposing eight and eight on every head of state who would allow himself to make unauthorised changes in the money supply. I can imagine this Solon erecting a high gallows on the market square of the state capital with the inscription:

'To this gallows will go, without regard to person or status, anyone who, by arbitrarily increasing the money supply, cheats the population out of a part of the purchasing power represented in the money!'

And finally, I can also imagine that this draconian measure will fulfil its purpose, so that the money, untouched by the state, will circulate in that quantity which traffic produces in the way I described earlier, and which will merely contract and expand again according to the twitches of the balance of payments. In such a country there would be a perfectly healthy currency, even if not a gram of gold were available for payment purposes. It would be shown here that a currency under the sign of the gallows, i.e. protected by draconian penalties against any abuse by the authorities - let us call it 'gallows currency' for the sake of brevity - is completely equal to the gold currency.

But I cannot help myself, dear James: I am only able to imagine such a currency in abstracto, only theoretically, not in living reality. Every state system goes through lines in which the temptation to lay hands on money becomes so great that all moral and economic objections no longer arise against it.

Even if the gallows, the symbol of the protection of money, were here threateningly erected, it would be of no use, for the power of the state would pull it down at the critical moment. If there is no commandment for the simple citizen in need, who is surrounded by penal laws, how much less for the sovereign state.

There is, after all, no simpler and more ineffective way of taxing the people than by taking away part of their purchasing power by increasing their money - the state will seize the money machine in order to make it work according to its needs. And there will then always be theorists who turn black into white and wrong into right by recognising the state as the master of money in learned deductions and stamp the money, which in reality only traffic is capable of producing, as a creature of the state and its arbitrary legal order.

For this reason, my son, because human institutions are regulated and occasionally abused by weak or short-sighted people, the paper currency, which in itself is quite useful, has always proved inferior to the gold currency. For this reason, even in its most perfect and best-secured form, namely in the form we have just called 'gallows currency', it would sooner or later fizzle out. Of course, the gold standard can also be abused. But by forcing the state to recognise a certain quantitative relationship between money and gold and not to violate it, it carries an element of self-protection.

It is immune to a certain degree from the poison of pernicious doctrines and negligent state pragmatism. That is why all the great trading nations always return to the gold standard after they have experienced in their own economies, in shorter or longer periods of monetary mismanagement, what it means to experiment with the yellow.

Hereby God be commanded!

Your old dad.

Seventh Letter

*Balance of payments and central bank
Discount, gold, foreign exchange and reserve policy*

Berlin, September 19th 1921

What, dear James, is the practical superiority of the gold currency over all non-metallic currencies? To put it briefly, it consists in the unsurpassable elasticity it gives to the circulation of money. In a gold-currency country, the circulation of money contracts automatically whenever the country's balance of payments is passive, only to expand again automatically as soon as the balance of payments becomes active. This process of alternating contraction and expansion of the circulation of money is brought about by the so-called 'gold movement,' i.e. by gold flowing out of the country in one case and flowing into the country in the other. Since gold in the gold-currency country is a component of the means of payment as a whole, its outflow reduces the money substance in circulation and the purchasing power embodied in it, while its inflow increases both. This elasticity, which gold gives to the national money, works so promptly that the balance of payments of the country always balances itself automatically with its help, and that there can be no stronger activity or passivity at all. Accordingly, the exchange rates in a gold-currency country can only rise or fall insignificantly. They can only ever oscillate between two closely spaced poles, namely between the pole at which gold imports begin (the lower gold point) and the other pole at which gold exports begin (the upper gold point).

'What a fine and reliable traffic regulator!' you will think.

And certainly the value of the gold movement can hardly ever be overestimated. Yet, by itself, it is not enough to balance the balance of payments with the speed and ease that is desirable. A healthy transport economy in a country with a healthy monetary system is extremely sensitive.
It reacts to the slightest irritation, and the movement of gold, which for all its reliability still has a certain clumsiness about it, is still far too clumsy for the normal case. As close as the two gold points at which gold moves over or under are to each other - the difference between them in gold-currency countries is about 1/2-3/4 per cent - and as little, therefore, as the exchange rates can rise above or fall below their mean level, a healthy economy still feels this slight fluctuation in the value of money as far too great a disturbance and as a complication in its calculations.

When we think back to the beautiful days, my son, when Germany enjoyed a genuine, right gold currency. we will remember the fact that at that time the exchange rates only bumped against the upper or lower gold point in rare exceptional cases, although the German balance of payments was almost never completely in equilibrium.
As a rule, exchange rates at that time fluctuated only by a few thousandths around the midpoint, around the so-called gold parity, i.e. around the price that a certain quantum of gold cost in German money according to the coinage law. For the 7 1/3 grams of gold contained in an English sovereign, this price was about 20.43 marks, and the rate of the sterling bill in Berlin usually deviated from this midpoint by only a few pennies. The upper gold point of 20.51 marks was only reached in exceptional cases, and the lower point of 20.34 marks was only reached once, to my recollection, in 1904.

This means that gold only had to act relatively seldom as a regulator of the balance of payments, because other balancing means had taken over this task from it; balancing means that acted more quickly than the cumbersome gold, which only reacted to exchange rates of 20.51 or 20.34. These are faster and therefore more effective balancing means. These faster and therefore milder means are old acquaintances, namely interest, credit and the commercial exploitation of both through arbitrage.

The most important and elementary of these three factors is interest, because it is the motor that sets the other two in motion. Interest is the most effective regulator of a healthy economy. Wherever we look, it is always somewhere in the background as a driving force. In the case of money, we have already become acquainted with it as the magnet which sometimes accelerates, sometimes slows down the circulation of money and thus adapts it to the needs of production. It is the factor which gives money the necessary elasticity in internal circulation; not by changing its quantity - interest is not able to do that - but by making existing money roll faster or slower by means of the high or low premium which it places on the intensive use of money, on the energetic utilisation of existing purchasing power. (In the case of paper money, one must say: 'fluttering')

Now that we are dealing with foreign trade, we again find interest on our path, as the light Ariel that relieves the ponderous Caliban 'gold' of the worry of balancing the balance of payments; and indeed interest does this by magnetically attracting or repelling credit, and sometimes alone, sometimes together with the latter, inducing arbitrage in the most movable commodities (securities, precious metals, coupons, speculative staple articles) to direct the movement of commodities in that direction which is suitable for settling the differences in payments between countries.

For the real means of world payment - do not forget this for a moment, my son! - is and remains the commodity.

It has now become customary, and not only in gold-currency countries, to take control of the interest rate in view of its importance for payment transactions, i.e. to pursue a purposeful 'interest rate policy'. As a rule, this task was entrusted to the same institutions in whose hands the other supervision and regulation of monetary transactions lies, namely the central banks.
In this way, it was hoped that all the elements which determine the national monetary system and its relations with foreign countries would be united in one hand, so that the same body which controls the internal circulation of money would not only manage the centralised gold supply of the country and oversee the international movement of gold, but would also be able to exert a decisive influence on the other important factor in the balance of payments, the interest rate.

The central banks exert this influence by raising and lowering the interest rate in accordance with the state of the balance of payments as indicated by the exchange rate, thereby allowing the trade credit, which they can grant as the largest reservoir of money in the country, to flow sometimes more abundantly, sometimes more sparsely, and in this way also directing the interest rate of the open money market in a direction corresponding to the balance of payments.

This activity is called 'discount policy' because they prefer to grant their credit by discounting commercial bills of exchange.
Thus, the central bank is the authority which does not exclusively maintain the connection between domestic and foreign payments - the multifaceted 'market' plays a decisive role in this - but it does have a decisive influence on it. For it has no less than four means of power in its hands to correct the national balance of payments in the respective

sense required. It has at its disposal the means of interest or 'discount policy', furthermore that of 'gold policy', thirdly, at least if it considers it desirable, the important auxiliary instrument of foreign exchange policy', and finally 'reserve policy' which under certain circumstances can become of quite considerable importance.

Let us consider, albeit briefly, the effectiveness of these four components of central bank policy in their relationship to the balance of payments and the external value of money; I will go into this in more detail when we have dealt with the subject of 'currency' and will deal with central banks as economic institutions.

If the state of the exchange rates indicates that the balance of payments is passive, and that the country is therefore immediately indebted to foreign countries, the central bank is accustomed to apply its discount policy as the first countermeasure. It raises the interest rate it demands from its borrowers to such an extent as is necessary to induce some of the borrowers to pay off their debt to the central bank and to look for substitute credit on the open money market or at private banks.

This also makes interest more expensive, so that many a businessman prefers to do without any credit for the moment and to make intended purchases only within the narrow limits of his own means, or to procure the necessary funds for this purpose by partially increasing his stock of goods. Thus, the propensity to buy slackens and the supply of goods increases. Consequence: A lowering of the price level, i.e. a cheaper buying opportunity for foreign countries, which first acquire the easily movable categories of goods (securities, speculative staple articles, etc.) by way of arbitrage, in order to then, depending on the degree of price reduction, also resort to more cumbersome categories of goods; until the domestic debt to foreign countries is balanced by the counterclaims thus created, i.e. the balance of payments is brought back into its equilibrium by exporting goods.

This is at least the purpose of the central banks' discount policy, which is often more instinctive than rational, but which they do not always achieve. For in times of boom and over-speculation, the open market very often fails to follow. Nevertheless, the discount policy is an extremely effective tool among my colleagues and among the economists of the world, and if you take the trouble, dear James, to study the report of an English monetary commission set up in 1917, the so-called 'Cunliffe Committee', which is well worth reading, you will find a song of praise for the discount policy. It says in one passage: 'The increase in the bank rate and the measures to make it effective in the market led with necessity to an increase in the national rate of interest and to a restriction of lending activity. ... The result was a fall in most prices on the domestic market, which hindered imports, but stimulated exports and thus compensated for the unfavourable balance of trade.'

But, as I said, in spite of the good censure given to it here, the discount policy often remains ineffective, and in this case it must be replaced by a sharper means, the gold policy. Since the direct way of curbing the desire to buy by means of interest has not succeeded and exports have not been increased to the necessary extent, the exchange rates reach the so-called upper gold point, the export of gold thus becomes worthwhile, and the central bank proceeds to the dispatch of bullion or coin gold, which at first, like any other commodity, redeems a part of the national debt by establishing a counterclaim. If the bank hesitates with the shipment of gold, it is forced by the specialists of the precious metal trade to hand over gold for export purposes by presenting notes. If it were to refuse the gold, this would mean the end of the gold currency. The amount of gold handed over would reduce the metal hoard, the note cover and therefore also the bank's borrowing possibilities.

Even if the market were willing to pay any interest on the bank loan, however high it might be, the central bank would refuse to lend to it in view of its reduced gold stock, and would even have to refuse to renew maturing loans. And through this, the purchasing power in the country experiences a very sensitive reduction.

The export of gold thus works in two directions: firstly, by generating foreign credits like any other export and by reducing the national debt accordingly, but then, and mainly, by the intensive repercussions it has on the volume of purchasing power, thus on the price level and thus again on exports.

The foreign exchange policy works in a similar way to this gold policy. It consists in accumulating a large stock of foreign means of payment in the form of bills of exchange and, when the exchange rate rises, to come to the aid of the market with them. Foreign exchange, since in this case it is almost always denominated in gold, is to be regarded as equal to gold, and its outflow therefore generally has the same effects as the export of gold. Some central banks prefer foreign exchange to gold because it is easily transportable, interest-bearing and, if necessary, can be used without loss of time in the country of origin.

Personally, I am not a friend of surrogates in any field and prefer gold to gold substitutes. Moreover, every central bank must reckon with the fact that one day it will suffer the same fate as the Deutsche Reichsbank with its English foreign exchange, which at the outbreak of war suddenly ceased to be gold, but sank to the level of cellar bills, because the English acceptors were not allowed to redeem them according to wartime law.

Finally, the fourth and last, very effective but relatively rarely used means in the service of the balance of payments is the reserve policy. This consists of the central bank of the country forcing the private banking community to increase its cash reserves (current account balances or deposits) when exchange rates are unfavourable. The effect is the same as in the case of a restriction of credit activity, except that it is even more prompt: the purchasing power in the country decreases to the extent that the central bank calls in and stores money - prices fall, exports increase, and the balance of payments improves.

This policy is understandably very unpopular with us bank directors. We do not like to give away our money just when we can best use it.

Consequently, only a central bank backed by a very strong negation, independent of the private banks, can apply the reserve policy. The Bank of England makes use of it from time to time in a special way, by selling its Console stocks on the Stock Exchange and using the money thus collected to strengthen its reserve. The English private banks, which have to give this money directly or indirectly, are naturally not at all delighted with such a policy. But their influence on the 'Old Lady' is not nearly as great as that of the continental bankers on the central banks of their respective countries. They may growl, but they pay.

With the help of these four means, dear James, every central bank in a gold-currency country is able to maintain the balance of payments in equilibrium without the exchange rates fluctuating more than very slightly. This is a great advantage for the country, but it is due far less to the skill of the central bank than to the fact that the gold currency prevails in the country. If the central bank were lacking, it would not do too much harm, for every gold currency protects itself.

Through the automatic outflow and inflow of gold, it keeps the price level at that level which is necessary in each case to force the world means of payment, the commodity, to balance the balance of payments. All that a central bank can do beyond this self-protection of the gold currency is to bring about the movement of commodities necessary for the establishment of equilibrium in the balance of payments by somewhat milder means, so that the rather crude means of gold migration need seldom come into operation, and consequently the exchange rates need not rise to the upper gold point or fall to the lower one.

This is, after all, a not inconsiderable advantage that a well-organised central bank is able to provide for the country. On the other hand, if one considers the enormous misery that a central bank administered according to the wrong principles or misused by the state can bring upon a country, one cannot help wondering whether this advantage actually justifies a country burdening itself with an instrument that represents such an extraordinary source of danger, and whether a gold-currency country could not also manage quite well without a central bank.

In any case, it is infinitely better for a country not to have a central bank than to have a mismanaged one.

>	With love

>	Your old dad.

Eight Letter

Once again the 'gold mania'
Gold, paper and currency

Berlin, September 22ⁿᵈ 1921

It is neither an outdated prejudice, dear James, nor an erroneous doctrine nor an economic 'gold mania' that leads cultural people back again and again to the gold currency after they have undergone a long Odyssean voyage on the stormy sea of non-metallic currency.

As true as it is that in the monetary system of a country it is not in and of itself the material of which the individual monetary tokens consist, but the quantity of these tokens that is important.

The fact is irrefutable that the stability of value of money and all the rights expressed in it is de facto higher if gold forms the basis of the national currency.
Let us imagine two countries, one of which has the full gold currency, the other a paper currency.
We want to assume that both countries have an equally clear notion, that in the country of the paper currency, no arbitrary paper economy, no unscrupulous or thoughtless inflation policy is pursued, but that the right to purchase goods embodied in money is strictly respected, and consequently any arbitrary creation of such rights with the help of the banknote press is fundamentally avoided.
In both cases, therefore, we are dealing with a stable, healthy currency; here with a healthy gold currency, here with a healthy paper currency. What is the state of the currency in these two countries, i.e. the valuation of the national money on the world market, as expressed in the exchange rates?

The balance of payments is decisive for the movement of exchange rates. If the balance of payments is passive in a country, i.e. if the country has to make more payments to foreign countries than it has to receive from them, the price of foreign currencies and bills of exchange rises and the value of the country's own money on the world market falls. For the country with the passive balance of payments must, in order to be able to pay off its debt, buy more foreign means of payment than are offered to it at the normal price, while there is no demand for its own money, because the foreign country owes it nothing. Passive balance of payments means, whatever its origin, a fall in the value of the country liable to pay, and this in the country of the gold currency just as in the country of the paper currency. The constitution of money cannot change the validity of this iron law in the least.

The means by which the passive balance of payments is eliminated and the currency restored to its normal level is also exactly the same in both countries. Here as there it consists in an increase in exports (or, which is exactly the same in effect, a reduction in imports), so that an export surplus results for the country liable to pay. Since the foreign country must settle this surplus with its money and bills of exchange, the foreign means of payment, which were originally lacking and were sought in vain at rising prices, are now available; the demand for them slackens, their price falls, and the normal state of the currency is restored.

The difference, however, begins with the technical part of the problem. Even if the economic law that the balance of payments is balanced by the movement of goods applies equally to all countries, the method by which this movement of goods is brought about is by no means the same in all cases. On the contrary, there is a whole series of variations. And it is not at the discretion of the financial and commercial circles or of governments whether they want to apply this or that method in a given case, but the most suitable method in each case imposes itself on them by force. Man is not the master of the movement of commodities which brings about the settlement of payments, but he is the servant of that movement which still carries out its own laws. And these laws are different in a country with gold currency than in a country with paper currency.

Where the gold currency prevails, things regulate themselves very simply, one might say mechanically. Here there is always a commodity which has the tendency to flow out of the country in the case of a very slight deterioration and, conversely, to return again in the case of a very slight improvement. We have come to know gold as this migratory commodity, always ready to jump. It has its fixed price in all countries with a gold currency.

In England, for example, as long as the gold currency was intact, the price was 77 shillings 10 1/2 pence for an ounce.

Now, as soon as the exchange rate of a gold-currency country, let us say, to stick to our example, England, deteriorates, it becomes advantageous for foreign countries to buy gold there, because the 77 shillings 10 1/2 pence that an ounce costs can be had below normal price. So gold is pushing out of the country with irresistible force.

This emigration of gold in the case of a passive balance of payments and its return in the case of an active balance of payments has - as I have explained to you in my earlier letters - all kinds of extremely important consequences for the purchasing power of the money circulating in the country, consequences which, for their part, contribute to accelerating the adjustment of the balance of payments. But we do not need to dwell on these consequences today, because all we need to do at the moment is to visualise the balance-of-payments regulation that is particularly characteristic of the gold standard.

The first and most important peculiarity of this currency is that in a country where it prevails, the exchange rates can never deviate by more than 1/4 or at most 1/2 per cent from their normal level, because if there is the slightest tendency of these rates to deviate further from the normal level, gold, which is always ready to jump, irresistibly pushes out of or into the country and forcibly pushes the exchange rates back to their old level. The value of a gold-currency country can therefore never fluctuate by more than a fraction of a per cent; it has a fixed, reliable level, and all claims payable in this value can be regarded as absolutely stable in value.

This, however, is not only in itself a tremendous advantage for a country intertwined in international trade and credit, but also has far-reaching consequences for the question that concerns us here, namely, the adjustment of the balance of payments. A country whose currency is regarded as a 'rocher de bronce' in international trade always has credit, and with the help of this credit and of a fine trusty bank, arbitrage, very considerable differences in the balance of payments can be regulated without the export of goods in the proper sense, the export of gold or of heavy movable goods.

We thus arrive at the result that in a gold-currency country the balance of payments can very easily be kept in equilibrium because its currency is stable, and that on the other hand its currency is stable because its balance of payments can always very easily be kept in equilibrium, in the extreme case by sending gold.

As is so often the case in the economy, here too there is a reciprocal relationship and one moment is both cause and effect of the other.

What about the balance of payments in a country with paper currency? The running weight 'gold', which has a regulating effect by simply shifting its resting point, is absent here or is only present very exceptionally. (If it were always available and ready to balance, it would not be a paper currency country, but a country with gold currency or at least with gold marginal currency).

Consequently, the fixed anchoring of the currency is also missing. For there is no commodity other than gold for which all the relevant countries are prepared to pay a certain normal price.

The exchange rates fluctuate disproportionately here because they only stop rising or falling when as many goods have flowed into or out of the country as the balance of payments requires to restore its equilibrium. And most goods react only very sluggishly to the command emanating from the exchange rate, at any rate much more sluggishly than gold.

However, even in the paper currency country, the two important traffic elements 'credit' and 'arbitrage' offer their good services. But they, which we have come to know in the country of the gold currency as extremely fluid, of almost mercurial mobility, lose this property to an extraordinary degree under the rule of the paper currency.

Whereas there they were still much faster than gold, which is also very lively, here they are usually even slower than the cumbersome normal commodity.

This is due to the fact that in the paper currency country the element of risk is attached to them like a lead weight. Since the exchange rate tends to deteriorate accordingly with a strongly passive balance of payments, every foreign lender and arbitrageur must reckon with the possibility that he will be paid in an inferior currency when the loan falls due or when the final settlement of the arbitrage transaction is made.

And if the lender secures himself against this risk of loss by demanding repayment in the stable-value money of his own country, the borrower bears the risk.
Consequently, credit and arbitrage do not react to very small interest or price advantages, as is the case in gold-currency countries, but only when they are beckoned by such a high interest rate or such a large additional price that the value risk can be accepted.

In a country with a relatively healthy paper currency - and this is the only one we are talking about here - there is certainly the possibility that the state or an institution commissioned by it (the central bank) will secure a stock of easily movable goods in order to send them abroad in the event of a possible balance of payments passivity, even before the exchange rates have deteriorated too much. The accumulation of a large stock of gold foreign exchange must be left out of consideration here; it practically amounts to an accumulation of gold, into which the foreign exchange can always be converted, except in the case of war, so that we are dealing here with the already mentioned variety of the gold currency, the gold marginal currency.

The same applies to other gold values, such as the English consols in normal times. Here we have only to think of neutral commodities which can easily be transformed into foreign claims by arbitrage or outright sale, such as silver, platinum, copper or grain. If the negation (or the central bank), in spite of the danger of loss connected with such articles, constantly operates with large stocks of this kind, or if it in some other way ensures that quickly realisable reserves are available in the country for the case of a strong foreign debt, it can keep the exchange rates relatively stable. It can also bring about the same effect, as we saw earlier, by systematically reducing the circulation of money. But such a policy is extraordinarily difficult, far more difficult than a transition to the gold standard, and therefore, to my knowledge, has never been attempted in practice.

Thus we see that the gold currency, apart from its main advantage, which is that it protects the country of its validity from being flooded with paper and therefore from a deterioration of money from within, has the second great advantage of securing for the country a stable currency, a constant external value of its money. Even a paper currency, however good and technically skilfully regulated, is not able to compete with the gold currency in this respect.

That is why all countries, having had their experiences with paper, sooner or later return to the gold currency, although theoretically it is actually indifferent what the money tokens are made of, in which the people's rights to purchase goods are embodied.

    With love

        Your old dad.

Ninth Letter

Internal and external value of money
'Double bottomed value of money'
Invoicing in foreign currency

Berlin, September 24th *1921*

Just in these weeks, dear James, in which we are both so intensely occupied with the valuta, our much-tried Germany is passing through the intermediate stage of a valutarian abnormality which is equally interesting for the layman and the economist.

This abnormality does not consist in the fact that the value of the Reichsmark has recently deteriorated enormously. The recent decline of the mark is rather to be seen as a quite natural, even self-evident process. For if the currency of a country that has to pay billions to foreign countries is not backed by gold, it must necessarily undergo a devaluation process in the course of the payments. But one would think that the money of a country, even if its inherent purchasing power sinks, must under all circumstances have a certain value, regardless of whether this value is half or one tenth or one hundredth of the legal gold pari.

In fact, we are surprised to see that the German Reichsmark today has not one value, but two values, namely a domestic value and a quite different, considerably lower foreign value.

The domestic value, i.e. the purchasing power of the mark in Germany itself, has fallen over time to about one-twelfth of its pre-war value, and prices and wages have risen accordingly to an average of twelve times their pre-war value.

The foreign value, on the other hand, i.e. the purchasing power of the mark abroad, has fallen far more, to about one twenty-fifth of its pre-war value. This can be seen quite clearly from the exchange rate on New Bork and from the price of gold. Abroad, the mark has been devalued twice as much as at home.

This is an abnormality that is very rarely observed with such ferocity. For it actually contradicts all economic laws. Above all, it contradicts the fact that the commodity, through its inflow and outflow, constantly strives to adjust the internal value of the national money to its external value. The external and internal value of money are normally kept in equilibrium by foreign trade, and a very simple consideration tells us that in principle it cannot be otherwise.

If the purchasing power of money in a country falls to a tenth, i.e. if prices here rise tenfold, all foreign goods appear cheap because their price has remained unchanged. Accordingly, a strong importation sets in. You will always see, dear James, that a depreciation of money at home is first followed by an increase in imports and a passive balance of trade. But the additional import must be paid for, and that in foreign money. As a result, there is a strong demand for foreign bills of exchange and money, so that their prices rise, which means nothing other than that the valuation of the national money abroad, in short the 'external value' of the money, falls accordingly.

If the external value of money falls to one-fifth of its original value, i.e. if one has to pay five times the price for imported goods, the foreign goods, measured against the ten times more expensive domestic goods, still appear cheap, and their importation continues.

Consequently, the rise in the price of foreign exchange, or rather the fall in the external value of money, continues until the latter has fallen to a tenth of its original value. For only then has the foreign commodity become ten times more expensive for the domestic buyer, and only then does importation come to a standstill, because the level of prices at home and abroad is equal.

We see, therefore, that the balance of payments of a country does not find its equilibrium until the exchange rates have deteriorated to the same degree as the national money has lost purchasing power; in other words, until the external value of the national money has sunk to the same low as its internal value. The external value could not normally fall any lower, for that would otherwise have meant a rise in foreign prices above the domestic prices and would have led immediately to increased exports; and thereby -the external value would have been raised again.
But neither could it fall less than the internal value of the national money, for the increased importation, which in this case continues, produces a debt to foreign countries and a demand for foreign exchange, which finally pushes the external value down by force to the low point of the internal value.
The internal and external values of money thus strive for agreement. Foreign trade, in its various manifestations, enforces this correspondence again and again and does not allow itself to be deterred from its obligation to bring the two fluctuating monetary values towards a common centre, even by customs barriers and export bans.

I know, dear James, that with what I have just said I am putting your trust in me to a somewhat severe test. For I myself have just discovered that the purchasing power of the mark abroad is only about one twenty-fifth of its prewar value, while in Germany it is still about one twelfth of that value; that one and the same banknote can therefore buy twice as much here as abroad. This fact, which no national economic theory can eliminate, is in fact incompatible with the fundamental correspondence between the external value of money and its internal value, as I have claimed.

Moreover, it cannot even be said that this is one of those well-known exceptions that confirm the rule. For the divergence of the two values is by no means of recent date, but can be traced back for quite some time, almost as long as we have had a distressed currency.
The only difference is that the relationship between internal and external value changes continuously, with one having the greater purchasing power and the other the greater. At the beginning of 1920, for example, the external value of the mark was barely half its internal value. But a few months later, in the summer of 1920, the opposite was the case: one German note could buy considerably more abroad than at home.
And today things are again roughly as they were in February 1920. The two categories of value always swing past each other, and even if they meet temporarily when they rise and fall, there is usually a considerable distance between them. What is normal here is not agreement but divergence.

But how does this divergence between the internal value and external value of money rhyme with the theorem that the two values are constantly striving for agreement?
Well, it rhymes very well with it, as soon as one reads the theorem correctly and puts the emphasis on the word 'strive'. The result is the very simple fact that the internal value and the external value of a currency constantly try to meet at a certain point, but that they always swing past this point, that is, they always move upwards and downwards

away from the common mean value, as soon as the monetary system in the country is as it is at present in Germany.

The facts are as clear as can be. When the devaluation of currency money in a country has reached a certain degree, let us say nine-tenths of the normal value, the internal and external purchasing power of money strive, in the manner described at the beginning of this letter, to meet on the new basis of one-tenth.

For a time, it is then possible for exchange rates to rise fifteenfold, while prices in the country have risen only sevenfold. But this anomaly is not permanent. Very soon the exchange rates will fall, about twelvefold, while domestic prices will rise, about ninefold; until one day the two values will meet at the new par corresponding to the real depreciation of money, namely tenfold.

This meeting is unavoidable and even occurs rather quickly if - precisely if - the assumed precondition is correct, namely that the value of the national money is really one tenth of its former value, no more and no less.

However, this condition only applies if the real value of the national money is fixed on its new basis, anchors here, so to speak. And that is just as little the case in Germany today as it is in most of the value-sick European Eastern states.

In all these countries, the printing press continues to work unabated, the money supply increases and the real value of the national currency sinks accordingly. If the real value has just amounted to one tenth of the old gold value, and if the external value and the internal value of the currency, i.e. the exchange rates and the prices, have just begun to adjust themselves to this tenth, the real value is already sinking to one twelfth under the influence of the printing press. And before these two values have even come close to this new parity, the parity has already fallen again, to one-fifteenth, to one-eighteenth, to one-twentieth. #

Each new fall, however, not only prevents the correspondence of the internal value with the external value of money by continually shifting the common point of rest towards which they are striving, but it even introduces a new, aggravated disturbance into the process of equalisation of values; it soon pushes the internal value, soon the external value, in a direction that is opposed to equalisation and thereby causes the gap between the two works, which has only just narrowed, to assume considerable dimensions again.

We have to think of this process in broad outlines as follows: as soon as the money press pours new masses of money onto the market, i.e. as soon as new purchasing power is created, a shock occurs either on the market of goods or on that of foreign bills of exchange. For either the newly created purchasing power turns preferentially to the domestic goods market, in which case all prices rise here, and one speaks of a new 'inflation'.

Or the new purchasing power turns preferentially to the market of foreign goods and the market of foreign means of payment, then the exchange rates rise, and one speaks of a new 'decline in currency'.

In the first case, therefore, the internal value of money deteriorates, in the second the external value. But whichever of these two values deteriorates, in any case the gap between them is widened and the approximation to the real value of the currency is made more difficult. This process is repeated and intensified to the extent that the printing press comes into new activity and inflation increases in the country.

Here we have the real reason why there is not one money value in Germany today, but two sharply separated money values. The printing press continues its disastrous work again and again after short intervals, thereby rushing new purchasing power - or, to speak exactly: purchasing power transferred from the old, rightful money holders to the new money holders - soon onto the commodity market, soon onto the foreign exchange market, and thus causes the divergence between the internal and the external value of money.

The divergence has the natural tendency to diminish continuously and finally to disappear altogether. But before this can happen, a new wave of inflation thwarts this tendency and drives a new wedge between the two values.

It is therefore, if I may say so, a quite 'normal abnormality' that in a country where the process of demonetization has not yet been completed, two fundamentally different monetary values coexist.

The consequences of this abnormality may seem grotesque to us, but they are inevitable. If in Germany today the foreigner can buy everything for half the price the national has to pay, this is the natural consequence of the fact that the external value of the mark is at present (certainly not for long) half as great as its internal value. And when the newspapers report that the Czech on the Polish border prefers to be shaved on Polish territory for 30 Polish marks instead of doing it in his own country for two crowns, we are looking at the opposite situation: the Czech crown is currently worth far more abroad than at home. For two crowns, one can be shaved only once at home, but twice or even three times in Poland.

Since the actual reason and the lawfulness of the tension between the internal and external value of money are only rarely recognised, attempts are made from time to time in all countries afflicted by this peculiar disease to eliminate the tension by artificial means or - which is particularly popular today - by decree.

In Germany, for example, whenever the external value of the mark is particularly low compared to the internal value and foreign exchange has to be paid far more expensively than the real value of the mark, the export trade is asked not to issue invoices in marks but 'to invoice in foreign currency'. Foreign countries should therefore pay not in remittances but in bills of exchange, i.e. not in marks but in dollars, pounds and guilders, thus relieving the German market of the necessity of covering its demand for these currencies on the foreign exchange market. If, as a result, demand falls here, then - so it is argued - the prices of foreign means of payment fall, i.e. the external value of the mark rises again to the level of its internal value. That sounds quite plausible.

But anyone who realises that the tension between domestic and foreign value, although an abnormality, nevertheless has its good economic reasons, will be quite sceptical about the success of 'invoicing in foreign currency'.

And indeed, the efforts to affect the external value of money through the mode of payment are as childish as they are futile. In reality, it makes no difference at all whether American debtors pay Germany in marks or dollars.

If they pay in marks, the corresponding dollar amounts are missing in Germany, and the German demand for them increases the exchange rate of the dollar and thus worsens the external value of the mark.
In return, however, the Americans must buy Mark notes, thereby improving the external value of the Mark by exactly as much as the German demand for dollars worsens it.
If, on the other hand, the Americans pay in dollars, a corresponding German demand for dollars can of course be satisfied without the exchange rate rising and the market value

falling accordingly. On the other hand, however, the American demand for marks ceases to exist, and therefore there is no improvement factor that would otherwise have raised the market value; in this case, too, advantage and disadvantage cancel each other out.

Technical aids and regulations, my dear James, cannot eliminate the evil of the 'double-bottom value of money'; just as organic disturbances are never remedied by mechanical interventions, but rather aggravated.

Whoever wants to bring the external value and the internal value of a currency into harmony and fix the monetary system on the basis of its real value must see to it that the printing press comes to a standstill.

Then, but only then, will the abnormality that one and the same national money is subject to two different valuations disappear along with so many other evils.

 Concerned

  Your old dad.

Tenth Letter

Balance of Payments and Reparations
Valuta and Fiscal Policy

Berlin, September 28th 1921

There are times, dear James, when it is extraordinarily difficult to maintain a clear view of the economic context. These are regularly times when some political or financial event of world-historical magnitude pushes itself into the foreground in such a way that it covers the entire mental field of vision. Then even intelligent people are often no longer able to distinguish which economic processes must be attributed to this tremendous event and which to other causes. They are then inclined to see the root and origin of all abnormal phenomena solely in that world-historical event, whose enormous shadow darkens all contemporary feeling and thinking. Germany is currently going through such a period of mental hypocrisy. There is hardly an economic event that the educated German does not see as a direct consequence of the all-dominant problem of 'reparations', the annual payment of several billion gold to the countries of the Entente.

Thus, there is not the slightest doubt in the minds of most economists that the acute fall which the German currency has undergone in the past quarter has been the direct result of reparations. Germany has had to pay a gold billion to foreign countries from mid-May to August 31, and to prepare for further large payments in the following period. At the same time, the exchange rate of the dollar in Berlin rose from 60 to 120 marks, the exchange rate of the pound sterling from 260 to 460 marks, i.e. the purchasing power of the Reichsmark abroad fell to less than one twenty-fifth of its pre-war value.

That these two processes - reparations and the fall in the value of the currency - are closely connected seems to be so self-evident to most people that they would shrug their shoulders in pity at an economist who wanted to cast doubt on the connection.

And indeed: within a few months, after the German Reich had to pay 1 billion gold marks in dollars, pounds and other foreign currencies; it had to buy these means of payment on the foreign exchange market, since they were only available to it in the smallest part; what was more natural under these circumstances than that the foreign currencies, corresponding to the strong demand with low supply, went up by leaps and bounds, and that at the same time German Reich marks were sold on all world markets at knock-down prices in order to procure the urgently needed foreign means of payment?

The causal connection between reparations and the collapse of the currency must seem quite self-evident even to those who know that payments from country to country are only apparently made in bills of exchange and other means of payment, but in reality in goods. For if the payment of 1 gold billion is equivalent to an export of goods in the same amount - unless credits intervene to help - German goods must be made very cheap so that foreign countries will buy them in the necessary volume.

The importer abroad naturally does not buy when Germany has a debt to pay and needs his bill of exchange for this purpose, but when the German goods appear cheap to him; otherwise he refrains from buying, however urgently Germany is dependent on him. And so it seems to follow from this logical train of thought that the fall in exchange rates is the direct and unavoidable consequence of reparations.

And yet... and yet...

I maintain, and will immediately prove, that the fall in the value of the currency was not the result of the reparations, but the result of a mistake in raising the reparations sum.
No payment to a foreign country, even if it were ten times as large as the sum now involved, would worsen the value of the paying country, if in making the payment the due straight, reasonable and natural course is taken.
We must carefully distinguish here, dear James, between two fundamentally different things, namely between the possibility of raising a certain sum and between the other possibility of transferring the raised sum abroad. There are, of course, payments that exceed a country's capacity. I do not want to get into the question of whether or not this is the case with the annual payments imposed on Germany, because the question has nothing to do with our subject matter, especially since Germany actually raised the critical billion in the case that concerns us. But the possibility always exists, of course, that a country, with the best will in the world, is not in a position to make a prescribed payment. However, the question of 'transfer' must be strictly separated from this question of 'procurement'. For here there is no impossibility. Once a country has succeeded in raising a sum of money for a foreign country in its own country, the technical transfer of the sum abroad does not pose the least difficulty. It then takes place in the simplest way imaginable, even quite automatically, without any difficulties on the foreign exchange market. There is no question of a currency catastrophe.

A practical example will make the matter clear to you:
Let us assume that a country in which the franc currency prevails has to pay 1 billion guilders to Holland within a certain period of time. For this purpose, it must first raise an equivalent amount, say 2 billion francs, domestically. If

it does not succeed in doing so, because such high taxes and bonds cannot be collected, the country must declare itself insolvent; not because 1 billion Dutch guilders cannot be paid in a short time, but because it is unable to do so. It is not because 1 billion Dutch guilders cannot be raised in such a short time, but because its economy is incapable of raising 2 billion francs. If, on the other hand, it succeeds in providing these 2 billion francs, be it through taxes, be it through bonds, be it through both types of procurement, then the country is faced with the task of managing the conversion of francs into guilders. How will this task be solved?

It is solved in a most simple way, as we see at once when we visualise the whole transaction in its details.

The first financial measure, as we have seen, was the raising of 2 million francs through taxes or bonds. By this amount, the state weakened the purchasing power in the country. It has withdrawn large sums from the money market, so that some of the banks are forced to sell shares, bonds, etc. from their holdings, while other banks have to restrict their loans, which in turn forces many industrialists, merchants and capitalists to sell securities. The result: strong price pressure on the securities market, with the effect that international values and securities of world renown flow abroad, where the securities markets are still in better shape. A further part of the sum left to the state is lacking for the wholesalers, importers and commodity speculators, who consequently see themselves forced to reduce their stocks, which also causes a price pressure in the field of world goods (cotton, metals and other staple articles), which causes goods to flow abroad and keeps further large quantities of goods, which under other circumstances would have flowed into the country, away from it. In the same way, all other economic areas are affected by a severe shortage of money, which forces sales and prevents purchases, so that finally the whole price level in the country is under a pressure which causes goods of all different kinds to flow abroad with fine unchanged high prices. But all these effects, staple articles and other goods must be paid for abroad. Thus, large quantities of foreign means of payment are on offer, and the state, which has to pay 1 billion guilders, need do nothing more than buy these offered means of payment with the help of the 2 billion francs procured beforehand and exchange them abroad - with the help of foreign exchange arbitrage - into guilders.

Is there anything simpler than this process? The goods that can no longer be bought domestically because the state has deprived the economy of 2 billion francs in purchasing power flow - they have to stay somewhere - abroad, and the purchase price that the foreign country pays for them makes up the 1 billion guilders that the state needs for its payment. So in reality, the state pays with the goods that it forces its population to export by issuing taxes or bonds. The whole thing, once the proceeds of the taxes and the proceeds of the bonds have been received, takes place completely automatically, without the slightest technical lubrication, and without any shocks on the foreign exchange market. A skilful financial policy will even be able to procure foreign exchange at very favourable conditions, because as a result of the strong export of goods there is a corresponding supply of foreign bills of exchange. However - this is the downside - there will be a not inconsiderable fall in prices in the country, because the falling price is the magnet that attracts foreign demand and thus promotes exports. In this case, the commodity is induced to perform its service as an international means of payment directly by the moment of price movement instead of by the diversions via the exchange rate. But the fall in prices does not take on any catastrophic forms, but stops immediately as soon as its economic purpose, the promotion of exports, is achieved.

For every foreign bill of exchange that exports send to the state, the latter gives the corresponding amount of francs, which immediately exerts its purchasing power again and supports the price level. If, at the end of the whole operation, the state has received the required 1 billion guilders, it has also returned the 2 billion francs that were withdrawn from circulation, so that the purchasing power in the country returns to its original level.

This example shows us, dear James, that the 1 billion gold marks paid by Germany in August cannot possibly be to blame for the recent currency crisis. If the right financial policy had been applied, the result should have been a sharp fall in prices in Germany, with a simultaneous stability of the exchange rate. Instead, we have experienced just the opposite: prices have gone up considerably and the exchange rate has deteriorated catastrophically. The necessary export of goods has not been brought about in the natural way via prices, but in the abnormal way via exchange rates, with the disastrous result that a gaping chasm has opened up between the internal and external value of the mark. And the reason? The Reich procured the sums necessary for the payment of reparations, but not by the legitimate means of taxation and borrowing, but by the illegitimate means of the printing press.

By failing to withdraw sufficient purchasing power from the market - only very inadequate amounts of treasury bills were placed on the money market - the Reich prevented prices in Germany from being set on an 'export footing'. As a result, no goods could flow out and no foreign exchange material could be procured. So the Reich had no choice but to offer such fantastic prices for foreign exchange that the external value of the mark fell by half. Only in this way, indirectly, did the price of German marks finally fall on the world market, which was necessary to induce foreign countries to buy. This reduction in price had to be enormous if it was to have any effect. For a price pressure that is not a natural market product, but is brought about by the sharp artifice of the exchange rate crisis, with brute force, so to speak, exerts only a very slight attraction on the foreign buyer's desire to buy, because the exchange rate risk and other risks may considerably reduce the benefit of the foreign buyer or even turn it into a loss.

Export goods only react to the price pressure exerted by the exchange rate if the price falls extraordinarily low below the comparative prices of the foreign country. This means not only an immediate loss for the country that has to pay, in our case Germany, which has to give half its products away in this way, but at the same time creates a hostile atmosphere abroad, which perceives the abnormally cheap prices as 'dumping' and 'skimming' and opposes them.
The fact that Germany is not voluntarily dumping, but is acting under the constraint of an incorrect financial policy, is naturally even less clearly recognised abroad than at home.

So here again, dear James, we come up against the arch enemy of any healthy economy, inflation. If mankind were even vaguely aware of the disastrous effects that the printing press exerts even in areas that seem to have nothing to do with it, every conscientious statesman would rather wither his hand before offering it for the operation of such an infernal machine.

And I myself... well, I didn't need to write you this letter.

With love

Your old dad.

Eleventh Letter

Valuta and 'dumping'
Anti-dumping measures

Berlin, October 1ˢᵗ 1921

As we have seen, there is nothing more natural, dear James, than that the value of money in a country should split into an internal value and an external value deviating from it, as soon as the quantity, composition and purchasing power of money are constantly changed by the continuous printing of notes.

For, depending on whether the purchasing power embodied in the new slips of paper is asserted in the home country or abroad, it drives up either the price level or the exchange rates, thus disturbing the correspondence between the internal and external value of the national money.

In politically and economically calm times, the new purchasing power tends to operate first at home and increase prices here, so that the money in the hands of the country's children already loses value if it is still valued and paid for abroad at its previous value. Conversely, in times of political disruption, a general mood of panic and, in particular, profound mistrust in the development of the value of the country's money. In such times, with persistent inflation, the newly created purchasing power tends to turn to foreign capital investments and means of payment, thereby pushing the foreign value of money deep below its domestic value. The movement of goods gradually corrects this disparity, but the correction is painful for the home country and no less so for the foreign country. For it is perceived at home as a shortage of goods, abroad as 'dumping' and leads to customs wars and other international entanglements.

Since Germany is now experiencing such times of a onesided low foreign value of its money and, as a result, an involuntary export of its money, the question arises whether both, namely monetary disparity and export of its money, cannot be eliminated by suitable measures; for instance, by artificially accelerating the approximation of the still relatively high internal value of money to the lower external value, which will take place in any case over time.

Aids to such an accelerated correction are available. For example, a general wage increase in the country can force an increase in the price level, i.e. a reduction in the value of money at home, and thus indirectly put a stop to exports at exaggeratedly cheap prices. Or, by levying export taxes, it is possible to increase the price of national goods for foreign buyers to such an extent that there is no longer any question of exporting at a loss.

In theory, such a fight against dumping, which is perceived as harmful, seems very appropriate. In practice, however, it turns out time and again that artificially suppressing natural consequences of economic processes is an impossibility. The perniciousness of such efforts is clearly evident in this very case.

For let us consider the case that an artificial price increase in the country or a high export duty actually succeeded in considerably restricting the export of goods. The first consequence that would become noticeable would be a shortage of foreign means of payment on the foreign exchange market, since foreign countries naturally pay less as soon as they buy less. But we have seen that there is an extremely strong demand for foreign means of payment on the foreign exchange market, indeed that precisely this demand, which emanates from the flight of newly created purchasing power from the country, is the actual cause of the rapid decline in exchange rates and thus also of the dumping that is to be combated. This demand is in no way weakened by the price and customs policy measures against dumping, but rather strengthened.

If, as a result of the decline in exports, the sought-after means of payment on the foreign exchange market are only available to a reduced extent, it is inevitable that this imbalance will again considerably worsen the exchange rates, thus further weakening the external value of the national currency. And this devaluation must necessarily continue until the suppressed export of goods begins again and supplies the foreign exchange market with the missing quantity of foreign means of payment.

Ergo: If it is not possible to plug the source of the disparity between the internal and external value of money, i.e. to prevent the flight of inflation-born purchasing power from the country, then the disparity itself and its necessary consequence, the centrifugal export, cannot be eliminated.
On the contrary, any attempt to artificially curb the exports only leads to a further aggravation of the disparity, an increased tension between the external and internal value of money.

Foreign countries are also powerless in the face of dumping. Its import bans and defensive tariffs can protect a certain country or industry from dumping competition, but only by diverting it to other countries or other industries.
Even with the most rigorous measures, foreign countries are not able to stop it completely. As soon as the country under the sign of inflation wants or has to make payments abroad,

no one can prevent the world means of payment 'commodity' from providing its payment service, and that at prices that are deeply below the price level of the world market.

Let us consider the course of a foreign struggle against dumping. Let us assume that the largest foreign trade states had agreed to keep out exports from a country with a unilaterally low external value of money and consequently with export dumping prices by means of a prohibitive tariff of 300 per cent, three times the value of the goods. Let us further assume, to choose the worst case, that it is not possible for the exporting country to secure other sales territories in place of the large importing countries thus barred. What is the consequence? In the first stage, of course, a complete standstill in exports. For however cheap the goods may be, a customs surcharge of 300 per cent, i.e. a quadrupling of their price, makes them unsaleable without further ado; the customs duty acts like a boycott.

As a result, the foreign currency market of the boycotted country begins to lack foreign currency, and the demand in the absence of supply causes the exchange rates to rise sharply, say by 100 per cent. The disparity between the internal and external value of money increases accordingly, but without any appreciable increase in the foreign exchange material on offer, for even in this second stage the foreign customs blockade does not allow any goods through, or at best only goods with such a high sentimental value that the foreign buyers willingly accept the price premium.

The inevitable consequence is a further rise in exchange rates, a further increase in the tension between the internal and external value of money.
Until finally the third stage is reached, namely, the stage in which the exchange rates (or the tension) reach that point at

which the three-hundred-percent duty of the foreign country becomes ineffective, because now the national money has become so cheap for the foreigner that he still buys considerably below the world market price, even if the duty is included. And now the goods are flowing abroad again as if the customs duty did not even exist.

The foreign country can do nothing against dumping by force. Instead of achieving the desired end, it merely ruins the currency of the dumping country. And thus not only this country, but also the foreign country itself is seriously damaged, because to the extent that the external value of the money in the 'dumping' country falls, every import there is made more difficult.

For the foreign goods become more expensive for this country by exactly the same amount as the price of the foreign bills of exchange with which the goods must be paid increases. The prohibitive tariff, therefore, does not kill the export of the country against which it is directed, but, on the contrary, the export of the foreign country - taken as a whole - which has imposed the tariff.

If we now, dear James, in order to go to the end of the problem, put to ourselves the question of what would happen in the (practically quite impossible) case of the whole of foreign countries shutting themselves off against imports from the dumping country by radical import bans, the answer is obvious.

There are then only two possibilities: Either there will be such a fall in the value of goods in the dumping country that export prices will fall to a minimum, thus creating a significant premium on imports by stealth abroad, and legitimate trade will be replaced by smuggling. In this case, the import bans prove to be ineffective.

Or, if importation is actually stopped - a very unlikely condition, since exportation also extends to abstract rights, e.g. capital shares, as well as services - then the exportation in the dumping country effectively ceases.

But not as a result of any change in the mode of payment in which the dumping country effects its voluntary or forced payment to the foreign country, not as a result of the substitution of the means of payment 'commodity' by any other means of payment.
But simply because the dumping country no longer pays at all.

Since it is now deprived of any possibility of exporting commodities and thus of generating the foreign exchange material needed for payment purposes, it can no longer raise any free means of payment, no matter how far its currency may fall. Despite the best will to pay, it is in fact insolvent. Thus, by slaying the dumping-price export, the foreign country has merely deprived itself of the payments it would otherwise have received.

The practical application in the case of German reparations is that as long as the foreign country insists on payment, it must also put up with the corresponding German export. And as long as Germany procures the means for reparations at home by issuing notes, i.e. by inflation, its export of reparations must necessarily have the character of a dumping-price export.

Today the unprejudiced observer is presented with the foolish picture that all countries demand payments, but at the same time reject the commodity in which alone these payments can be made.

So little do their leading financiers and economists know the ABC of economics, and so little do they recognise the compelling force of economic laws, that they believe they can replace these laws with their dictates and streams of ink!

It is a pity that you and I will not live to see the day when our great-grandchildren burst into Homeric laughter when they read about this folly in their textbooks!

That's it - I can't see any more ink today!

Your old dad.

Twelfth Letter

Back to the gold currency?
Expediency and possibility of return

Berlin, 5 October 1921

All countries, dear James, which today are groaning under the scourge of the decline in the value of the currency, will very soon be faced with the important question: 'Back to the gold currency or not? '
And this question will split into two sub-questions for them, namely, firstly, is the return advisable and is it worth the financial sacrifices that might have to be made for this? And secondly, if this question has to be answered in the affirmative, is the return possible at all without comprehensive organisational preparations and enormous economic upheavals having preceded it?

How the answer to the question of expediency will turn out cannot for a moment be in doubt. For the complete disruption of the monetary system, which has occurred everywhere where gold has been turned one's back, has made the superiority of the gold currency over the paper currency, in spite of the theoretical equivalence of the latter, palpably clear. The superiority of the gold currency, as we know from the previous letters, is threefold.

First of all, it guarantees a sound monetary constitution simply by the fact that it is there. It works, as the English say, 'in being'. Even if it is a limping gold currency, as it was before the war in all the so-called gold-currency countries except England - because everywhere a paper pyramid was built up on the gold base - it nevertheless affords a valuable protection against all too daring monetary experiments and against excessive inflation. Even where the numerical correspondence between money in circulation and gold reserves, which characterises the full gold currency, does not exist, but only the rather questionable principle of one-third coverage prevails, gold sets certain, rather narrow limits to the money supply in the country, so that an arbitrary flooding of the country with money tokens is excluded. Also, wherever it has been adopted, the gold currency exercises a kind of self-protection which makes it difficult for governments to break with it at will. It very quickly creates a gold tradition, a kind of benevolent 'gold fetishism' that makes even governments inexperienced in monetary economics shy away from attacks against the gold currency and guarantees the continuance of this inflation protection as long as political catastrophes do not bring about a dictatorship of foolhardiness.

In addition, there are the valuable active services that the gold currency provides to the value of the country's money abroad and thus to the country's international trade relations. Where the gold currency prevails, the exchange rates, which express the value of the country's money in foreign currency, can only fluctuate by fractions of a percent, because when the upper or lower 'gold point' is reached, gold immediately flows out or flows in. In this way the circulation of money in the country is brought into the most exact conformity with the requirements of the balance of payments, so that the exchange rates quickly return to their normal level. At home and abroad, everyone knows the value of domestic money in relation to foreign money, which gives foreign trade and capital transactions the security without which they would degenerate into speculation to the detriment of the country.

The third service that the gold currency performs for the country is derived from the first two. Since it protects the monetary system against inflation and anchors the currency at a fixed normal level, it makes the country highly creditworthy. Even a small additional interest bid by the country's banks attracts large amounts of foreign capital, whereas in a country with a strongly fluctuating currency even a high additional interest rate has no effect, because the foreign exchange risk threatens to eat up the interest benefit.

In a gold-currency country, therefore, the balance of payments is kept in equilibrium not only by gold imports and exports, but also by credit (and the arbitrage closely connected with it).
And in peacetime there is hardly any need for money, be it public or private, which the foreign country does not readily satisfy if the credit-seeking country has the gold currency.

The question 'Back to the gold currency or not? ' will therefore probably be answered everywhere with a convinced 'yes'.
But what about the possibility of this in countries that have devalued their currency by fourteen fifteenths or ninety-nine hundredths through enormous masses of paper?

Well, the possibility, dear James, is there everywhere, even in the countries most devastated by inflation, provided only that a return is made to sensible financial management.
The gold standard is an undemanding plant and will thrive even in arid soil, if only it is healthy. All that is necessary is for the countries that are homesick for the gold standard to manage their finances as every careful householder should, namely, in such a way that expenditure does not exceed income. For then there is no need to resort to the printing press. And wherever this does not happen, the gold standard will be established of its own accord at the slightest desire for it.

This process takes place in a very simple way. As soon as the printing press in a country is finally shut down, the value, the foreign currency, which has continued to deteriorate with strong fluctuations, comes to a standstill.

For when the money tokens and the purchasing power inherent in the money tokens are no longer exposed to arbitrary change through the appearance of ever new masses of notes, the prices in the country are fixed on that basis which corresponds to the now stable monetary value. Goods flow more calmly out of the country and into it, a certain equality of level with world market prices is established, and a consolidation of exchange rates takes place, whose pendulum swings, hitherto so violent, become smaller and smaller. However, these oscillations do not stop completely, because there is still no element that reacts to every oscillation, no matter how small, and brings the pendulum to rest by shifting it accordingly. But it is recognisable that the oscillations take place around a certain centre point, and that is the point which corresponds to the new world value of the national money.

Determining this point is a matter of experimental foreign exchange policy. Some central office in the country always buys foreign exchange when the exchange rates are below the presumed midpoint and gives it away again when the exchange rates exceed this point.

It can happen that this very simple procedure is not successful at the first attempt, for example, that the central office sees its stock of foreign exchange exhausted very quickly because the exchange rates are far more often above than below the midpoint, the new gold parity.

Then this is a sign that this parity has not yet been determined quite correctly, and that it is in fact somewhat higher than anticipated.

One must therefore continue the experiment and look for a new midpoint until one finds it where the outflow and inflow of the exchange material are in balance. Once this point, this new parity, has been established, and if it has then been possible, through continued foreign exchange purchases, to accumulate a stock of exchange which the occasional outflows can no longer exhaust, then one has - the new gold currency. For the central office can then convert its stock of foreign bills into gold at any time by discounting or selling them abroad and having the equivalent value remitted to it in gold.

However, this is not yet a 'full gold currency,' but only a gold edge currency, i.e. a currency that has a core of paper money and an edge of gold, which guarantees the value equivalence of the paper money with the newly determined gold pari through outflow and inflow.

But for the beginning such a gold rand currency is sufficient. It fulfils its purpose of keeping exchange rates stable, placing all the country's external relations on the secure basis of a fixed monetary value and restoring the country's international creditworthiness. Large countries, such as the old Austro-Hungarian Monarchy, managed for decades with such a gold rand currency.

Gradually, one can move to the full gold currency. The central office will increase its foreign exchange holdings, draw the gold amounts in which the bills of exchange are denominated at maturity or even before - by way of sale or discount - until one day it feels strong enough to take the step called 'resumption of cash payments'. The central office, which will expediently be identical with the central bank of issue, where such a bank exists, declares itself ready to hand over gold against notes to any holder of note money on demand.

According to all experience, a stock of gold amounting to one third of the paper in circulation is sufficient to ensure that the gold is sufficiently redeemed. In this case, too, we are not dealing with a full gold currency in the orthodox sense, for this requires that every banknote in the country be covered piece by piece by gold. Nevertheless, it is the normal gold currency which meets practical requirements, as Germany had it until the outbreak of war.

How much gold is needed to set up such a gold currency in Germany, based on the principle of one-third coverage? The most adventurous ideas about this are widespread. In fact, a gold currency can be established in Germany with a gold stock that is only slightly larger than the gold stock that the German Reichsbank already has today.

A little calculation will quickly make this clear to you, my son.

In Germany, around 90 billion marks of paper money have been put into circulation to date, at the beginning of October 1921. Of this, approximately 10 billion are in Belgium and France, where they were exchanged for francs after the end of the war.
Another enormous amount is in the hands of international speculation. It is estimated to be between 30 and 40 billion, but we want to be cautious and put it at only 20 billion, especially since large sums have flowed back to Germany in the last few weeks. (Before Germany proceeds to a currency reform, it will have to exchange these notes for bonds and finally withdraw them from circulation). This leaves about 60 billion that are actually in circulation in Germany.

Today, the Reichsbank holds more than 1 billion in gold. Only a few weeks ago the value of a paper mark was about the twelfth or thirteenth part of a gold mark. As can be seen from the general price movement, however, its value has recently fallen sharply, to about the fifteenth part of a gold mark: at least this is its internal value, which we want to regard as decisive, disregarding the far lower external value.

The 1 billion gold marks in the possession of the Reichsbank are thus offset by about 4 billion gold marks in paper money. We can also say that the 60 billion paper marks in circulation are offset by about 15 billion paper marks in gold at the Reichsbank.
The one as well as the other expresses the same fact, namely that the German money in circulation today is covered with about 25 per cent in gold, and that the Reichsbank would have to increase its gold holdings from 1 billion to about 1 1/3 billion in order to achieve a third coverage.

Germany can therefore return to the gold currency today and resume cash payments if the Reichsbank increases its gold holdings by one billion gold marks and if - this 'if' is of course very significant - the banknote press is immediately shut down.

If the latter does not happen, this is not tantamount to a necessary failure of the return to gold, but it only has the consequence that the monetary basis on which this return can take place deteriorates more and more. It will not be possible, as at present, to convert 15 paper marks into one gold mark, but 100 or 1000 or even more paper marks will be merged into one gold mark.

Inflation does not make monetary reform impossible anywhere or at any stage, however advanced it may be. It only worsens the conditions for reorganisation. Even Russia can reckon in gold within half a year if it wants to. Here, however, the exchange of Soviet roubles into gold roubles can hardly be done in any other way than by weight: 1 kg of ten-ruble notes equals 1 gold rouble.

For me, dear James, there is not the least doubt that old European countries which claim to be great powers or even only middle powers will reintroduce the gold standard within a few years.

For trade and change will only then return to their normal channels, freed from dumping, usury and speculation, and world credit will only then fully resume its function as a regulator of the balance of payments, when the currency of the countries regains its old stability of value: and this the currency can only secure in the long run when the golden bar is again in place, which protects the monetary system of the countries from arbitrariness and dilettantism.

Which means I'm putting the pen down for this one.

>With love

>>Your old dad.

Part III: The Central Bank

First Letter

*Concept and origin
Girobank and central bank
Metal receipt
Banknotes*

Berlin, June 1st 1922

Have you, dear James, ever thought about why the economic institutions of mankind have such an extraordinary capacity for persistence and tend to outlast the political institutions by far? Governments come and go, administrative systems change, entire states come into being and disappear again, but the institutions that economic man has created remain.

Events of world-historical significance exert no influence on them; the profound effects of wars between nations and revolutions slide off them like water off an oil-soaked cloth. The old Roman Empire has been dead for 16 centuries, but the commercial institutions it created, the legal concepts it shaped for commercial intercourse, are still alive today.

Where Babylon and Nineveh once stood, sheep graze; but the complicated banking system of those days has survived through the millennia, as have the giro transactions of the ancient Egyptians and the grain futures trading of the biblical economic dictator Joseph.

Where does this come from, my son? How is it to be explained that the Bolshevists in Russia, who politically turned the lowest to the highest and overthrew the holy Baal 'property', had to stop at the transport facilities?

For the sake of principle, they did try to transfer banking, that odious symbol of high capitalism, from private to state ownership and to centralise it in the Bank of the People's Deputies.

But this had such disastrous consequences for the whole of commercial life that they soon gave up the attempt. They are now in the process of returning banking to its old channels.
And when a few decades have passed, there will be nothing left to remind us in economic terms of the greatest sociopolitical upheaval that has ever taken place in Europe.

One must beware of the temptation to attribute this toughness of transport facilities to their absolute unsurpassability. Everything that man has created is a product of compromises he has had to make: Compromises between will and ability, between knowledge and prejudice, between the urge to innovate and sluggish adherence to the established.
That is why there is nothing in the world that could not be better and more expedient. No railway network in Europe is so perfect that one could say that no improvements are conceivable; on the contrary, precisely the most important connections, the routes between the main centres of traffic, are defective because they do not run in a straight line but in a winding manner, which results in losses of time and energy.

Nevertheless, the railways must remain as they are, because traffic has become accustomed to them and has even adapted to their deficiencies to such an extent that these deficiencies can now no longer be remedied without damaging the most important parts of the economy.

It is exactly the same with the other transport facilities. No matter how many imperfections they may have, they cannot and will not be dispensed with, because they have not only become organic components of the economy, but also because considerable interests, cherished habits and popular prejudices, which want to be protected, rush against them. And so economic institutions hold on by their own weight, by virtue of a law of inertia that is far more effective here than in the fields of political-national development and state administration.

To this law of inertia, dear James, we must attribute the fact that the institution of central banks proves to be of greater permanence in the countries where it once exists than the state which created it.

The Austro-Hungarian Monarchy is in ruins. But the central bank it established still exists, and when the liquidation stage it is currently in is over, four or five new central banks will be active in its place, because none of the successor states of Austria-Hungary wants to do without an institution to which trade and commerce in the country concerned have become accustomed. The prejudice that a central bank is as much a part of a modern state as a mint and a treasury, and that it simply cannot exist without a central bank, also plays a role.

This is, of course, a misconception. Central banks are by no means indispensable, and especially in countries whose monetary system is based on a sound foundation, they are superfluous. Nevertheless, they offer a number of conveniences to the economy of those states which know how to use them wisely, and this fact, in conjunction with the economic law of inertia, means that they always rise up again, like the Little Man, when an economic or political upheaval has once thrown them to the ground.

The fact that they cause infinitely more harm than good as soon as they are irrationally managed or consciencelessly put at the service of certain interests does not detract from this tenacity.

On the contrary, the possibility of occasionally misusing this important instrument for special purposes is only one more reason for governments to maintain the institution of the central bank. Especially since most of them have only a very unclear idea of where the legitimate use ends and the illegitimate one begins.

I am very doubtful whether most of the central banks in existence today would have been established if their founders had known what a central bank is allowed to do and what it is not allowed to do. For the tasks that were assigned to the institutions when they were set up almost everywhere go far beyond what a central bank can do without causing damage.

I am not even thinking of those purposes that were envisaged here and there but which one did not dare to mention to the public, i.e. those purposes that are better described as 'ulterior motives'. I am not thinking, for example, of the particular ulterior motives pursued by the Napoleonic Consulate with the Bank of France and by the Tsardom with the Russian Imperial Bank. In both cases, the consideration was that a central bank of issue would be able to finance state actions of all kinds, including warlike ones, and thus free the state from the odium that would attach to it if it itself wanted to see state paper money in circulation; a train of thought that, of course, was never admitted to the public.

As I said, I am not thinking of such secret side intentions when I say that most central banks were assigned tasks at the time of their foundation that are incompatible with a healthy national economy.

Rather, I have in mind only those intentions which were loudly proclaimed as such at the time of foundation, and of which their promoters believed that their realisation would be possible for a normally managed central bank without further ado and without bad consequences for the economy.

But since the founders were mistaken on this point, and the central banks can only fulfil some of the tasks assigned to them per nefas and only in violation of important general interests, it must be said that most central banks owe their existence to a misunderstanding.

You will perhaps be surprised, dear James, that I begin my attempt to bring the nature and effectiveness of central banks closer to your understanding with a statement that must arouse doubts in you from the outset about the raison d'être of central banks. But we are faced with the undeniable fact that almost all European central banks have carried out a predominantly harmful activity in recent years. We are faced with the fact that the banks have partly ruined the currencies of their countries, partly seriously endangered them, but at least deprived them of the stability of value without which there is no law and no equity; for a country that deals in money of variable value is like a merchant who weighs with uncalibrated weights of varying mass or measures with an adjustable metre-measure.

But we are also faced with the fact that this harmful activity of the central banks is by no means a new phenomenon which could be excused with the World War and accepted as a one-off exception without therefore rejecting the principle as such; but that we are dealing here with a well-known phenomenon which recurs periodically, i.e. not with an acute but with a chronic disease.

This was noted more than a hundred years ago by one of the few authorities on money and banking, Ricardo, who coined the succinct phrase: 'No bank has ever had the unlimited power to put paper money into circulation without abusing it'. '

Ricardo believed that it was not the function of central banks per se, but merely the human weakness of overworking the banks that was harmful to the economy.
Consequently, he demanded that the powers of the bank managers be restricted in a certain way, which is what happened later with the Bank of England.

I myself believe, however, that it is the principle itself rather than the abuse of the principle that must be held responsible for the damage done to the central banking system, because the tasks with which the central banks are burdened are in themselves in part an economic absurdity and in many cases virtually an invitation to commit an abuse.

What are these tasks?

With what intention and for what purposes are central banks established?

I could answer briefly: so that they help out parts of the economy in need of credit with loans, for which they procure the necessary funds by putting their notes into circulation.

But this answer would neither be complete nor would it correctly reflect the train of thought that led to the emergence of central banks. For the idea of the central bank is by no means the result of a straightforward, strictly logical thought process.

It did not spring from the head of the economic reformers one day, like Pallas Athena from the head of the Olympian Zeus. Rather, it has a complicated history and has emerged in stages, so to speak.

There is no question of a preconceived plan that was realised on some historical date by some historical person, so that one could say, for example: The central banking system of modern times came into being when the Bank of England was established in July 1694 according to the ideas of the Scotsman William Patterson.

Rather, the central banks are the last link in a longer chain of institutions, one of which has always crystallised out of the other, so that we are dealing here with the end product of a longer development. On the leading rope of this development, economic mankind has quite gradually, and more by chance than according to plan, arrived at the institution of central banks.

I will briefly describe the course of events and the logical connection between them.

Naturally, we must start from money. You know, my son, that money is the indispensable mediator of every traffic in goods; that it embodies a legal claim to consideration which has been acquired on the basis of a service, and that it thus interposes itself as an intermediate link between all services and considerations.

You know, moreover, that money circulates when its respective owners immediately assert the claim embodied in it, so that it moves to and fro between buyers and sellers; and that it rests when its owners temporarily refrain from asserting the claim embodied in money, because they prefer to realise this claim, which represents a certain purchasing power, only at a future time.

There are always people who let their money 'rest' in order to make provisions for the future, a procedure that is called 'saving'.

On the other hand, there are people who wish to receive the money today, which will only flow to them later due to services yet to be rendered, because they believe they can use it advantageously now. So there are two groups facing each other, one of which has money in the present which it will only need in the future, and the other needs money in the present which it will only have in the future. What could be more obvious than for the two groups to make an exchange in which one group, which saves money, gives its idle money to the other group, which needs money, on condition that it receives it back at a certain time in the future?

Such an exchange causes the dormant money to become circulating money, and the consequence is an enrichment of the whole economic community. For the group needing money must, after the agreed time, repay not only the money received (loan) but, as a rule, a certain premium (interest), and in order to be able to do this, it must, as the saying goes, 'put the money to work'.

That is to say, it must produce quality goods from the raw goods it has bought for the money it has received, with the help of physical or mental refining labour, for which it is granted such a high claim to consideration, that is to say so much money, that it can not only repay the loan plus interest, but still retain a surplus for itself.

Production and consumption are thus stimulated by the exchange described above, which we call a 'credit process', and a country in which this credit process has become so common that there is hardly any dormant but almost only circulating money, must necessarily come to a high commercial prosperity. The interest which compels borrowers to productive labour is a stern master who tolerates no idleness.

Since in most countries what we call 'commercial prosperity' is regarded as a desirable state - in contrast to the Buddhist ideal of Nirvana - early efforts were made to organise this credit process and to facilitate it through special institutions. Already in classical and pre-classical antiquity there were countless bankers and savings banks - in Egypt these were the temples - which transformed dormant money into circulating money by balancing surplus money and the need for credit.

Eventually, these bankers and savings banks covered the entire ancient cultural world as if with a net. And then it turned out that this organisation could be put to good use for other purposes: one could simplify the cumbersome transfer of money from place to place by depositing a sum of money with a banker, for example in Alexandria, who then ensured that an equally large sum was paid out in the same or equivalent money at a banker connected with him, for example in Antiocha or Ctesiphon.

In this way the 'credit banks' generally became 'deposit and exchange banks'. For the convenience of this transfer of money finally led to the bankers being used as cashiers, i.e. payments were made only through their intermediary, namely by means of bills of exchange, cheques and money orders. Some old-fashioned copies of such instructions are still preserved today.

The habit of carrying the money to the banker had a number of other advantages. For example, it turned out that a sum of money deposited with the banker could be exploited much more quickly than was the case when it remained in the hands of the owner. By giving and receiving instructions, the same sum could change hands several times in one day, even if they lived in quite different places, provided only that their bankers maintained a representation in one and the same central place. The circulation of money was thus considerably accelerated by the cash management of the public at the banker's and of the bankers at the central banker's, i.e. the purchasing power of the individual monetary token was exploited more intensively, whereby commercial activity was stimulated to the highest conceivable degree. It also turned out, however, that the public avoided certain dangers associated with cash payments when using this method of payment. Thus, as soon as one paid by money order, one no longer had to anxiously check with each individual payment that the money marks corresponded to the regulations. There was no need to check whether they contained the right amount of precious metal if they were coins, or whether they were issued by an authorised body if they were paper money. A bank order always meant a guarantee of proper money.

This guarantee function of the banks, dear James, then led one step further again, first in those countries whose governments pursued an unscrupulous monetary policy. Here, the merchant country saw itself constantly threatened by the experiments that the state conducted with money, either by lowering its fineness or by issuing note money in arbitrary quantities, from which the purchasing power of the individual note suffered. The merchant never knew how much the money in which he promised or expected payment would be worth on the day of payment; in particular, this made his dealings with foreign countries very difficult.

The solution was to make use of the guarantee function of the banks. Anyone who wanted to protect himself against the devaluation of money deposited a large sum in good money or in gold or silver with a bank expressly designated for this purpose and then made his payments only with instructions to the bank.
Since most respectable merchants adopted this practical payment system, i.e. maintained an account at the bank, 'transfer orders' (giro slips) very soon took the place of instructions (cheques), i.e. one paid by having the amount written off from one's credit balance and credited to the recipient's account.

Now the state could do whatever it wanted with its 'Kurant-Money' and 'Paper-Money', the 'Banko-Money' retained its value under all circumstances and was highly respected as the special currency of honourable merchants at home and abroad. In this way, the credit banks and deposit banks were replaced by giro banks, the most famous of which were based in Venice, Genova, Amsterdam and Hamburg.

This type of bank, dear James, deserves our special attention, because it differs from the other banks we have come to know in that it actively intervenes in the shaping of the national currency.
Through the giro banks, the countries have received a second, private money, in addition to the official, state money, and a better money at that. It is very interesting to note that wherever traffic has created such a bank money, i.e. a private money, out of an act of self-help, this private money has been more stable in value, more respected and internationally more usable than the official currency money of the state.

The stable value of the bank money was guaranteed by the fact that every account holder could withdraw his credit balance in gold or silver if he wanted to. Consequently, the value of the bank mark - which, mind you, was not a monetary token at all, but only an abstract unit of account transferable from account to account - could never be worth less than the precious metal for which it was credited to the depositor and for which it could be exchanged back at any time.

We are dealing here with an ideal money, because its quantity and its circulation speed always had to be exactly as great as corresponded to the purposes of the traffic, which, with its deposits and withdrawals of precious metal, decided completely autonomously to what extent the economy was to be saturated with bank money.

However, this excellent monetary constitution was immediately broken as soon as it was decided to lend out a part of the metal stocks of the giro banks, i.e. to make a mixture of giro bank and credit bank out of the institutions.

For now it was no longer the circulation (through the issue and withdrawal of metal) that decided on the quantity of bank money, but the credit policy of the bank managers.
By lending out the metal and crediting the depositor with bank money when the same metal was returned, they increased the quantity of bank money existing in the account beyond the metal cover and thus beyond the will of the market.

And they did the same when they granted loans not in metal but in Banko-Money. In doing so, they committed the same mistake of arbitrary money creation that the state had previously committed. But since they kept it within fairly narrow limits, bank money remained superior to state money, even if it lost its absolute stability of value.

A further step was taken when some giro banks began to find the book transfer of all payments to be made in Banko-Money too cumbersome and tedious and therefore switched to using the bank receipts issued for the deposited metal amounts for payment purposes.

The payee was no longer handed a giro slip but a metal receipt representing a certain, usually rounded-off amount of Banko-Money. In this way, the abstract Banko-Money became concrete paper money.
Many deposit banks, especially in Scotland, also used to issue such notes, and the receipts of the English goldsmiths who provided banking services in the Middle Ages and into more modern times were an extremely popular form of money before the Bank of England was founded.

And with that, my dear James, we have happily arrived at the central banks. For the debt certificates that the giro banks, deposit banks and goldsmiths put into circulation were basically nothing more than banknotes to be redeemed on demand. By introducing note circulation instead of giro circulation or alongside it, the giro banks became note banks all by themselves.
Thus the oldest of the central banks still in existence today, namely the Bank of England and the Bank of Scotland, were initially a kind of giro bank with the right to issue notes.
They were founded because towards the end of the 17th century the mischief of 'tilting and rocking' the silver currency money in England and Scotland assumed such proportions that the coins lost about 25 percent of their original real value, and trade and commerce longed for a bank similar to the famous Amsterdam one in order to obtain

book accounts and notes against metal deposits, the value of which could not be diminished by any government arbitrariness.

In addition, of course, other desires were attached to the foundation of the bank, namely the same desires that had already prevailed with the giro banks and had turned them into credit banks in general:

With the help of their book credits and bank notes, the banks were to provide the entrepreneurs with means of circulation, i.e. purchasing power, as soon as the population did not want to give as much purchasing power as they wished to receive; or, to stick to my earlier expression: as soon as the population did not give as much 'resting money' as they wished to convert into 'active money' and use it productively.

Thus, in a sense, the central banks have grown out of two different roots. One root reaches deep into the history of the development of banking and makes the central banks appear as the organic further development of the giro banks. The other root has its origin in the desire for credit on the part of entrepreneurs. The more the history of banking approaches modern times, the more the first root withers and the second root strengthens.

The desire of tradesmen to obtain credit with the help of the central bank, which the self-reliant economy cannot or will not grant them, is the most important factor in the birth of the newer central banks, recognised and favoured by the state, which believes it has found here a convenient and harmless aid to its policy of promoting trade.

Only a few governments have had the necessary acumen to recognise that this aid is by no means harmless, but embodies an extremely dubious principle, namely the principle of the arbitrary creation of money; and that wherever this principle has been adopted in principle, there is an urgent danger of abuse, because there is no reliable criterion for the extent to which the issue of notes for credit purposes can be pushed without harming the national currency. When and for what purposes a central bank is useful and when it is not, there are such extraordinarily different, and in fact predominantly erroneous, views on this that it is not surprising that most of the existing central banks have done more harm than good in the course of their effectiveness.

This has finally led to the fact that independently thinking people often reject the whole principle of the central bank and flatly reject this institution in every form. You will see from my next letter, dear James, that I do not go that far, but rather consider central banks useful under very specific conditions and in very specific forms.

But this much is also certain for me: it is incomparably better for a state to have no central bank at all than one built on false basic ideas.

Which brings me to the end of our chat for this time.

    With love

        your old Dad.

Second Letter

*The scope of tasks of the central bank
Legitimate functions
The savings idea and the emergency service*

Berlin, June 5th 1922

If, my dear James, in the first part of this letter I attempt to describe to you very briefly the conditions under which a central bank can have a beneficial effect on the national economy, I must ask you not to think for a moment of the central banks that exist at present; for not a single bank, not even the Bank of England excepted, corresponds to the model of a central bank as it must be constituted if it is always to bring only benefit and never harm to the country.

The tasks which are set for a central bank today are in all countries of such a nature that no institution can fulfil them without violating some important economic law.

The circle of tasks that may be assigned to a central bank without violating the dictates of economic reason is narrowly limited and easy to overlook. Any child can tell at a glance whether a particular task given to a bank is within the bounds of economic law or not. The touchstone for this consists in a single short question, which is: 'Can the bank carry out the task in question without altering in the slightest the quantity of money available in the country, or does the carrying out of the task entail an arbitrary increase or decrease in this quantity of money?' If the answer is: 'The money supply remains untouched', then the bank can confidently carry out the function assigned to it. If, however, the answer is the opposite, then it is a function that is fundamentally and under normal circumstances unacceptable.

For the quantity of money in circulation in the country coincides to the penny with the legal claims to services and goods which have been acquired by previous services and have not yet been asserted at the given moment; and the sum of these legal claims may not be increased or diminished by any arbitrary act of a bank, however well-intentioned. Why this must not happen, and what the consequences are if it happens nevertheless, I have explained to you in detail in my letters on 'Money'.[1]

There is no question, then, that a central bank is quite useful if it has the task of regulating and facilitating the circulation of money in the country without changing anything quantitatively.
A central bank may therefore easily take parts of the circulating money, if it consists of gold and silver, and replace them with its own notes, which can be sent from place to place more easily than the heavy metal, and which, above all, can be adapted far more precisely to the individual turnovers of the traffic.

An English 50 pound note weighing 2 grammes gives the same turnover as 50 individual gold sovereigns weighing about two-fifths of a kilogram. And a 5 shilling note is on the one hand more handy and transportable than the corresponding amount of silver, nickel or copper, and on the other hand more expedient than a 5 shilling coin of gold would be, which could only be the size of a fingernail and would therefore have to be lost frequently.
Equally useful is a central bank which, on the basis of the sums of hard money deposited with it, opens book accounts for the depositors and manages the payments which these

---

[1] See Part I of this book.

depositors make to each other by writing up and down from these accounts.

If an institution limits its activity to these transcriptions (giro function), it is not a central bank, but a giro bank. It only becomes a bank of issue if it combines this function with the issue of banknotes, i.e. if it makes payment by transfer or by handing out banknotes, as desired: in the first case the institution carries out the cash management for its depositors all by itself, in the second case it leaves this work to those who want to make use of its banknotes.

A central bank is also extremely useful when it uses the sums of money deposited with it in cash to grant loans to businessmen in need of loans. Here, of course, it benefits less by virtue of its note privilege than by virtue of its capacity as a credit institution, i.e. not as a note bank but as a bank per se.

Its right to issue notes, however, has an effect here insofar as this right guarantees a certain solidity of management and usually also state control, i.e. a trustworthiness that cannot be assumed without further ado in the case of another bank; this allows the deposits to flow in more abundantly and creates a more extensive credit possibility than would otherwise be the case, so that indirectly it is again the special character as a bank of issue that allows the institution to grant extensive credit, i.e. 'dormant' money in the form of loans. That is, to convert 'dormant' money into 'active money'.

In all these cases, the benefit of a central bank cannot be denied. In other cases a benefit can also be stated, but not necessarily, but only under certain conditions and with certain reservations. I am thinking here above all of the much-mentioned advantage of national savings, achieved by the use of a metal substitute as a means of circulation, as well as of the emergency service which paper bank money can render a nation in times of the greatest distress.

I presume, dear James, that you know your Adam Smith, and especially that chapter of his Wealth of Nations in which he deals with the history of the Bank of England. Here we find the parable that has become famous, which describes the replacement of metal money by the bank note as being as useful to a nation as the replacement of country roads and farm roads by means of a 'road of desire'.
If it were possible, Smith thinks, to accomplish all transport in the lusts instead of by the usual routes of conveyance, all the roads now reserved for traffic, and which deprive a large part of the arable soil of agricultural cultivation, might be utilised as corn and pasture lands, thus enriching the country by many square miles of useful land.
It would be a very similar enrichment for a country if a part of the metal money, which is tied up in circulation as 'dead assets', were replaced by paper and released in this way, so that it now represents 'useful assets' and can be exchanged for any goods.

Smith himself, however, immediately makes the restriction that a traffic 'carried by the Daedalus wings of paper money' does not have the same secure foundation as a traffic resting on the solid ground of gold and silver. And this restriction is indeed appropriate. For even if it is in itself quite indifferent whether the payments of a country make use of hard money or paper money - or, in other terminology, whether the economy is metallistic or nominalistic - there is nevertheless the grave concern that the paper economy lacks the natural elasticity inherent in the metal economy.

In the latter, the automatic outflow and inflow of metal always maintains the money supply in exact accordance with the demand for circulation; thus, unwelcome fluctuations in the purchasing power of money are prevented. Theoretically, it is certainly possible to replace this natural elasticity by a skilful monetary policy, i.e. by alternately increasing or decreasing the paper money supply, and thus by an artificial elasticity.

But practice has shown that such a monetary policy almost always suffers shipwreck because of the inadequacy of human insight or the weakness of monetary policymakers in the face of the selfish wishes of authoritative economic circles.

The so-called 'emergency service' of the banknote is even more questionable. The banknote can perform this service because, in contrast to metal money, it can be multiplied at any time and to any extent. The arbitrary multipliability of the banknote - as of any kind of paper money - is its weakness and at the same time its strength. Its weakness insofar as every arbitrary increase of the national money changes the monetary value, falsifies all rights and duties expressed in money and severely shakes the foundations of all traffic.
Its strength, on the other hand, lies in the fact that, thanks to its rapid multiplication, it can help the state to overcome momentary crises of fate. Every state goes through days in which its existence depends on the immediate procurement of money, this is especially the case with the sudden outbreak of war. Then it is said: Necessity knows no commandment.

The fact that an arbitrary increase of money by issuing large quantities of notes means a shaking of all legal foundations, subjects the population to a kind of most severe compulsory taxation and virtually expropriates wide circles in favour of the state, does not then weigh as heavily as the advantage that the state gets over the momentary crisis.

It is better that the state should remain alive, even with the help of a breach of law - which it may be able to cure after the crisis has been overcome - than that it should perish under strict observation of the law.

This train of thought, dear James, naturally leads to the fact that even those people who basically do not want to know anything about the banknote as a too dangerous substitute for metal money, come to terms with it as a helper in times of need. And it would indeed not be so bad if one could fix the monetary economy to the formula: Basically metal money, in the case of the greatest need an addition of paper money.

But unfortunately this formula is not useful. For a population that has become accustomed to paying exclusively with metallic money resolutely refuses to regard and use paper money, which is foreign to it, as an equal means of payment if it is to be imposed on it in the days of a catastrophe. During the Seven Years' War, Frederick the Great of Prussia repeatedly considered the plan of replacing the circulating thalers, guilders and ducats with paper. But the population, accustomed to hard money, would have regarded the notes, to which they were completely unaccustomed, with the greatest suspicion and would have concluded from their issue that the outcome of the war would be unfortunate.

The king therefore had to stick to hard money willy-nilly; the fact that he considerably debased this money did not bother the population (although factually there is no difference between debasement through coin debasement and debasement through note printing), for hard money was a familiar means of payment to them even in the new, poor quality.

Therefore, a state which regards banknotes as an indispensable factor in its readiness for war and crisis must accustom the people to banknotes from a long way off. A people who know the use of the banknote makes no distinction between the normal covered note, which is a metal certificate, and the uncovered note of the crisis period, which is note money.

So we could consider the central bank a useful institution from this point of view as well, if an important concern did not impose itself on us. That is the danger of abuse. It is to be feared that a state which regards the arbitrary printing of notes as a permissible political tool will use this means not only in the case of extreme danger to life, but also on less important occasions; and that once it has used it, it will not return with the necessary energy and speed to the legitimate and harmless means of obtaining money. The issue of notes, as soon as it springs from a will of authority or a policy of expediency and not from the will of autonomous traffic, is an insidious poison.

And even if one accepts this poison - just as one accepts the scourges of war, compulsory economy, state upheaval, etc. - at a moment when the fatherland cannot be saved in any other way, one must nevertheless demand its immediate eradication from the body of the people as soon as that moment has passed.

But since the issuance of notes is, as it were, a 'place at the table' for those who make use of it, a temptingly convenient substitute for statesmanship and financial skills, the renunciation of this treacherous poison requires a strictly honest mind, a strong arm and a high degree of economic

insight, i.e. things that a state rarely has at its disposal at the same time.

Let us briefly summarise what has been said: The activity of a central bank is useful and in no respect questionable if its purpose is to substitute an easier-to-handle means of payment for the cumbersome metal, be it notes which circulate in place of the metal money deposited with it, or giro transfers which are made on the basis of this metal deposit. Furthermore, the central bank has an unrestrictedly useful effect when it uses sums of money deposited in cash, whether in kind or in the form of fully-covered notes or credit notes, to grant credit, whereby it must of course be presupposed that it observes the basic rules of banking credit transactions just as strictly as a bank without note privilege.

As long as a central bank confines itself to the functions of money distribution, cash management and the granting of credit (in the sense of making available money stocks usable), it promotes the economy without triggering harmful side effects.

A central bank is only conditionally useful if it serves the idea of savings, i.e. if it first replaces metal money with notes, but then does not keep the metal as collateral, but makes it economically usable; for example, by sending the metal abroad and leaving the equivalent value to the state, which is now in possession of foreign credit balances, without anyone in the country having given up a penny of purchasing power.

In this case, the nation as a whole has been enriched - to the amount of the new foreign assets - by using a less valuable means of payment instead of the metal. This is permissible and harmless as long as the management of the central bank is able to maintain the circulation of money in the country at exactly the same level as it would be if the metal were still in circulation.

The danger, however, that this condition will be violated, and that an incompetent, careless central bank, or one abused by outside authorities, will leave more or less money in circulation than the circulation in the country would hold if it were left to itself, is so great that I, for my part, would regard such a central bank as a constant threat to the national monetary system.

Nevertheless, the basic possibility of a metal-saving and yet harmless central bank cannot be denied, and there are even situations in which, faute de mieux, such a bank must be welcomed, at least temporarily.
Finally, a central bank can be considered useful from the special point of view of a crisis reserve.
But here the strongest reservations are in order, and I draw your attention with the greatest emphasis, dear James, to the fact that in this case it is a question of a purely political usefulness, which under certain circumstances is bought with the most serious economic dangers.

Every state should see to it that it creates crisis reserves of a different, albeit more costly kind, for instance in the form of special metal stocks, which may only be touched in times of greatest distress. It is better to renounce the principle of savings and to accept the reproach of a certain wastefulness than to conjure up the danger that the systematic habituation of the population to the banknote will one day lead to an unconscionable flooding of the traffic with note money.

For the crisis reserve consists in making the people familiar with the note with the preconceived intention of abusing this familiarity in an emergency. That is why I see the central bank as a very bad crisis reserve. But I admit that a bad reserve is still better than none at all, and that therefore a state, which unfortunately has not been given a financial constitution suitable for all cases of change, cannot do without a central bank as a crisis reserve.

You see, my son, what compromises one must make under certain circumstances. But -then one must pay all the more scrupulous attention to the fundamentals, so that one never confuses compromises born of necessity with economic laws.

    With love

        Your old father.

Third Letter

The 'Elasticity' of the Currency
The Commodity Exchange as an Index
A False Principle

Berlin, June 9th 1922

We have seen, dear James, that there are a number of tasks which a central bank can perform for the benefit of the economy without this benefit being accompanied by disadvantages or creating questionable possibilities; and that there are other tasks which justify the existence of a central bank, but which are associated with certain dangers and place a high degree of responsibility in the hands of the bank managers and the supervising statesmen. All these tasks, the harmless as well as the more precarious ones, have one thing in common, that they are clearly outlined and give no cause for misunderstanding. Everyone knows what it means when a central bank has the purpose of facilitating payment transactions, performing cash services, making available funds usable by way of credit, saving gold and silver or serving as a crisis reserve.

In addition, however, central banks are also assigned tasks that are not clear and unambiguous, where one person thinks one thing and the other another, and on the implementation of which the greatest differences of opinion prevail. It even happens that demands are made on the central banks which arise from fundamentally wrong economic views, and the fulfilment of which is consequently a logical impossibility from the outset.

We will have to deal in detail, dear James, with the most important and least known of these views, which are merely the result of a gross misunderstanding and are responsible for the fact that central banking is in danger of losing all its credit, especially among the most astute economists. For it is possible that you yourself are caught up in this view. It is very widespread and describes the task of the central banks as making the national money elastic, i.e. adjusting it in quantity to the changing needs of the economy.

Those who ascribe this purpose to the central banks assume that the quantity of precious metals at the disposal of the individual countries is neither large enough to cover the justified demand for money, nor is it as flexible as the variable volume of production requires. In this respect, the notes of the note banks are a welcome addition. With their help, the short gold and silver cover of the economy could be extended and the circulation of money could be excellently tailored to the respective need by increasing the quantity of notes issued when demand increases and decreasing it again when demand decreases. Just as the human chest rises and falls according to the changing strength of the breath, so, according to this view, the circulation of money in the country, supplemented by paper, rises and falls according to every breath of the economic body.

This sounds so convincing, dear James, that most economists take it for granted, and that the heads of almost all central banks see the main task of their institutions in providing the economy with the amount of means of payment that corresponds to the change in the intensity of traffic. They live and weave in the idea that between the quantity of hard money in a country and the natural demand for means of payment there exists a quite unavoidable dichotomy, and this because the quantity of hard money has a fixed extent, whereas the demand for money has a variable extent, thus an elastic demand is opposed to a rigid supply. We can visualise this idea very well in numerical terms:

The circulation of hard money in any country amounts once and for all to 1 billion; the demand of the economy, on the other hand, amounts in normal times to only 3/4 billion, rises periodically to 1 1/2 billion and in critical days to 2 billion.

Thus, once in a while 1/4 billion too much money circulates in the country, and at other times 1/2 or a whole billion too little.
This dichotomy between supply and demand and the disturbances that naturally result from it can be eliminated in the simplest way if there is a central bank that absorbs the surplus 1/4 billion of hard money in calm times and pumps the missing half or whole billion into the economy in the form of banknotes in turbulent times.

This is the function which seems to most central bank managers to form the main content of their activity, and which seems to them infinitely more important, more useful and more responsible than cash service, payment mediation, metal saving, etc.

The prevailing view is that the central bank faces the economy in much the same way as a doctor faces a patient: like the latter, it has two main duties, firstly to make a diagnosis, to take the pulse of the economy, so to speak, and secondly, on the basis of this diagnosis, to proceed to therapy, i.e. to eliminate either an excess of blood or a shortage of blood.

Consequently, the bank's responsibility is twofold. Everything depends on it observing correctly, recognising the state of the economy correctly, and then actively intervening in the required manner, i.e. supplying the economy with precisely the quantity of circulating capital it needs in order to function normally.

Any too much or too little would be disastrous for the whole country and would show that either wrong observation or wrong treatment had taken place.

Starting from this basic view, the central banks treat the economic body entrusted to them according to certain methods recognised as expedient by theory and practice. Here, just as in medical science, fixed rules have developed, and in particular the symptoms from which an increase or decrease in the need for means of payment can be read are the same for almost all central banks. What the clinical thermometer is to the doctor, the rise or fall of the quantity of good commercial bills is to them.

The circulation of bills of exchange, it is almost universally argued, shows with unsurpassable clarity how great the respective monetary need of economic life is, and a well-managed central bank, i.e. a bank that knows how to distinguish the solid commercial bill of exchange from the less solid financial bill of exchange and from the dizzy riding bill of exchange, therefore has nothing else to do than to ensure that its circulation of bills of exchange automatically adjusts to the monetary need thus documented.

This could best be achieved by a consistent discount policy. If the amount of bills in circulation in the country increases to such an extent that the economy, represented by the commercial banks, can no longer absorb it with the available funds, this is a signal that further funds are required; the central bank must then itself buy or discount the part of the bills not absorbed by the circulation and pay for it with its notes, which thereby flow into circulation and bring about the desired expansion of the money in circulation.

If, on the other hand, the amount of bills in circulation decreases, i.e. if the sum of the bills submitted to the bank for discounting falls short of the sum of the maturing bills from the preceding period, the procedure is to be reversed: The bank must then withdraw the notes with which the maturing bills of exchange are paid and which are not necessary for discounting new bills of exchange and not re-issue them, whereby the money in circulation is reduced in accordance with the reduced trading activity.

This theory of elasticity, dear James, is fundamentally wrong. However, not in its presupposition: that the monetary system must be elastic and adapt itself to the extent of commercial activity is correct, and that is why this theory sounds so convincing.

But it builds on the correct premise a fundamentally wrong conclusion. Precisely because the monetary system is supposed to be elastic, one must not give it, as far as it consists of metal, an appendage of paper which can be stretched at will, but must leave it as it is, because it possesses in itself the highest conceivable degree of elasticity, and indeed an elasticity of a twofold kind.

If you have, as I hope, absorbed the contents of my earlier letters, you know that traffic generates the money it needs to manage its turnover, either in a circulatory or in a quantitative way. In the former case, if the amount of money in circulation up to now is not in proportion to the volume of traffic, it brings the existing quantity of money into more rapid circulation by transforming money which is in a state of rest into working money. The external incentive for this transformation is provided by the price, which makes it appear more useful to the producing circles of the people to use money for the purchase of raw materials, auxiliary material and labour than to let it lie barren in the money cupboard. And the most effective incentive to the conversion is offered by interest, which is the premium for someone leaving his money lying dead in the box, whose purchasing power he himself does not want to or cannot exercise, to other people who want to step up production under the incentive of the price.

Thus a lively gainful activity procures the necessary money by setting the totality of the country's money in faster motion, as a wagon driver increases speed by making the wheels of the wagon rotate faster.

In addition to this, traffic also adapts the national money to its volume in a second, quantitative way, in that it sometimes draws money into the country and sometimes expels it abroad. Here, too, price and interest act as regulators. A relatively high price, which indicates that demand is greater than supply, and thus that commercial activity is too small in relation to purchasing power, draws foreign goods into the country, thus making the balance of payments more passive than it would otherwise be, and causes money to flow abroad to cover it, whereby the purchasing power in the country is reduced and prices fall accordingly.

A low interest rate, which also indicates that more purchasing power is available and offers itself for production purposes (as loan or equity capital) than the pores of the labour economy are capable of absorbing, leads to a flow in the same direction; also here the balance of payments becomes passive - this time as a result of the tendency of capital to migrate to countries with higher interest rates - so that metal money flows out of the country.

And in the opposite direction, i.e. the quantitative increase of the circulation of money through the importation of metal money, interest and price act as soon as their level indicates that the purchasing power is proportionately lower than it corresponds to the degree of intensity of production.

For it is precisely in this, my son, that the superiority of a metallic currency over a non-metallic one consists, that it brings the national money not only circulatory, by regulating its velocity of circulation, but also quantitative, by increasing or decreasing the quantity of money, thus from two sides, into accordance with the needs of the economy, and does so completely automatically, so that there is no place here for human error and human arbitrariness.

Hold this quite firmly, dear James: a metallic monetary system is in itself as elastic as can be demanded, and needs no increase in elasticity from outside. The two elementary factors of the economy, 'interest' and 'price', ensure that there is never more or less money circulating in the country than corresponds to the economic need, and everything that man can do here lies in the negative field: he can ensure that interest and price are not disturbed in their money-regulating function, that therefore, as a result of arbitrary measures, false interest and price rates do not arise and the overall economic picture is falsified. There is neither a need nor a possibility for positive measures. A central bank, therefore, which is assigned the task of making the monetary system elastic by contraction and expansion, is condemned from the outset to unfruitful activity.

In the best case, which is very rare, such a bank will do no harm, namely, if its management is clever and sensitive enough to obey the instructions given to it by the market through price and interest, and always to keep just as much money in circulation as would circulate if it, the bank, did not exist.

In most cases, however, it will harm the economy, because its management will be inclined to enforce its own conception of the money requirements of traffic, i.e. to follow a policy which deviates from the automatic regulation of the economic organism.

It must therefore be said that, from the point of view of elasticity, a central bank is at best superfluous, but usually harmful. This harsh judgement must be made even if the central bank is guided by sound principles in its efforts to adjust the money supply to the demand for circulation.

For even in this case it will never regulate the circulation of money better, but often worse, than the economy automatically does under the influence of its elementary laws. Correct principles in the assessment of the need for circulation are, however, a great rarity among central banks. As a rule, the banks are rather under the determining influence of theories which are quite aberrant and which give rise to a fundamentally false picture of the economy and its respective monetary needs in the minds of their managers. And among these aberrant theories is that of the signalling capacity of the exchange of goods.

I myself, and you too, my boy, have grown up with the economic axiom that the need for money in commercial transactions can nowhere be better read off than in the exchange of goods. As soon as production and trade become more lively and need more money to cope with them, the prevailing view is that the number of bills of exchange with which the manufacturer pays for the raw materials and the merchant for the finished products swells sharply, more sharply than is commensurate with the financial resources and the willingness of the bankers to discount.
In this increase of the quantity of bills of exchange over and above the amount of money available, the theory sees the most reliable sign that traffic is once again in need of new quantities of money, and the central banks, which have almost all adopted this theory, see in the quantity of good

merchant's bills of exchange that come into existence the very criterion of the need for money. The sum of the merchant bills which free circulation is unable to absorb and which are therefore offered to the central bank at a discount, either directly or through the intermediary of a banking institution, determines the sum of money which the central bank believes it must put into circulation by means of note issue.

This view that the exchange of goods is the measure of the legitimate need for money and the index of the elasticity of the means of circulation is just as false as the view of the nature of the elasticity of money itself; and it is not made any more correct by the fact that the prevailing doctrine at our universities and commercial colleges regards the exchange of goods as the decisive factor in determining the extent of the issue of notes. In reality, the commercial bill of exchange has nothing whatsoever to do with the legitimate monetary needs of the economy. I myself, who have seen many thousands of bills of exchange come into being, see in the appearance of a new bill of exchange nothing more than a sign that two persons are involved in a certain production or trade process instead of one.

A thousand times I have observed that whenever the manufacturer or merchant himself had the capital he needed for a transaction - whether as full owner or as co-owner or manager - the transaction in question was carried out in cash without a bill of exchange coming into existence; that, on the other hand, whenever it was not the manufacturer A or the merchant B but a third person C who possessed the necessary capital, a bill of exchange was issued and accepted, the purpose of which was to transfer the capital from the hands of C into those of A or B. The 'economy' as a whole has always been a 'business' in which the capital is transferred from one person to another. The 'economy' as a whole had just as much or as little capital and just as great or as small a need for money in one fold as in the other.

The only difference was that in one case the money was found with A or B, who wanted to use it, in the other case with C, who did not want to use it, but either let it rest or lend it to a third party, which was usually decided by the amount of the remuneration (interest) offered to him.

And so I have become accustomed to seeing in a strong supply of bills of exchange not the sign of a correspondingly strong legitimate need for money in the economy, but only a sign that it is not the entrepreneur but other people who have the money in their possession for certain undertakings, mostly purchases of goods; that, in other words, commercial activity is built up to a great extent on credit rather than on personal property.

I have not allowed myself to be disturbed in this view by the fact that in many branches of business it has become virtually customary to pay with bills of exchange instead of cash.

For the motive which gives rise to a bill of exchange is not important, but only whether capitalist C is in a position to hand over in bills of exchange the money which factory owner A and merchant B want to use for the purchase of goods or not. If the people of the C class have sufficient money at their disposal to satisfy the claims of the A and B classes or of the commodity creditors of these classes, it is irrelevant whether the bills of exchange documenting the transfer of money owe their origin to a private agreement, or to a commercial custom, or perhaps to a syndicate compulsion.

The very fact that business practice and trade custom determine whether thousands of bills of exchange are created or not proves how little the 'economic need for money' has to do with the respective circulation of bills of exchange. Sometimes the circulation of bills increases because a few large cartels have decided to demand payment with a three-month acceptance; sometimes because the merchants and manufacturers want to profit from the low rate of discount on bills that prevails on the money market, which in turn shows that numerous capitalists and banks are inclined to convert their dormant purchasing power into active purchasing power, their treasured money into money on loan; soon because a tax or other expenditure imposed on tradesmen forces them temporarily to use foreign money to a greater extent. In all these cases the higher circulation of bills of exchange merely proves that an exchange of money has taken place between different classes of the population. It says nothing about the causes of the exchange of money.

Of course, there are also cases in which an increase in bills of exchange is the direct consequence of an absolute increase in commercial activity, and these cases even form the majority. But here, my boy, beware, for heaven's sake, of a misunderstanding: do not think that the increasing circulation of bills of exchange represents an appeal of the economy to some authority, a cry for help, as it were, by which the general public is called upon to assist the increased commercial activity with increased funds! You would be attaching quite the wrong significance to exchange transactions in general and to sound commercial exchange in particular if you wanted to believe this. The best way to protect yourself from such an error is to visualise the meaning of the emergence of such a 'cyclical exchange' in a practical case.

If the manufacturer A or the merchant B put their acceptance on a three-month draft drawn on them by their supplier X, this happens because the supplier is prepared to defer the corresponding debt sum for three months, either because he does not need this sum and can therefore leave it to A and B for three months, or because he has made an agreement with C, the 'discounting agent,' according to which the latter lets him have the sum on loan. The prerequisite for such a solid commercial exchange is therefore that someone has a surplus amount of money and gives it away. Otherwise, supplier X would not be able to draw a draft on A or B, that is, he would not be able to allow his customers to remain three months in arrears with payment. Rather, he would have to insist on immediate payment in order to be able to pay his own suppliers, employees and workers. Somewhere in the economy there must be a 'dormant' amount of money that can and will be transformed into 'active' money through bill discounting. Therefore, you must never see in an increase in bills of exchange a 'cry for help' from the economy in need of money, but quite the contrary, a certificate from the economy that surplus money is available to an extent that allows the manufacturers and traders to strengthen their operations.

The fact that each new bill of exchange is matched by a corresponding amount of available money is precisely the sign that it is a solid commercial bill of exchange originating from legitimate trade and not a riding or cellar bill of exchange.

This meaning of the bill of exchange, however, is reversed into its very opposite as soon as one sees in every bill of exchange that appears on the market the symbol of a corresponding lack of money and the call to eliminate this lack of money; as soon, therefore, as supplier X, without having his own reserves or a backer C willing to lend, draws a bill of exchange on A or B because he believes or believes to know that public opinion sees in his bill of exchange a 'legitimate monetary need' of the economy and will therefore already see to it that some instance satisfies the monetary need. In this case, the bill of exchange does not come into being because a reserve exists within the economy and seeks investment, nor because the increasing liveliness of business transactions justifies its creation - for a bill of exchange is only legitimate if there is a disconteur for it - but simply because X has concluded a transaction with A or B, trusting in the help of some body outside the economy, which otherwise could not have been concluded. The bill of exchange is therefore no longer, as it should be by its nature, a certificate of the economy that surplus funds are available which allow the manufacturers and traders to increase their turnover, but quite the opposite, a certificate that such funds are not available, but are rather to be conjured up by some trick.

But the national economy, dear James, does not know any magic wands, which practice money that does not exist. And if a central bank is set up in a country to play the role of a magic wand, so to speak, and to pour out money on the economy which the latter wishes to receive, because otherwise it cannot expand its scope of business at will, then this central bank is set up on a false principle and is a product of the superstition that an authority authorised by the state can produce money outside the living economy.

We both know, however, that this is not possible, but that only circulation is capable of generating money. Every attempt by a central bank to produce money by printing slips of paper and to hand it over to trade and industry in exchange for bills of exchange which the latter have put into circulation in speculation on the money-generating power of the bank fails because of the multiplication tables of the laws of economics. It is only a deception of the eye if the spectator believes to see new money gushing forth from the magic horn of plenty of the central bank. For what gushes forth is old money, a part of the country's long-standing purchasing power, which is diluted to the extent that the bank stretches it out with its notes backed by bills of exchange. To use an illustration, the central bank is the roller mill in a wire rolling mill: on the left, a thick iron rod is pushed between the rollers, and on the right, a thin iron thread emerges from it. No matter how long the iron thread may be, one can never say that the existing iron mass has been increased by rolling it into wire.

And so one must not say of national money that it has been increased by the activity of the printing press, but only that this activity has 'rolled it out'.

The money which the central bank hands out to the bill collectors as the representatives of the economy supposedly in need of money is nothing other than a part of the money of this economy itself, gained through a dilution process which the holders of money and money claims clearly feel because the purchasing power of their money is reduced, i.e. the prices of goods rise.

If the bad boys tempt you with theories to the contrary, do not follow them, my son. You would infallibly go astray.

    With love

        Your old dad.

Fourth Letter

Banking theory and currency theory
Balance of payments and money elasticity
Treasury bills and private bills of exchange

Berlin, June 14th 1922

As long as there are central banks, dear James, which not only perform the functions of money distribution, cash management and utilisation of available cash stocks, but also have the privilege of money creation through note issuance, they will be at the centre of the dispute of economic doctrines.

Two main directions of central bank theory can be distinguished. The first is based on the observation that the economy has a great need for money at times and a smaller need at other times, and assigns the central banks the task of satisfying this changing need by expanding and contracting their circulation of notes.

This is the theory which wants the central bank to be included as an elasticity factor in the allegedly otherwise too rigid monetary constitution of the country. The other view is that a healthy monetary system, i.e. a monetary system that is closely enough connected with the currency of the other most important countries to allow foreign money to flow into the country and national money to flow out of the country, is elastic in itself and does not require regulation by the central bank; that the central bank must therefore be careful never to see more or less money in circulation than would be in circulation if it did not exist itself. Economics still calls these two directions by the names given them in England more than 100 years ago by Tooke, John Lloyd and Ricardo, namely the first as 'banking theorythe ,' second as 'currency theory'.

After my previous letter, you will not be in doubt for a moment as to which of these two theories you are to regard as correct and which as false. It is the 'banking theory' that has given birth to the double superstition that, firstly, one can read off the 'money demand' of the economy from the quantity of solid commercial bills of exchange, and secondly, one can satisfy this money demand by issuing 'new' money if the 'old' money is not sufficient for this purpose. This error, that a banking transaction, namely the discounting of bills of exchange, in a certain sense forms a monetary index, that another banking transaction, namely the issue of notes, must be guided by this index, and that consequently the sound commercial bill of exchange forms the best cover for notes, in short, that the monetary system is an object of banking policy, this error has given its name to the direction in question.

Similarly, the name of the 'currency theory' is derived from its fundamental theorem, which is that money itself - and in this school only the metal or the metal certificate is regarded as 'money' - decides on its quantity, and that never more or less money circulates in the country than corresponds to the given state of the economy. (We have seen that this self-regulation of the quantity of money in circulation takes place quantitatively, through the outflow or inflow of money, and circulatory, through the increase or decrease of the velocity of circulation).

Consequently, according to this doctrine, the central bank must behave purely passively and do nothing more than accept metal when it is offered to it and give it back again when it is demanded of it.
If it fulfils this basic condition, it is at liberty to replace metal with notes temporarily and to the

extent that traffic permits, but in this case the notes represent nothing more than receipts (certificates) for deposited metal that can be reclaimed at any time.

At the centre of this struggle between the two main directions of monetary theory has always been the balance of payments. Banking theory makes it a main pillar of its doctrinal edifice, arguing as follows: Every economy is subject to contingencies which easily force it to make heavy payments to foreign countries. A bad harvest which results in large grain imports, a war which makes it necessary to maintain an army abroad or to grant subsidies to a confederate, and many other possibilities generate a debt to foreign countries which leads to money exports and causes a shortage of money at home.

In such cases, the central bank has the duty to eliminate the domestic money shortage, which manifests itself in the form of an increased deposit of bills of exchange, by increasing the issue of notes. The occurrence of a strongly passive balance of payments can easily be read from the exchange rates; as soon as these deteriorate to an unusual degree, this is the sign of a significant outflow of money and thus a signal for the central bank to make increased quantities of notes available to the market, because the bills offered to it are in this case of 'legitimate origin'.

The 'currency theory' contradicts this with all its energy. It denies, and rightly so, that a passive balance of payments entitles or even obliges the central banks to increase their circulation of notes; the banks do not thereby lead the economy towards recovery, but on the contrary prevent the self-healing that would otherwise automatically occur.
For the lack of money, which occurs as a result of a passive balance of payments and the outflow of money caused by

it, is nothing other than a medicine, albeit a bitter one, which heals the economic body from within; the lack of money restricts the possibility of purchase in the country, thus reduces prices, thereby promotes foreign demand and export and, through this export, eliminates the passive balance of payments, i.e. the source of the evil, thus restoring the disturbed equilibrium.

This harsh but beneficial medicine should not be rendered ineffective by replacing the money that has flowed out with notes; for in this way one prevents the fall in prices and the export, so that the passive balance of payments does not disappear, but on the contrary becomes worse under the influence of the artificially high prices.

Indeed, the persistence of a passive balance of payments, i.e. of bad exchange rates, was the typical characteristic that the self-healing power of the economy had been paralysed by a wrong central bank policy and an artificially increased money supply, and that the doctor had been replaced by the quack.

Of course, the battle of the two doctrines did not quite take place in the pointed form and also not using the parables that I have chosen here to make the contrast quite vivid for you.

The bottom line is this:
The 'banking theory' believes that money is too inelastic for the needs of the economy and requires, so to speak, an elastic deposit; that bad balances of payments, as a result of this inelasticity, cause money shortages and economic crises; and that, in order to avoid these crises, an increase in money by means of note issue is absolutely necessary. On the other hand, the 'currency theory' maintains that money is elastic in itself and does not need any artificial supplemen-

tation; that passive balances of payments correct themselves quickly and entirely of their own accord; and that the aggravation of their passivity over a certain period of time comes from nothing other than the quantities of notes put into circulation by the banks.

More succinctly still:
The passive balance of payments is not the cause but the effect of the arbitrary multiplication of money.

Many centuries of experience have proven the 'currency theory' right. A country has never suffered from a strongly or persistently passive balance of payments, from excessive money exports and the resulting economic crisis, if its monetary system was healthy, i.e. if there was never more money circulating in the country than was generated and held by circulation itself, without tutelage by the central bank.

If money flowed abroad, it did no harm. For either the economy compensated for the deficiency by faster circulation of money, which is synonymous with faster production and greater efficiency; or the reduced money supply produced a price pressure which was not too great, but only just great enough to stimulate foreign countries to make purchases and to bring the balance of payments back into equilibrium.
In one case as in the other, the disturbance was removed by increased exports, sometimes as a result of increased efficiency, sometimes as a result of reduced prices. And in both cases money proved to be sufficiently elastic to protect the economy from crises, unless these were rooted not in monetary but in physical causes (bad harvests, epidemics), or in political moments (war, revolution), or finally in economic mismanagement (credit fraud, industrial litterateurism).

Conversely, every country has suffered from a strongly and persistently passive balance of payments, from excessive money exports and from severe economic crises when its monetary system was sick, i.e. when considerably more money was circulating in the country than the circulation could automatically produce and hold.

The additional money spent, by raising prices, not only reduced the value of money and was socially destructive, but by raising prices it also prevented the balance of payments from being balanced through exports. Only when the exchange rates had risen to such a level, i.e. when the national money had devalued abroad to such an extent that even the increased domestic prices appeared cheap to foreigners and encouraged them to buy, could the balance of payments return to equilibrium; but now on the basis of an enormously deteriorated monetary value, a completely ruined currency.

Metal money had disappeared from circulation, into foreign countries or into hiding places, because of its intrinsic value, which no central bank policy, however bad, could take away. The only notes circulating were those that were perhaps an object of speculation abroad - often not even that - but not money with which to balance payments. The monetary system now lacked elasticity, i.e. the ability to increase or decrease automatically, depending on the state of the exchange rates, through inflow and outflow; and the circulatory stretching ability had also been almost completely lost as a result of the general mistrust of the national currency. The arbitrary issuing of notes, falsely called 'elasticity', had killed the natural, real elasticity of money.
Fortunately, the cases in which a country feels the effects of a policy oriented according to the 'banking principle' so drastically are not all that frequent.

European continental states go through such a period on average once every 100 years, usually following wars or revolutions.

The economy whose 'legitimate claim to money' the central bank then has to satisfy is not private commerce with its commercial exchange, but the state war economy or the economy of the financial dilettantes, whom the revolution has brought to the helm, with their public debt bond.

The supporters of the banking principle, however, do not want to see this debt bond placed in the same line as the sound commercial bill of exchange. They regard only the latter as the legitimate representative of an economic claim to money, the treasury bill, on the other hand, as a pretender which, since it has no direct relation to the economy, only arrogates to itself the claim to money. It is easy to understand why such a distinction is made: anyone who allows the state power behind the treasury bill access to the issuing desk of the central bank has to admit, willy-nilly, that the banknotes are not money of economic origin but non-interest-bearing special-purpose bonds to cover the deficit in the state budget and are thus pseudo-money; that they do not form an organic component of a sound currency but a foreign body in this currency. But this does not alter the fact that factually there is no difference between the claim to money in the form of the private bill of exchange and that in the form of the treasury bill, and that both can assert a claim to the monetary tokens of the central bank with exactly the same right or entitlement.

Yes, one could even think that the claim of the treasury bill would be the more privileged one, mind you, the economically privileged one.

For in the case of the private bill of exchange it may well be doubtful whether it has an economically sound origin and does not only owe its origin to an accidental need for money of a frivolous merchant, brought about for instance by gambling losses.

Even the giro of a large bank does not remove this doubt. On the other hand, in the case of a treasury bill submitted to a central bank for discounting, there can be no doubt that it represents a 'legitimate monetary claim of the commercial economy' inasmuch as the state, if it had not created the treasury bill, would have been compelled to raise the corresponding amount through taxation or borrowing, thus withdrawing it from the economy and reducing its purchasing possibilities.

By discounting the treasury bill at the central bank, therefore, the purchasing power of the economy, as the supporters of the banking principle understand it, is strengthened in every case; in the case of discounting a private bill, it is strengthened only if it is of productive and not speculative origin. Every banknote issued on the basis of a treasury note spares the gainful employment in the country and makes possible for it turnovers which otherwise could not take place, so that the apparently purely fiscal creation of money is in reality a creation of money for the benefit of the economy, just like the banknote issued on the basis of a bill of exchange.

And so the theory of the 'legitimate claim of the commercial economy on the money-creating power of the central bank' leads straight to the mischief of money creation on the orders of the state and thus to its own absurdity.

Whether the conversion of bills of exchange into money is carried out on a large or small scale, i.e. whether the possibilities of banking theory are consistently exploited to the utmost or only timidly used, makes no difference in principle.

A wrong principle remains wrong even if it is followed with moderation; only that in this case the evil consequences naturally do not show themselves so clearly.

However, it cannot be emphasised strongly enough that every issue of notes is accompanied by evil consequences, which cannot legitimise themselves in any other way than through the creation and bank discounting of corresponding cross-bills, irrespective of whether these originate from commercial transactions or from the treasury, irrespective of whether they have the so-called 'legitimate business' or a state deficit as their origin.

The money that enters the market in the form of newly issued notes is never 'new purchasing power', but always old purchasing power withdrawn from circulation by invisible means, and the enlarged circulation of notes does not, in the name of the state, embody new purchasing power. The increased circulation of notes does not embody one iota more purchasing possibilities than the previous smaller turnover, but at best the same purchasing possibilities at higher prices.

Have I been clear enough?

Your old father.

Fifth Letter

The Unlimitedness of the 'Legitimate Need for Money' Investment Credit or Operating Credit? Ambivalent Banking Policy

Berlin, June 19th 1922

In my last letter, dear James, I casually remarked that the pernicious consequences of the central bank policy oriented according to the 'banking principle' only reveal themselves in their full force relatively rarely, namely on average about once every hundred years.

This fact must actually be disconcerting. For central bank managers have always been supporters of the aforementioned principle and thus of the view that the issuance of banknotes should be guided by the 'needs of trade and industry'.

Logically, this imposes on them the obligation to discount every commercial bill that is offered to them and does not exactly bear the characteristics of fraud or recklessness.

But the so-called 'legitimate need' of money in the economy, if no obstacles are placed in its way, is absolutely infinite, and if a body exists which is prepared to discount every sound commercial bill, that is, to meet every credit demand of a proper businessman, one would think that there was not paper enough in the world for the bills of exchange which are created on the basis of this willingness to discount, and for the notes which are issued on the basis of the bills thus created.

I have some experience in commercial life and know how boundless business enterprise is when it is allowed to run wild.

Nevertheless, I am always shocked when I think of the incalculable number of transactions that are planned, discussed, prepared and carefully calculated, and which are only not carried out because the necessary capital is lacking.

Mind you, I am not thinking here of the wild project-making of the elements who habitually hazard with other people's money. Rather, I am thinking of the very sensible, often even excellently clever business intentions of serious men, which, if they were carried out, would usually represent an economic enrichment of the country; I am thinking, for example, of the exploitation of the many thousands of valuable patents which are granted in every country - naturally alongside many more worthless ones - and which can never stand the test of their usefulness only because nowhere is there even remotely as much capital as the inventors claim.

The tremendous motor power of the ebb and flow - to pick out a single example - would long ago have been made usable by electrical means all over the world if it did not require more capital, i.e. the provision of more subsistence resources for millions of workers, than the world economy can provide apart from the requirements for its current programme.

How then, when an authority appears which considers it its task to 'satisfy every legitimate monetary need' with the help of the banknote and thus to help all those excellent projects to be carried out which have hitherto been stuck in the embryonic stage of development? Must not a deluge of credit claims descend upon this authority and force it to issue unmeasured quantities of notes?

You will probably object here, my boy, that the claims of the economy described are a matter of pronounced investment credit, which is embodied in bonds, long-term bank loans and the like, and not of operating credit, which is clothed in the form of bills of exchange.

And since it is one of the recognised principles of central banks not to fix their funds - if only for technical reasons - in permanent loans, but only in short-term acceptances secured by the so-called bill of exchange limit, which are due in three months at the most, those claims cannot be a burden on the central banks. If you make this objection, you show that you know about credit theory.

In practice, however, I have to reject it for two reasons: Firstly, a so-called 'business loanwhich is ,' habitually renewed after three months by repeatedly taking the same or even a constantly increasing amount of bills from the bill acceptor or his bank, is not a business loan at all, but a permanent loan, which can be used at will, possibly also for investments. (We are touching here on the important subject of chain operating credit, for which we now have the apt term 'revolving credit', and of the 'petrified bill of exchange,' about which I would have much to say; but all in good time.

Secondly, and this is the key point, one must not make any distinction at all in economic practice between operating credit and investment credit. The money which the entrepreneur needs for explicit investment purposes, and which therefore no central bank in the world would advance to him, is, from the point of view of the merchant who supplies him with building materials, machines, etc., and from the point of view of the manufacturer who buys and processes the raw materials necessary for this, equally explicit operating money.

If the merchant and the manufacturer pay for their purchases with three-month bills of exchange, these bills of exchange, although the goods paid for with them are ultimately transformed into fixed assets, fall without further ado into the category of 'legitimate commercial bills of exchangeand if ,' the central bank discounts them, i.e. advances the merchant and the manufacturer the money for their purchases, the latter are in a position to grant credit to the ordering entrepreneur, namely an investment credit.

They can grant this credit for years to come, they can even convert it into a fixed participation, for the bill credit which they enjoy with the central bank directly or through the intermediation of their bank account is as a rule replaced by a new credit of the same kind when the bill matures.
They can deal with it as with a part of their own capital. In this way, many, indeed most, business loans are automatically transformed into investment loans, and a central bank need only buy any desired quantity of bills of exchange from the solid merchants and industrialists well known to it, in order to help carry out all those projects of which I have just spoken, and which it would never have financed directly. The result, however, is an enormous flood of banknotes, caused by nothing other than the legitimate and even obligatory satisfaction of the legitimate exchange credit claim of the transport industry according to 'banking theory'.

The peculiar thing now - and here I return to the starting point - is that despite these connections and despite the broad-minded view that almost all central bank managers have of the extent of their credit obligations, a flooding of countries with banknotes is so exceedingly rare and usually only occurs in cases of national distress, i.e. emergency.
This is partly due to the fact that in all countries legal limits have been set for the issue of notes, which every bank must respect, no matter how legitimate the demands of the economy may be and how urgent they may appear. For even if the pernicious effects of excessive note issue ('infla-

tion') tend to befall a nation only once every hundred years on average, they are nevertheless so severe, indeed downright disastrous, that legislators have erected firm dams against the flood of notes.

Even where legislation is influenced by the 'banking principle' and believes in the necessity of making the monetary system as 'elastic' as possible, the memory of the last preceding inflationary period nevertheless works in the direction of a salutary restriction of the quantity of notes. I will discuss the various types of this restriction later.

But the legal limits imposed on the issue of banknotes do not fully explain the restraint of the central bank managers, indeed they do not even seem to be the main reason for this restraint. Otherwise, in normal times, the circulation of banknotes would have to remain close to the legal limit, or at least not significantly below it, and furthermore, in times of a boom and an increased need for credit, the bank managers would have to make representations to their negatives about raising the limit.

But both are very seldom the case. At the Bank of England, for example, which is only entitled to issue a very small amount of non-metal-covered notes, the directors not only never applied for an increase in this quota before the war, but for decades they have not even used the quota, rather they have always insisted that only gold-covered notes are in circulation; even today the gold stock exceeds the note issue.

The German Reichsbank was also very cautious before the war. Although it was entitled to issue any amount of notes within the very broad framework of the one-third cover, which I will speak about later (up to a certain amount tax-free, beyond that against payment of a five-percent levy), it always strove to limit the circulation of notes and fought the rush of credit claims with energetic means of defence, which I will also discuss later.

Similarly, all other central banks, including the Bank of France, have repeatedly increased the quota of banknotes in circulation, but until the war, circulation very rarely exceeded the metal supply by more than 30 per cent, although 200 per cent was permissible.

It must therefore be stated that a certain restraint was observed everywhere and that the banks, although based on the banking principle and managed in the spirit of this principle, visibly compromised with the currency principle.

This would not be at all surprising, but would only prove that in the course of time one has become aware of how elastic a circulation-created monetary system is in itself, and how unnecessary, indeed harmful, an artificial increase in its elasticity would appear, if the central bank managements of all countries did not repeatedly counter this view.

In fact, there is an extraordinary and difficult to explain contradiction between the words and the deeds of the bank managements, between the theory and the practice of banking policy.

While in normal times the banks show a commendable moderation, restrict the issue of notes as far and as long as possible, and fight the demands of the economy on their willingness to lend with a whole arsenal of defensive means as soon as the issue of notes would thereby be considerably increased, their presidents always emphasise anew that every 'justified credit claimwhich ' approaches them in the form of bills of exchange will be satisfied, and that it is the task of the central banks to supply the economy with funds to the extent that the traffic situation requires. In other words, bank managers act according to the currency principle and talk according to banking theory. This is a contradiction that can be observed in almost all banks, and it cannot be explained in any other way than that a healthy instinct usually prevents the management from overlooking their highly questionable conception of money. The contradiction is by no means new.

Even the classics of money and banking have noted it. Bagehot, for example, writes in his famous book 'Lombard Street': 'Although the directors of the Bank of England at that time (meaning the time around 1800) fell into erroneous views, they acted on the whole with peculiar prudence and moderation.
But when they were questioned in 1810 about the reasons for their actions, they gave answers that have become almost classical by their nonsense'. And long before Bagehot, Ricardo said: 'It will scarcely be believed, after fifty years, that the directors and officers of the Bank (of England) have in our time seriously asserted in Parliament and its committees that the issue of notes by the Bank of England has no influence on the prices of commodities, bullion or foreign exchange, nor can it have any such influence. 'This is Ricardo's damning verdict on the monetary understanding of the same bank managers who, in spite of their views, which would have corresponded to rampant inflation, nevertheless pursued a relatively prudent note policy and thus achieved that the pound sterling, in the most difficult period that England has ever gone through, only temporarily lost in value and not by more than 15 to 25 per cent.

I would almost like to assume that this dichotomy between word and deed, which can be found at all times and in almost all countries, is deeply rooted in the nature of the central bank itself. The principle of increasing elasticity, on which central banking is mainly based, is inherently fragile and, if followed as consistently as theory demands, will inevitably lead to a monetary catastrophe. Therefore, the principle must never be applied consistently, but must be weakened in practice in such a way that the economy does not suffer too considerable damage from the error of the principle.

Central bank managers must therefore be skilful tacticians who apply the principle to the extent necessary to maintain faith in it, but again not to the extent that its evil consequences become apparent to the unarmed eye.
While they thus practically perform a kind of egg-dance around the theory of elasticity, they must nevertheless firmly affirm the correctness of this theory, for it is, after all, the basis of the central bank, and to combat it would be to deny the raison d'être of the bank.

At least that is what the bank managers seem to believe or instinctively feel, because the functions of money distribution, cash management and the utilisation of available cash, against which no objection can be raised, do not seem to them to be sufficient for a central bank. But the latter is a mistake. A central bank can very well limit itself to the three main functions and a few secondary ones and still be a large, even powerful institution.

Proof:
The Bank of England, whose importance is based precisely on the exercise of these functions, and which plays so little role as a factor of elasticity that it can almost no longer be called a 'central bank' in the usual sense. For its notes are - with the exception of the war period - as a rule fully covered by metal and are basically nothing more than certificates of a metal deposit. The bank thus corresponds more to the concept of the old giro bank than to the concept as-

sociated with a central bank, and as soon as it will have excluded cash payment again, it will best be described as a 'giro bank with an attached conversion fund'.

But as long as it does not find the courage to destroy the superstition that it has to increase the elasticity of money with its notes and to satisfy every legitimate credit claim, its directors will have to dance along with their continental colleagues.

By the way, you do not need to tell these gentlemen what I wrote to you in this letter about Bagehot and Ricardo and their judgement of the central bank directors, should you ever speak to one of them. They do not like such reminiscences, even if they only refer to their predecessors.

> It's late: so good night for today!
>
> Papa.

Sixth Letter

Money substitution and money addition
Credit crisis
The 'justified' credit claim

Berlin, June 24th 1922

Two truths of life, my dear James, must precede this letter, so that you may adjust yourself properly to it.

First:
There is no principle in practical economic policy that may not be violated once in a while, and that is when its violation causes less damage than would be feared from its strict observance.
The popular saying on this subject is somewhat generalised: No rule without exception.

Secondly, if defective institutions exist which cannot be easily abolished because of the economic law of inertia, one should try to extract from these institutions whatever benefit can be gained from them, even if it can only be done by pushing against a recognised economic rule.

Hardly any other field demands the application of these two principles to such an extent as central banking. Sometimes compromises have to be made, or, as the saying goes, 'just boiling water'.

The central banks which we see before us today owe their origin not so much to the desire to possess an institution for the distribution of money, for cash management and other useful functions, but almost without exception to the endeavour to make money 'elastic' and to artificially satisfy traffic demands which cannot be satisfied within the framework of the existing money supply.

We have seen that this endeavour is based on a false premise, because money cannot tolerate any increase in elasticity and paralyses every arbitrary increase - and also decrease - of its quantity by changing its purchasing power in the opposite direction.
But the central banks are there, and the peoples have become accustomed to them, along with their organic errors.

Their abolition would make their advantages disappear along with their faults: And so practical considerations dictate that we come to terms with them, gradually pushing them more and more away from the generation of money and towards the mediation of payments, as has long been the case in England, and in the meantime also taking advantage of their mistakes as far as possible 'to make the best of it', as the American would say.

And central banks can indeed provide such benefits quite often. Since not everything outside the central banking system is as it should be, and since our entire economic organisation is flawed, it happens that error can be compensated for with error, i.e. that economic disturbances can be mitigated by exploiting the basically false principle of elasticity of the central banks.

Thus the economy of the main trading countries suffers from the alarming defect that it is built up far too much on short-term credit. The consequence of this is that whenever any circumstance arouses distrust, makes lenders fearful and causes the cancellation of numerous loans, the economy is most seriously damaged and many a branch of industry which works particularly heavily with credit is virtually ruined.

The fears that create such a mood of crisis can be 'justified or groundless, and the crisis itself can last a long time or pass quickly, depending on its cause. In such cases, the central bank, with its right to issue banknotes, is not infrequently able to save the situation by stepping in for the fearful lenders and providing substitute credit to the economy until calm returns and capital offers itself again.

In this case, the economy's flawed credit constitution is healed by the bank's essentially equally flawed credit policy. The iron heals the wound that the iron has inflicted.
The bank's stepping in with additional money, which, strictly speaking, it would not be allowed to issue, can even be justified to a certain extent from the point of view of monetary theory.

Namely as follows:
You know that every credit transaction, every lending of money to a third party, represents an acceleration of the circulation of money:
Money, which would otherwise be in a state of rest, is added to the circulating money by this process, which is equivalent to an absolute increase in money (and is indeed one of the means by which the economy itself generates the money it lacks). If this process is now reversed, i.e. circulating money is put back into retirement, this amounts to an absolute reduction of money. And if the economy has an instrument at its disposal which, like the central bank, can compensate for this reduction in money by a planned increase in money, then one may make use of it for the momentary advantage of the life of traffic without asking at length whether the principle according to which it carries out the increase is in itself correct or not.

But great insight and restraint are needed here, so that the advantage of being able to cure one economic error by another is not bought with the disadvantages which an artificial and arbitrary creation of money normally entails.

These disadvantages come into play immediately with all their severity if the bank management neglects to immediately withdraw its notes from circulation when private willingness to lend returns and when the dormant money supply is again 'activated'. If their notes were previously harmless substitutes, they will now become harmful additions if they are not recalled. It takes a lot of perspicacity and firm will to carry out this recall in the right proportion to the revival of the old credits, consistently and unperturbed by any 'legitimate claims' of circulation.

Wherever a central bank exists in a country that works excessively with credit, it should be welcomed as a 'crisis reserve', even if it owes its existence to a false principle. Its notes then represent an insurance policy for emergencies and spare the country, which is suffering from an overstretching of the credit principle, from having to use desperate means at the outbreak of a credit crisis and, in fine perplexity, to create a special emergency money ('emergency notes'), as the Americans issued several times before they had their centralised central bank system.

But here again there is the danger that the central banks will fail to recognise the symptoms of such a credit crisis in which they are entitled to intervene, and will consider themselves entitled to intervene even when there is no question of a credit panic at all, but only of a manoeuvre on the part of commercial circles to obtain increased credit.

It is rather difficult to distinguish when a credit shortage has its origin in the withdrawal of old loans, i.e. in the return of working money to dormancy, and when it is based on the increased demands of an enterprising merchant class. Where an economy is highly dependent on credit, in the course of time it becomes customary for credit to mature on certain dates, usually the first of the quarter. On these dates, the payment obligations crowd together in such a way that the outward appearance of a crisis is easily created, although in reality it is only a question of payments which, for the sake of convenience, have been transferred from the previous business period to the beginning of the new period, and for which every prudent merchant should have made provision by setting aside a part of his quarterly income.

If a central bank follows the policy of regarding this periodic accumulation of payments, which seems to it to be a crisis, as a signal to issue large quantities of notes, i.e. to make money available to the market which it would have to bring in itself if it behaved properly, it accustoms business to rely on this quarterly aid and to manage its own money carelessly. The consequence is that the justified 'claims' of the entrepreneurs on the quarterly dates have the tendency to grow constantly, like the claims of a spoilt child who can count on the fulfilment of every one of his wishes. And when, for some reason or other, the central bank is unable to supply the market with as large a quantity of notes as it demands, then there is a crisis - a crisis which has its origin not so much in market conditions as in a wrong banking policy.

The fact is, however, that almost all central banks regard and satisfy the regularly recurring demand of the economy, which swells strongly in lively times, as the most justified demand imaginable. Take a look, dear James, at the banknote statements of the large European central banks and follow the movement of banknote issuance. Everywhere you will find that - at some banks more, at others (Bank of England) less strongly - the quantities of notes suddenly swell at the end of the quarter, because the entrepreneurs and the commercial banks close to them habitually procure the money for the forthcoming payment dates by depositing bills of exchange with the central bank.

The latter willingly hands over its notes because it knows that after the so-called 'overcoming of the deadline' the demand for credit will dwindle and the notes will flow back to it. The process seems completely harmless to bank managers, even to those who are aware of the evil consequences of any excessive note issue: For the issue of notes, which immediately return to their hands with -the reliability of a boomerang, is in their eyes no real note issue at all and remains, in their view, without any influence on the economy.

But this is a mistake.

In reality, the whole structure of the economy is changed by the habitual supply of 'forward notes' to traffic. If this supply were omitted, every businessman would have to accumulate money in view of the coming payment date, i.e. leave available purchasing power unused. But since the central bank relieves him of this precaution, he can leave the market with considerably larger sums than would correspond to his monetary power and the natural abundance of money in the channels of circulation. Demand is thus increased beyond its economically justified level and has the effect of raising prices, i.e. reducing the value of money.

The fact that banknotes issued at the end of September or the end of December return to the issuing office in the first few days of October or January does not change anything.

Although these banknotes are not in circulation for nine tenths of the year, but are at the bank, they are economically considered to be in circulation. They have exactly the same effect on the value of money as if they were permanently in circulation, as if they formed a fixed component of the circulating total quantity of money, of which certain partial amounts are also not active, i.e. do not pass from hand to hand in a transaction-mediating manner, but 'rest'.

And whether a certain amount of money rests in the pockets and safes of private individuals or in the vault of the central bank is indifferent as long as the possibility exists that it will pass from the state of rest to activity in case of need.

If, therefore, a bank of issue is not in the habit of issuing any notes at all during the greater part of the year, but issues 1 billion on the dates, this has exactly the same effect on the monetary system as if the bank had constantly issued 1 billion notes. Not the lowest and not the average, but the highest amount that the bank habitually issues is decisive for the national currency.

Therefore, the term policy, which the central banks pursue and consider harmless, is in reality far more alarming than an occasional, even very extensive intervention in times of panic and crisis. In the latter case, the banknotes are only a substitute for the money that has suddenly been withdrawn from circulation and is now lying idle.
The term notes, on the other hand, are an addition to the natural circulation of money and act accordingly.

    God be with you!

        Your old father.

Seventh Letter

*The triple dam against inflation
Discount policy
Direct or indirect defence?*

Berlin, June 30th 1922

In the course of this epistolary lecture, dear James, you have probably already become aware of the fact that the central banks, as far as their money-creating function is concerned, are products of compromise: since they neither completely fulfil the task assigned to them by one theory of making the monetary system elastic enough to satisfy all 'legitimate' monetary claims, nor do they fulfil the demand of another theory of respecting the autonomy of the monetary system.

In fact, central banks vacillate between these two postulates, one of which always makes the fulfilment of the other impossible, always striving to promote the economy by issuing money and yet leaving the national currency untouched.

Since these two endeavours cannot be reconciled, the activity of the central banks is a continuous violation of one or the other postulate. Until one day circumstances arise which appear to be force majeure and imperatively demand from the bank a large-scale supply of money. Whereupon the bank throws all theoretical concerns about money overboard, unreservedly professes the 'banking principle' and makes the national money so 'elastic' that it loses most of its purchasing power and becomes an object of speculation instead of a store of value.

That is why in all countries dams have been erected to protect the monetary system from being flooded with notes by the banks in the fulfilment of their assigned tasks and to ruin the currency. We can also use another image and call those protective measures the 'anchor' which does not allow the central banks to drift out on the high seas of inflation, but keeps them in the safe harbour, at the right distance from both the shore and the open sea, i.e. at the right point of compromise between the two fundamentally different theories which meet and fight each other in our central banks today.

To be sure, we must distinguish between two kinds of anchors - or dams - depending on whether they originate in the law, which is designed to protect the currency from frivolous or imprudent bank directors, or in bank policy, by which purposeful directors prescribe for themselves guidelines for their practical conduct and at the same time create a tradition which also binds their successors to a certain extent.

There is - or at least there used to be - a radical strand of banking theory that rejects any legal limit on banknote issuance as incompatible with the principle of banknotes and the tasks of central banks. This direction, even if its theory is wrong, is at least consistent.

For once someone has said A and committed himself to the questionable principle of elasticity, he must logically also say B and recognise no other limit for the issue of notes than that which the fabulous 'need' of the economy sees to you. One cannot demand on the one hand that the need of the economy should be fully satisfied, but on the other hand agree to any mechanical obstacles being placed in the way of this satisfaction of need. In fact, there was a time when the principle of freedom of issue prevailed.

In Scotland, for example, until well into the last century, not only was everyone in principle entitled to issue notes - I will come back to the important contrast between the multi-bank system and the monopoly of a single note-issuing bank later - but there was also no limit to which the individual note-issuing authority was bound, if one disregards the limit consisting in the right of every citizen to reject a note unless it is expressly declared to be 'legal tender'.

Practical experience has decided against this unlimited right to issue notes. It has been shown everywhere that, as was drastically said in England, note-issuing freedom is identical with swindling freedom, and that Ricardo was right when he said: 'Experience shows that neither a state nor a bank has ever had the unlimited right of issuing notes without abusing this right. ' That is why today there are legal limits everywhere to arbitrariness in satisfying the supposed needs of the economy.

We have to distinguish between three kinds of limits, three different dams, as it were, which the law sets against the flood of banknotes. First of all, there is an external dam that prevents the banknotes from exceeding a certain percentage of the metal stock of the central bank; usually 300 percent of the metal cover is the maximum (principle of one-third cover), more rarely 250 percent. Here the compromise character of our present-day central banking system becomes quite clear: one knows or suspects the importance of metal for the stability of value of money; but one does not have the courage to make metal (or the note fully covered by metal) the sole currency, but considers it harmless if in addition as many, but not more notes circulate as the traffic 'voluntarily' accepts without demanding their exchange into metal.

And since practical experience teaches that under normal circumstances never more than one third of all notes issued are presented for exchange into metal, the legislature in most countries has considered itself justified in declaring the circulation of notes up to this extreme limit to be harmless and permissible.
But it turned out that this limitation was not sufficient protection, and that symptoms of illness in the monetary system appeared even when the one-third coverage of the notes was still completely intact.

As a result, the legislators felt compelled to erect a second, inner dam in addition to this outer dam in the form of a 'quota', beyond which the issue of notes was not to exceed, even if the principle of one-third cover, i.e. the outer dam, still permitted further expansion. This quota has been fixed by the most diverse methods. In one country it was made elastic so that in an emergency it was possible to exceed it and the quantity of notes could penetrate as far as the outer dam. This was the case in Germany, where before the war a penalty tax of 5 per cent made the quota limit stand out sharply, but did not make it an absolute maximum.
In other countries, the quota was made rigid and impossible to exceed, either by maximising the quantity of notes not covered by metal (as in England and Sweden) or by maximising the absolute quantity of notes without regard to cover (as in France). Just as different as the method of contingency - here elastic, there rigid, here direct, there indirect, here relative, there absolute - was the limitation of the quantity.
The more a country was inclined towards the 'currency principle' and hard money (England), the smaller was the

quota of notes, the more it professed the 'banking principle' (Spain before the war), the larger was the quota.

Finally, the national laws usually set up a third dam to reinforce the other two, by prescribing to the central banks exactly against which documents they were allowed to issue notes without metal cover, and against which they were not. Almost everywhere, the commercial bill has been made the decisive cover because it is seen as the representative of the economy's 'legitimate need for money'.

In most cases, the number of signatures that the bill of exchange should bear in order to be able to serve as banknote cover (in Germany 'as a rule' three, at least two) is also stipulated by banking law. Only in England has such a reinforcing dam not been included, but the Bank of England has been given freedom in the choice of non-metallic note cover, a freedom of which the Bank very rarely makes use, since, as I wrote to you earlier, it normally only has metal-covered notes in circulation.

These are the three dams which the law of note issue has drawn. To these are added the measures of self-restraint which the bank managements have adopted and by which they protect themselves against being driven against the dams erected by the law by the 'demand of the economy', which is, after all, infinite if one traces it with the divining rod of the banknote.

Since these protective measures consist essentially in establishing principles for discounting commercial bills, the quantity of which is identical with the money demand of the economy, they are usually called the discount policy of the banks.

Now, as you are probably sufficiently aware, an infinite amount has been written about this discount policy, and it tends to occupy a large space in the economic section of the daily newspapers. But its principle is so simple that the abundance of literature on this subject only proves how much people tend to complicate the simplest questions by unclear ideas. What ingenuity, for example, has been summoned up to determine whether the central banks, with their discount policy, i.e. with their fixing of interest rates, should subordinate themselves to the market, or whether they should influence the interest rate of the free market by their policy and push it in a certain direction.

This question of whether the central bank should only 'state the interest rate ' or whether it should 'dictate' it is basically only the outflow of an erroneous view and loses all meaning as soon as one takes things as they are.

The erroneous view I have in mind here consists in the widespread opinion that a high interest rate has a weakening effect on the entrepreneurial spirit of the economy, while a low interest rate promotes business and increases its volume. Consequently, it is argued, a central bank that is threatened by the 'legitimate demands of the economy' overflowing its head need only tighten the interest screw, i.e. increase its discount rate, in order to cause the entrepreneurial spirit to decline and the demands on its willingness to lend and its stock of notes to shrink.

That is the basic point on which there is general agreement. The disagreement only starts where the practical implementation begins. One group believes that the free market shows the attentive observer exactly when the entrepreneurial spirit is going too far, since interest becomes more expensive when the demand for capital is excessive and in many cases makes the use of capital unrewarding.

The central bank, therefore, need only be careful and raise its interest rate in accordance with the market rate; in this way it strengthens the deterrent effect of the increase in interest and at the same time protects itself from too great a demand.

The other, on the other hand, thinks that the free market always shows the excess of entrepreneurial desire only when it is too late; here the interest rate increases in price a posteriori, at a far advanced stage, and forces the liquidation of the excess of business only when it is no longer harmless but tantamount to a crisis. That is why the central bank has to play the preventive game. It must not follow the market interest rate, but must influence it through its own interest rate policy and, if necessary, stiffen it through a strong increase in the discount rate, in order to paralyse business at a moment when it has not yet assumed an excessive volume.

This whole dispute, dear James, is about the emperor's beard, so to speak, because the premise on which both schools of thought agree is a mistake.

An increase in interest rates does not have the effect of shrinking the volume of business that is attributed to it. On the contrary, it is a common fact that in trade and industry more is never earned than in times of so-called 'expensive money,' and that in such times of increased earning potential the entrepreneur can pay a high interest rate more easily than a low one in a calmer business situation.

The high interest rate is precisely the sign that the use of capital has become unusually profitable and that it is therefore advisable for the businessman to take advantage of every possible credit, including the central bank credit, to the best of his ability. But in so far as the planned taxation of interest really has an effect, it is a most undesirable, anti-social and economically questionable one: in this case it strangles precisely the sound enterprise which works with little profit, and leaves untouched the unsound one, tailored to cyclical or gambling profit, in which the amount of expenses is of secondary importance.

Strong discount increases, therefore, whether they 'state' or 'dictate the ' market situation, have far less the effect of bringing business back to a healthy level than they do of increasing the speculative nature of business.

All this actually belongs more to a treatise on interest than to one on the central bank. However, I could not spare you this little digression, because otherwise you would hardly recognise what a really effective discount policy must be like.

But now I can hope that you see clearly in this respect, without my having to say much more. A discount policy of the central bank is normally only effective if it restricts these claims on the credit of the bank directly, by outright refusal of credit, and not if it seeks to limit these claims indirectly by discount increases, whereby it strangles precisely the legitimate business and only creates all the more scope for the illegitimate, speculative one.

Actually, I must always repeat to you, the principle of artificially strengthening the credit power in the country by expanding the circulation of money is mistaken from the outset. But once this principle has been adopted, the central bank must use another criterion for the extent and selection of its loans than the mechanical interest rate. In this case, the subjective moments of the type of business, the social and cultural benefits of the enterprises must decide on the yes or no of the granting of credit. Especially since the programmatic assertion of the central banks that their notes are available to every 'justified credit claim' who approaches them is a phrase without content:

My bank can dispose of the discount credit of the central bank in any amount, even if it uses it to finance stock market speculation, but a good master carpenter who needs money to buy wood does not receive the discount credit of the central bank, or at best only through the mediation of a credit organisation, i.e. considerably more expensive.

Only in one case can the discount policy in the traditional sense, i.e. the regulation of credit claims through interest, do good service:

Namely, when the credit system in a country is so subtly organised and has so many reserves, above all reserves abroad, that every half per cent increase or decrease in the interest rate leads to an inflow of loan capital from those reserves or to an outflow into the reserves.

Where this condition exists, the interest policy is usually - not always - effective without influencing the scope of entrepreneurial activity too much. It then raises and lowers the level in the capital reserve pools and induces the finely ramified organisation that serves those pools to help it with its credit policy. But this condition seems to me to be fulfilled in only one country today, namely England. Here, therefore, the interest rate policy of the central bank usually has the desired success.

Good night.

Your old dad.

Eight Letter

The one-third cover
Economic laws, state law and banking policy
The "Giralgeld" - Bank money

Berlin, July 4th 1922

Two questions of practical central bank policy, dear James, are the main ones that constantly occupy bank managers and bank theorists in all countries.

One question concerns the principle of one-third coverage per se. One wonders why it is that national currencies so often show clear signs of devaluation, although the notes issued are covered to one third or more by gold and can be exchanged for gold at any time.
Since this possibility of exchanging notes for gold ensures that each individual note has its full gold value, it is actually absurd that the part of the national currency consisting of notes should be valued lower than gold.

Nevertheless, it has been shown time and again in practice that the exchange value of such a currency, which according to the prevailing view is a 'gold currency', sinks below its gold equivalent as soon as an absolutely large quantity of notes has been issued, irrespective of the maintenance of the principle of one-third coverage and the free exchange of notes for gold and of gold for notes.

In this case, the devaluation of the national currency is never significant. But it is clearly recognisable in the exchange rate and at times rises to 1/2% or even a little above, which in a gold-currency country already means a quite sensitive depreciation.

Above all, however, it seems to mean an unnatural depreciation, for if a spoon can be exchanged for a lot of silver at any time, then according to Adam Riese it can never be worth less than a lot of silver.

There are, of course, good reasons for this peculiar process, and you can recognise the reasons very easily if you consider three things: First, how the issue of notes in itself, detached from the gold redemption obligation, affects the currency. Secondly, how gold redemption, as prescribed by law, corrects this effect. And thirdly, how central bank practice, i.e. the application of the law, corrects this correction once again.

First of all, the effect of issuing notes in itself. We know that it consists in a certain counterfeiting of prices, since the notes supply the market with a purchasing power which it would not otherwise have. (It is clear that enterprising businessmen must refrain from many a purchase if there is no office to discount their bills of exchange and to hand them note money which has arisen only on account of this discounting process).

The price increase that occurs is identical with a corresponding devaluation of money and proves the fact to which I must repeatedly draw your attention, namely that the purchasing power of the notes issued is not at all a 'new' or 'additional' purchasing power, but a part of the long existing, circulation-born purchasing power, which becomes thinner to the extent that it is stretched. If national money is treated as a rubber band that can be stretched out at will, it reacts to this arbitrary act just like a rubber band. The natural effect of the increase in money through the issue of banknotes is therefore a reduction in the value of money.

But now we come to point two, namely the legal requirement that every note issued must be 'redeemed' in gold on demand.

This makes the national currency a gold currency and each of its components gold-value. The natural effect of the multiplication of money, to reduce the value of money, is thus annulled.

Can the law of the state do this? Can a human law override an economic law?

Apparently no.

It can only remove the conditions under which the economic law becomes effective. And if we look at the processes connected with the issue of notes in a straightforward manner, we soon realise that the state law of redeeming notes in gold does not make the economic law of monetary devaluation effective by eliminating the origin of monetary devaluation, the multiplication of money. The processes follow one another as follows.

First act: issue of notes, appearance of supposedly new purchasing power on the market, price increase.

Second act: Deterioration of the balance of payments through reduced exports and increased imports of goods (since the price increase of domestic goods makes foreign goods appear correspondingly cheaper), deterioration of the exchange rates until the 'export gold pointis ' reached, at which payment in gold becomes cheaper than payment in foreign currency, finally gold export.

Third act: Strong presentation of notes at the bank for redemption in gold, which is needed for export. When this third act takes place, the state law of note redemption has paralysed the economic law of demonetization by reversing the multiplication of money.

For the notes issued, which have led to the devaluation of money, have flowed back to the bank, and the gold given in exchange has migrated abroad. However, not all the notes issued were presented for redemption in gold and thus withdrawn from circulation, but only as many notes as could profitably be exchanged for export gold.

But since the exchange of gold is only worthwhile as long as the exchange rates are at or above the export gold point, but every reduction in the value of notes results in an improvement in the value of money and therefore pushes the exchange rates down below the gold point, the presentation of notes ceases even before the entire quantity of notes issued has flowed back to the bank.

A part of the arbitrarily created notes thus remains in circulation. And accordingly, a certain deterioration of the value of money remains. The only difference is that this deterioration is no longer as great as in the first stage, when all the notes issued still burdened circulation, but is correspondingly smaller.

The exchange rates are worse than the normal level, the gold parity, but at least not so bad as to make an export of gold worthwhile. The state law has therefore only eliminated part of the precondition of the economic law, namely part of the increase in money, and in this way it could naturally only achieve that an appealing part of the effect of the economic law, namely the reduction in the value of money, ceased to exist.

**And now we come to point three, the central bank practice, which in some respects deviates from the initialled legal intention and thus complicates matters somewhat.
Almost not a single central bank honestly complies with the legal requirement to exchange its notes for gold at coin parity.**

The German Reichsbank, for example, before the war, when it was obliged to redeem its notes, very rarely gave away 1 kilogram of coined or uncoined gold of legal fineness for every 2790 marks of notes, as would have been the intention of the law, but instead tried to prevent the exchange of the notes wherever possible, by denouncing the withdrawal of gold for export purposes as 'unpatriotic', by threatening bankers and gold arbitrageurs who nevertheless presented notes with credit hardship, and thus in fact often succeeded in ensuring that their gold redemption obligation remained on paper.

If, however, they were forced to hand over gold, they rarely gave the note submitters the 1000 grams of gold of legal fineness that they had to claim for each 2790 marks of notes, but a few grams less by giving them worn coins that had lost part of their legal tender weight through natural wear instead of new, full-value gold coins.

Similar practices were common at almost all central banks, and even at the Bank of England, which still had the greatest respect for the meaning of the gold currency, it occasionally happened that only one counter was opened for the depositors demanding gold and the gold was slowly added to them, so that only very small quantities of notes could be redeemed on any one day.

Hence it is, my son, that the national currency, even in gold-currency countries, has often devalued far more significantly than was theoretically possible under the laws of coinage and banking.

In Germany, for example, where the export gold point was reached at about 20.50 marks for the pound sterling, the London cheque rate repeatedly stood at 20.60 and even higher - actually a logical impossibility, since at a rate of 20.50 a mass presentation of notes to the bank would have taken place, and at about 20.55 the entire gold stock would have had to be demanded from it.
In fact, the gold currency was heavily holed, i.e. more notes were artificially kept in circulation than the traffic wanted to absorb voluntarily and than could have remained in circulation if the banking law had been followed exactly.
If the banking law was only able to eliminate a part of the conditions under which the economic law of demonetization became effective, banking practice ensured that not even this part of the conditions was eliminated, but rather that the issue of notes was maintained above the maximum level possible under the banking law, - with the quite natural consequence that the national currency deteriorated accordingly. And so it is that in so many countries we have experienced the apparent absurdity of a gold currency legally consolidated by gold redemption and one-third cover, with a monetary value that nevertheless fluctuates and falls below parity.

This is one of the problems that both practitioners and theorists of central banking are constantly racking their brains over. The other problem, which I mentioned at the beginning of this letter, concerns the deposits of the central banks, which, since they are usually transferred from account to account in cashless payment transactions, are usually called 'giro money'.

And the question in dispute is whether these giro deposits, as a part of the national means of payment, are to be considered equal to the banknotes and are also to be covered with metal on a percentage basis, or not.
Just as every question carries half of its answer within itself as soon as it is posed correctly, this question also answers itself very easily if it is formulated precisely.

This is all the more necessary because the central banks giro money has two fundamentally different characteristics. For on the one hand they are capital which can be called in at any time, and on the other hand they are money which the holder can convert into notes at any time and then present for exchange into gold.

If one makes this distinction, one realises that one is dealing with a double question, which must correctly read:
How must giro money be covered in its capacity as capital, and how must it be covered in its capacity as money?

The first part of this double question answers itself without further ado, namely, that the giro money must be covered as capital in exactly the same way as any other deposit of a bank that can be recalled on a daily basis.
That is to say, they must have a certain percentage of cash money in reserve, which can be determined by experience. This cash may consist of notes wherever the banknote is a legal tender.

The answer to the second part of the question is not quite so obvious. As you know, the common view is that a high percentage of giro money must be backed by gold because, just like banknotes, it can lead to a demand for gold at any time.

The central banks themselves are also inclined to this view and most of them complain that it is a mistake that most banking laws (not all) do not make sight deposits subject to cover.

Economists support this view by pointing out that the sight deposits at the central banks are nothing more than a special kind of money ('giro money'), which is not itself legal tender, but can only be exchanged for it. Therefore, it had to be covered by the money that was valid as a definitive means of payment in the country, i.e. by gold in gold-currency countries.

So here we are, my boy, once again faced with the fundamentally so important question of what 'giro money' is. At the time, when I was chatting with you about money, I already put all emphasis on the statement that the current accounts of the banks and thus also of the central banks are not money, but only the accounting expression of the fact that money has passed the respective bank.

The money that appears on the debit side of the central bank's balance sheet as a current account balance has, at the time it was deposited at the bank, migrated into the bank's cash, has found some use that emerges from the asset side of the bank's balance sheet, and is now circulating in the economy again. If the current account balance, which came into existence when it was deposited, were also money, then one and the same sum of money would have split into two equal sums when it entered the central bank, i.e. it would have doubled. But this is an impossibility, since money is not an amoeba that multiplies by splitting.

In reality, the 'giral money' is nothing more than a trace left by money on its migration, and thus an expression of its speed of circulation. And if it seems as if it leads an independent life in the bank's books - since one can pay perfectly effectively by transferring it from one account to another - this is a deception of the eye. In reality, one does not pay with the current account balance, but with the money that one currently has deposited at the bank, and which the bank must make available again if the new owner of the current account balance wishes to receive the amount in cash.

If the bank does not need to procure the money because the new owner does not demand it, this is not proof that the current account balance has become money, so-called 'giro money,' but merely proof that the cash which the bank has currently received and credited to the current account is being left with the bank until further notice.

This fact does not change even if the current account balance does not appear to have been created by cash payment but by a credit transaction, i.e. by the bank crediting a person or a corporation with an amount on the current account. In this case, too, the bank can be forced at any time to pay out the credited amount in cash, and it then becomes apparent that it was only able to credit it because it had the corresponding cash amount at its disposal from some source. The peculiarity of the case lies only in the fact that here it was not the first recipient of the credit note but any third party who gave the cash amount to the bank. If this were not the case, but if the bank had actually 'created moneyby ' granting a current account credit to a borrower - for instance the state - the giro money thus created would have to be declared irredeemable.
Only irredeemable sight deposits are money.

If, however, the credit balances are redeemable, so that they can be withdrawn in cash at any time and the bank has to give notes for them, it turns out that the bank only creates new money now, at the moment of issuing notes, and therefore could not have created it at the time when the sight deposit came into existence. But since there are no current accounts for which withdrawal is excluded, there is also no 'giro money,' but only 'transferable cash balances on current accounts'.

The answer to our double question is, as you can see, very simple: current accounts do not need to be covered in any other way than any other bank deposits.

It is sufficient if they are matched by a cash reserve corresponding to the withdrawal risk, which is composed in exactly the same way as any other cash reserve. A special gold cover is not required. If the bank notes in circulation are fully covered in gold, the sight deposits, which are only a visible segment of the money circulation, are also covered in gold without further ado.

With love

Your old father.

Ninth Letter

Central bank or multi-bank
Metamorphosis of the banknote
The 'one-reserve system'.

Berlin, 10 July 1922.

How would you answer the question, dear James, as to whether a country should adhere to the principle of a single bank or that of multiple banks? Is it better for there to be a single, central, state-owned or state-represented central bank which combines all the tasks incumbent on central banking? Or is a systematic division of labour along geographical or functional lines preferable? Or is it finally advisable to let central banking develop as it wishes, to regard it as a trade like all others and to proclaim the principle of freedom of issue?

The question has long since been decided in favour of the central bank, and it seems hardly comprehensible to us today that there were times when the central banks were allowed to operate arbitrarily. When it was considered an encroachment on natural liberty when an institution such as the Bank of England was granted a monopoly on notes, although the monopoly only applied to a radius of 65 English miles.

We, who have seen where the wrong note policy of a single institution can take a country, are involuntarily horrified when we think that our country could be at the mercy of a multitude of central banks whose right of issue might not even be contingent.

We already find it alarming that in Germany and in America - though here only for a limited time - private note banks exist as remnants of an earlier period and conduct their own independent policies, and we see in this a breach of the principle of the single currency.

This view has its roots in the modern conception of central banking. We see the central bank as the right hand of the state, which realises its monetary and economic policy intentions through it, i.e. a public body of the highest political importance, and so we cannot consequently approve of a large number of banks pursuing policy on their own initiative, possibly even acting purely according to private economic principles instead of national economic principles.

But we must not forget that central banks today are something quite different from what they were in those days of central bank freedom, and also something quite different from what they would have to be today if they embodied a truly sound economic principle.

In an earlier letter I described to you how the banknote organically emerged from the metal deposit of the giro bank as a receipt for the deposit of a sum of money.
Why should a bank not be allowed to issue such receipts as much as it wants, i.e. as much as corresponds to the deposited sums of money?

Furthermore, it has been customary from time immemorial for a respectable bank to take advantage of the credit which it enjoys by accepting bills of exchange in which it undertakes to pay a certain sum on such and such a day, or even at sight.

Why should a bank not be allowed to issue such acceptances in round amounts and in series? And what are banknotes basically but such acceptances on the bearer in which the bank promises to pay the presenter in lawful money?

It is not at all surprising that two hundred and even a hundred years ago it was considered the good right of every bank to issue such notes, indeed that one could not even imagine a bank that did not issue notes.
When people spoke of 'banking' and 'banks' in the first half of the 19th century, they meant what we now call 'central banking' and 'central banks', simply because there were few banks that would have renounced the right to issue promises of payment in note form.

And so it is quite understandable why there was talk of an encroachment by the state on natural freedom when the banks were denied the right to issue notes.

Again, however, the state was perfectly within its rights when, around the middle of the last century, it saw in the banknote a promise of payment of its own kind, the issuing of which it was not allowed to arrange for everyone who was in a position to accept a commercial bill of exchange. For the character of the banknote had changed enormously in the course of time.

Originally it had indeed been a special kind of bank acceptance, differing only in appearance from a cheque or sight draft drawn on the bank. Those who wanted it took it; those who did not want it rejected it. If one could speak of a 'circulation' of these notes at all, then it only took place in commercial traffic and was also only limited to the district in which the bank had its headquarters.
Outside the district in which the bank was known exactly, no one thought of taking such a note in payment.

In other words, the note was more a credit instrument than a means of payment. Its circulation, insofar as it took place, was therefore an economically quite neutral process, like the circulation of a cheque, which every bearer can give to the bank and collect. The moment this credit instrument changed its character and became a distinct means of payment, because ever wider circles of traffic became accustomed to the convenient and easily dispatchable paper, the state necessarily had to change its position vis-à-vis the banknote. For it had become 'money' and as such fell under the state's sovereignty of coinage, even if it only circulated by virtue of custom and not by virtue of a compulsory acceptance.

Here the state became the advocate of traffic. You know, my boy, that traffic can only accept a certain amount of money, that it decides itself on this amount and tries to reject a plus that is forced upon it.
The issue of notes by the banks and the habit of the people of equating notes with money had the consequence that the economy became oversaturated with money and gave part of it to foreign countries.

And it did not hand over the banknotes, which were only valid in certain districts or at best in certain provinces, but the metal money. Gresham's old saying that the worse money always drives the better money out of the country thus came into full effect here. And the state could not allow that. It could not tolerate that in the case of a strongly passive balance of payments, the country was left without a metal reserve large enough to bring the balance back into equilibrium - by flowing abroad and automatically reducing the domestic circulation of money.

It is only regrettable that the state did not eliminate the freedom of banknotes because it brought a disturbing element into the monetary system, but rather because it wanted to make the banknote serve its own purposes. It seemed to him to be a useful instrument for his economic policy, the needs of which were not met by metal money, allegedly because it was not 'elastic' enough, in reality because the economy had different views about those needs than the state and did not want to give the necessary money.

Thus, over time, the banknote has become what it is today: a means of satisfying real or supposed needs for which one does not want to use the natural means of coverage of the bond or tax, a means, above all, with which the state covers any amount, no matter how high, in times of crisis and war, by withdrawing parts of the population's purchasing power without asking them.

For such purposes, the principle of the single bank is naturally superior to that of the multiple banks. Here the bank forms a lever in the hands of the state and is basically only a state organ itself, even if it is organised according to private capitalist principles.

But if we look at things not from the point of view of political expediency, but from that of economic benefit, it seems very questionable what is better, i.e. more beneficial, for the transport economy; a central bank, which can be abused by any sic volo sic jubeo of a superior authority without limit, up to the complete ruin of the national currency; or a multi-bank system of the old style, which is based on banking freedom and individual trust in the individual bank, and in which any attempt at abuse very soon reaches the limit where the traffic refuses to accept further quantities of banknotes.

The situation is different if one leaves aside the 'elasticity principle', which the central banks must serve today to the detriment of the currency, and thinks only of the legitimate tasks of the banks, i.e. the mediation of payments, utilisation of existing money stocks, etc.

Here the central bank is definitely superior to a fragmented central banking system. Institutions which serve to facilitate traffic and offer no possibilities of abuse, such as the giro and clearing, virtually presuppose a central office which functions as the 'bank of the banks'; and the existence of a national cash reserve, into which the available cash holdings of the banks flee in order to form an emergency fund for the time of a possible credit crisis, 'is also dependent on the existence of a large central bank. However, this central bank did not exactly have to be a central bank.

The institutions of giro, clearing and cash reserve have nothing to do with the banknote. But since central banks do exist and will probably continue to exist in most countries even when their influence on the national currency is diminished by the experience of the last few years, it is good to put them at the service of legitimate central bank business.

They can be very useful if they combine the traffic-promoting facilities of settlement and payment mediation with the function of a cash reserve and credit centre, but they have to pay attention to two things:
First, as a matter of principle: that they should grant credit, which they will expediently limit to the circle of banks, only within the framework of the existing reserve funds left to them by the commercial banks on behalf of the economy as a whole; for these funds, but not the credit desires of industry expressed in the offer of bills of exchange, represent the yardstick for the really legitimate needs of the economy

and at the same time show the limit to which the credit principle may be pushed without exerting harmful repercussions on the monetary system.

Secondly, in terms of business policy: that they remain aware at all times of how much depends on their prudence and ability to dispose, because they are the guardians of the last reserve in the country, a reserve whose performance is crucial in the event of an economic crisis wherever trade and industry are accustomed to working with short-term credit and have to fear the times of epidemic distrust with its attendant cancellation of credit and shortage of capital. The better the central banks are prepared for such crises, and the better they can face them without having to resort to the last, dubious resort of 'emergency notes', the more they will strip the modern 'one-reserve system of which ,' they are the apex, of its inherent dangers. To this end, they will do well to ensure that, in addition to their last reserve, there are a number of efficient intermediate reserves in the country which absorb the shock of a credit crisis and only allow it to reach the central reserve in a weakened form, thus acting as a buffer between the central bank and the economy.

You see, my dear James, that in the case of the central banks, which will probably remain central banks everywhere for the time being, it is not only a question of how their sphere of business is constituted, but also of in what sense and with what final aims they fill this sphere of business in practical day-to-day policy; and above all of what position they occupy within (or above) the credit organisation, and how they influence this credit organisation for their part. I shall therefore find the central banks again in our path when we one day deal with the special question of the so-called money market and banking, which shall happen in the not too distant future, if God grants me life.

I seal the last letter of this series with a fatherly kiss and remain in old love

Your dad.

Part IV: Monetary Crisis
Pictures from a money-sick country

First Letter

Theory and practice
Political Earthquake and Economic Molework

Berlin, February 2nd *1923*

With melancholy in my heart, dear James, I take hold of this white sheet of paper today in order to chat with you once again about economic matters after a break of months. I would prefer not to do so at all. The days of bitter hardship that the German people are now going through are weighing heavily on my thoughts and on my hand. I can only look at the inkwell with reluctance, because it reminds me of the hundreds of thousands of other inkwells with which Germany's misery is now being cranked around in just as many writing rooms, and it costs me an effort to touch a quill.

But you have asked me to explain to you the events that are taking place in our poor country today and which seem so puzzling and full of contradictions to you. You address me as a man who will one day be called upon to let the shuttle of money glide through the meshes of the economic fabric at his own discretion and under his own responsibility. You think that such a man, if he does not want to practise his profession as a dilettante, must absolutely have clarity about this. What is actually going on in Germany today.
At every turn you come across abominable, nonsensical phenomena that mock law and morality, whose origins you suspect but do not clearly recognise. You see all around you the signs of a political, moral and economic decay, of a far advanced material and ideal impoverishment, the ultimate, real reason for which is hidden from you.

For you thoroughly distrust the Volksstimme, which attributes all this to the heavy burdens imposed on the German nation by the peace treaty of Versailles. What else is there for me, an old man who has the triple responsibility towards you as father, teacher and predecessor in office, but to sit down in front of the hated inkwell and once again take on the role of mentor!

But which way should I go? I fear that theory will not lead us to our goal this time.

If economic chairs were sufficient to explain the chaotic conditions in our country completely, I would be able to save myself this letter and all the letters that follow. For I have already built up, as best I could, the systematic doctrinal edifice into whose cells the processes of our time can be logically arranged. So I could say to you today: Take my earlier letters in hand, my son, and think through thoroughly everything I have ever written to you about "money"; you will then find that all the riddles you think you are facing have already been solved in great outline. I might even be angry with you for asking where I have already answered.

But I am old enough to know that theory and practice, intellectual abstraction and concrete event, stand in a certain hostile relationship to each other. Admittedly, a certain process always triggers certain consequences.

And a bad economist is one who cannot recognise the lawfulness of these consequences and reduce them to a generally valid formula.

But even if he succeeds in doing so, even if he is able to predict with the greatest conceivable certainty that this or that measure will lead to this or that consequence on the basis of this or that event, there is still necessarily a discrepancy between the picture which he draws up prophetically and the actual course of development.

The event never quite coincides with the idea one has of it.

Why is that? The reason, my son, is that the idea, human thinking, follows a straight path and ignores all the bends and crossroads that can distract from the goal, while the fact undergoes a certain change at each of these bends and crossroads through the addition of new, co-determining moments.

Countless, constantly changing influences that cannot be overlooked in their overall complex, let alone determined in advance, push it out of the straight direction onto often quite strange side paths or place it in a political, social and economic light that completely changes its original appearance.

If the observer - for example, a certain James - suddenly comes across such a fact, bearing the traces of all the various influences, shimmering kaleidoscopically in a hundred colours, he will seldom succeed in recognising its first and actual origin, in determining its real cause of origin.

Even if he has been told beforehand that, as a result of certain abnormal processes, he must expect to encounter a certain event on his way, he will not come to the assumption that that fantastically colourful fact which he sees before him is identical with the predicted event.

Have I not pictured to you again and again in numerous letters what fate awaits a country in which one is blind to the economic truth, so infinitely important, that "money" is a legal claim which arises and expires out of intercourse, but can never be increased or diminished at will?

Well, my son:
The consequences I have pictured for you have occurred with the force of a natural phenomenon everywhere where the law embodied in money has been carelessly or criminally bent and money signs have been created at will; even here, in Germany. But you do not recognise these consequences for what they are; not as the effect of a quite definite cause.

You do not see the connection between the violation of rights that the state committed when it replaced the money born of traffic, the representative of well-acquired claims, with bank notes, the quantity of which was ultimately limited only by the production capacity of the high-speed presses, and the economic as well as moral decline, the frightening symptoms of which we see at every turn.

With the mental armoury of logic, I have tried to show you the natural consequences of such an unheard-of inflation of the circulation of money.

But the lawful decline which I have thus developed for you in logical trains of thought, and the lawful decline which I have developed for you in logical trains of thought and the factual decline which takes place before your eyes in plastic tangibility do not seem to be identical to you, because your thinking is confused by a series of co-determining moments. You think of everything that Germany has gone through politically and economically:

Lost war, disarmament, loss of territory, revolution, lack of work, "20 million people too many", (which is economically equivalent to having to buy and pay for enormous amounts of food abroad), reparations in cash and in kind, compensation payments, "sanctions'" etc. - and you ask me whether all these unfortunate moments must not quite naturally trigger the decay we are witnessing, and whether this decay should not also have occurred if we were still enjoying the same healthy monetary system today as before the war.

Certainly you admit that mismanagement in the field of monetary affairs must be accompanied by evil consequences. But the political loss of territory, power and military resistance must also have disastrous effects.

The domestic chaos that follows revolutions must also bring about profound changes in all spheres of national expression. And the victor's hand, which after a lost war lays heavy on the fortune and income of the vanquished, must, by impoverishing the latter to a greater or lesser extent, result in manifestations of social and cultural decline.

So which of the symptoms of disintegration that I see before me today must I attribute to the war? Which ones to the revolution? Which to the reparations? And which, after subtracting everything that can be attributed to those causes, finally remain, so that I can say with inner conviction: "Here I see before me the disastrous consequences of the amateurish monetary policy?"

To this question, dear James, which is so obvious that almost the whole of all peoples who have passed through war, political upheaval and monetary misery ask it, theory cannot give you an answer. There is nothing to be done here but to put the probe of exact investigation to each of the many symptoms in which the decline manifests itself. Actually, you should be able to carry out such an examination case by case by your own reflection, without my help, for it is not at all difficult.

You would probably even realise to your own surprise how quickly and easily one finds the solutions to seemingly intricate economic problems if one thinks straightforwardly and does not let the guiding rope of common sense out of one's hands for a moment. But I know that the path of sober and straightforward thinking is fraught with all kinds of pitfalls. There are a lot of prejudices, supposed "self-evident truths" and melodious phrases that even distract the logically thinking economist from the straight path and lead him into a tangle of contradictions from which he is no longer able to extricate himself. That is why I want to help you. Together we want to probe the symptoms in which Germany's economic and moral decay expresses itself today. With selection, of course.

For the symptoms are innumerable; we cannot set foot without encountering one. It is the same with an economic body as with a physical organism:

If there is a large focus of disease here, there is hardly a single organ left that performs its functions in a completely normal way. The diagnostician, however, will disregard the second-order disorders, which are only offshoots, and content himself with determining the nature and causes of the main disease from a few particularly striking symptoms. We want to proceed in this way.

However, I can already tell you the result we will reach today. We will recognise that the phenomena which we summarise in the collective term "Germany's economic decline" are exclusively outflows of mismanagement in the field of monetary affairs.

This will certainly surprise you.

For certain processes that we will encounter in our diagnostic investigation are considered by the vast majority, even by the majority of economists, to be of political, financial or social, but not monetary, origin.

However, this is only because at some point in their chain of thought, the aforementioned majority let go of the guiding rope of common sense and allowed themselves to be led astray by some prejudice or buzzword. The temptation to do so is indeed very great.

The man who experiences a tremendous earthquake and suddenly feels himself sinking into the depths will always be inclined to attribute this sinking to the earthquake, instead of investigating whether the ground on which he stands has not been undermined by some invisible mine-work.

Let us both, dear James, endeavour to pay less attention to the great political earthquake than to the imperceptible economic mining process which has undermined our soil.

Do not exclaim here:
"But the political earthquake has had effects, had to have effects, and no diagnosis, however exact, will be able to convince me that the economic changes I see before me have nothing to do with the earthquake!"

Should you nevertheless be unable to suppress this exclamation, read my reply right here:
I do not deny that every earthquake exerts effects in the country that has been affected by it, and that therefore Germany must also feel the consequences of the political catastrophe it has experienced. It would be foolish to claim otherwise.

What Germany has gone through politically since 1914 could not possibly remain without economic consequences.

But these consequences have nothing to do with the evils that are commonly in mind when we speak of Germany's decline. As soon as we apply the dissecting knife to the tremendous changes which we observe at every turn and which fill us with sadness and anger, in order to recognise their nature and their origin, it immediately turns out that they are either not at all or only very remotely connected with Germany's great political destiny, but all the more closely with the pernicious mole-work at the roots of the German monetary system.

And now on to joint vivisection on the living economic body!

> With love
>
> Your old dad.

Second Letter

Impoverishment.
Valuta premium and dumping export.
The pressure on labour income.

Berlin, February 6th 1923

So now grasp it tightly, my boy! Let us pick out a few phenomena from the abundance that are so striking that they leave their mark on our time, so to speak.

We need not dwell long on the choice. Since it is important for us to ascertain the causes of the decay, the characteristics of which force themselves upon us at every turn, it is quite immaterial whether we begin with this or that symptom - provided my premise is correct that they are all emanations of one and the same disease, and that therefore, if we trace each individual symptom back to its origin, we must always come across the same source.

If I, who am the talking part of both of us, ask you, the listening part, in spirit, which phenomena seem to you to characterise our German counterpart most succinctly, I believe I hear the answer:

What seems to me to be most characteristic is the general impoverishment that can be observed in Germany and, in addition, the process of restructuring which has the effect that in this impoverished Germany not all classes of the population are impoverished more or less equally, but that a large stratum of the disinherited is confronted with a smaller stratum of the enriched.

Let us deal with the first of these two phenomena today. First of all, we have to deal with an objection. There are quite a number of people who do not want to know anything about an "impoverished Germany", but rather claim outright that such a Germany is a deception. In reality, they say, Germany is as productive as ever, and the income of its population has not decreased, at least not significantly, but only shifted.

To which is then usually attached the cheap joke that income has not only shifted, but has also been shifted, namely to foreign countries. One can hear this view expressed particularly often by foreigners who speak with respectful admiration - and if they are competitors, with fear or envy - about the strength of German production and do not know how to talk enough about the gigantic scale on which the large German factories in the Rhineland and Westphalia have been expanded compared to the pre-war period.

Is this true? Yes, my son, it is true.

In most of the larger joint-stock companies with which my bank maintains relations, quite considerable expansions did indeed take place during and after the war.

But can we conclude from this that German industry as a whole or even the German economy, which also includes other elements - agriculture, trade, small businesses, crafts - is in a flourishing situation?

No, you can't.

Even a cursory glance at your daily surroundings will teach you that it would be downright grotesque to speak of a flourishing German economy.

I am not asking you to visualise how the German middle classes, white-collar and blue-collar workers live today and to calculate by how much their consumption has fallen compared to normal consumption ten years ago.

No, I challenge you to look at the consumption of the so-called wealthy classes, the factory owners, the wholesalers, even the banking world, which is particularly close to you. This is where luxury reigns, isn't it? Isn't this where people live lavishly?

I assume that you will answer with a resounding "yes", and now claim that nothing characterises the German decline more clearly than the "luxury consumption" of the privileged classes.

For how is luxury expressed here?

It is expressed in the possession of a car, which used to be part of the inventory of every better doctor; in the enjoyment of a caviar roll, which used to be available to every employee with a monthly salary of 500 marks, if he wanted to; in a family trip to Switzerland - a pinnacle! - which wide circles of the German middle classes used to regard as a trivial matter and did not undertake only because nearby Switzerland did not appeal to them.

I have to force myself every day not to burst out laughing when I see with what solemn and connoisseur-like expressions even my colleagues from high finance are today indulging in things that only a few years ago they hardly noticed as a matter of course.

Insofar as they have liaisons, they present them with semi-precious stones, such as agate and malachite, or even coral, with the same grandeur

with which they used to give them pearls and diamonds.

And the gentlemen draw annual incomes that are the envy of the whole nation!

To find the solution to this riddle, you only have to convert these fabulous incomes into gold marks. Then you will realise that the real income of those of the richest among us has been reduced in a very short time to a fraction of their former income.

And the same is true, of course, to a much greater extent of the other classes of the population. Among the middle classes, the decision to purchase a new article of clothing for each member of the family is as much a financial question as the purchase of a summer house was scarcely in the past, and the clerk who expresses the intention of marrying exposes himself to the danger of being examined as to his state of mind, because, judged by the standard of his present income, the savings of a whole life are not sufficient to meet the cost of furnishing the house.

"And the theatres? The fashion salons? The liqueur parlours? All those luxurious places that have mushroomed in the big German cities?"

I don't know whether you have this interjection on the tip of your tongue, but if it should be the case, let me tell you:

Those places of luxury are on the same level as the caviar rolls and coral jewellery I spoke of earlier.

They are, strange as it may sound, symptoms of impoverishment. They serve the need for luxury of the second and third rank and enjoy increased popularity because the

German can no longer afford luxury expenditure of the first rank. Those who are no longer allowed to make a maturity after Switzerland can at least still visit the theatre. And for the tenth part of what a new society suit costs, one can consume quite a respectable quantity of Asbach and sherry, brandy.

If you visit a village tavern, you will be surprised at the incredible quantities of thin beer that the poor villagers consume. Well, our new theatres, salons and liquor bars are the thin beer of the average German, whose income no longer allows him to drink Rhine wine. There are, however, many other factors that must be taken into account, such as the transfer of a large part of the national income from the hands that consume it in a culturally refined way into new hands with raw consumption habits; furthermore, that the German people as a whole no longer save today, but consume their income. But that's just in passing; I'll come back to it later.

I assume, however, that you are obstinate, dear James, and call out to me:

"You speak of income, I speak of production!"

Well, my boy, let us speak of production. I happen to have before me a statistical compilation of the "Frankfurter Zeitung", entitled "The Economic Curve". According to this, in 1921 the production of raw iron was 58%, that of steel 45% of the production before the war - despite the expansion of our large factories, which is so impressive to foreign countries.

However, for my part, I must call out a word of caution to you here. For it is not permissible to conclude from these and certain other figures from raw materials and semi-finished goods industries that total German production has fallen by 50%. Part of this decline is offset by the unmistakable increase in the production of end products.

It is interesting to observe how Germany is trying to compensate for the narrowing of its raw material base (as a result of the loss of ore, zinc and lead mines) by systematically switching to refining, and how the "labour" factor is increasingly displacing the "material" factor in German manufactures. But even if we were to assume that, as a result of this conversion to the end product, Germany today is not very far removed from its fine pre-war performance, this would not prove the slightest thing either for German national wealth or for German national income. For the two important questions then arise:

Who actually owns the works in which German labour is creatively active?

And: Who benefits from this creative German labour?

Well, to put it briefly:
Today, only a fraction of capital and capital gains are German.

By way of shareholding and the purchase of shares, a very considerable percentage of German "constant capital", as Marr calls it, has passed into foreign ownership. And foreign countries benefit from the fruits of this capital not only in proportion to their financial participation, but to a much greater extent. In addition to the foreign capitalists who, by virtue of their co-ownership title, have a claim to a pension from the German enterprise, the entire foreign country, insofar as it buys German goods, profits from the production strength of the German factories, because German industry is forced to sell its products considerably below world prices.

It is not a professional secret of the industrialists, but a well-known fact that foreign buyers who visit our industrial centres, trade fairs and staging areas only decide to buy if they are offered a price that, plus all expenses and plus all defensive duties that foreign countries have imposed on German goods, remains far, far below the world price.

Every now and then, the prices at which German machines, chemicals, toys, etc. are offered in Reval or Moscow, in Buenos Aires or Montevideo, become known; they are usually less than half the corresponding English and American prices. Germany is thus giving away half of its goods.

If healthy conditions existed in the foreign countries thus given away, they would be happy to receive cheap German goods.

One would calculate statistically how much the countries are enriched by the fact that they only have to give half as much national products in exchange for the inflowing German products as they would have to do under normal conditions.

But, as is well known, the conditions are not really healthy in any of the industrially developed countries.

Everywhere, industries have been artificially bred for which the preconditions are so unfavourable that they immediately come to a standstill when cheap competing goods penetrate and thus bring unemployment and hunger to the population, which has been "industrialised", i.e. alienated from the fields.

And so one perceives as harmful what one would have to regard as highly gratifying if one were not forced to pursue a producer policy instead of a people policy.

But no matter how those countries judge the penetration of cheap German goods:

For Germany itself, the sale of its products below their natural price is the main cause of its low real income and, consequently, of its slowed capital formation.

The German people as a whole, which receives for its exports only half of the foreign products which it ought lawfully to receive, cannot remotely withdraw that quantity of real values from current consumption and convert it into productive capital as it would be able to do under other circumstances; it cannot "save" in the normal way, because by surrendering fine labour below cost it can hardly obtain from abroad what it needs for bare living.

And since the price which the German product obtains abroad is partly decisive for its price at home, but this price is only worthwhile if production can be carried out at very low real wages, German labour wages are under permanent pressure. This pressure, in turn, makes it impossible for the German worker and employee to offer to German primary production, especially agriculture, an equivalent corresponding to the world price. The consequence is that the articles of daily use, for which the German consumer is virtually starving, flow abroad; if they are prevented from doing so, their production is restricted because it is not worthwhile in view of the weakened German purchasing power.

But why does Germany dump its goods on the world market? Is this a case of wantonness, a policy of arbitrariness unscrupulously pursued by all-powerful cartels? Abroad, this is often believed. But it is not true. Nor is it correct that Germany must sell at any price in order to import the raw material and that part of the foodstuffs for the proceeds which the German soil does not yield. For foreign countries need German coal, German potash, German dyes and countless other products of German industry just as urgently as Germany needs foreign wool and cotton, hides and tanning materials, oil and grain; and before the war the exchange of these commodities took place smoothly and without a German policy of skidding, although the production prices at that time were far higher than they are today because of the relatively good wages of the German worker.

So why is Germany dumping?

Germany is dumping, dear James, for no other reason than because it has abandoned its gold currency and committed itself to the devil of the printing press.

It is not German industrial policy, not German trade, but bad German money that is dumping.

With every sale that Germany makes abroad today, it has to pay a high levy for the fact that it no longer calculates in reliable money of stable value.

The foreign buyer who buys German goods, but does not know how many pounds or dollars he will have to pay for the marks he must remit to the seller when the goods arrive, charges himself a high premium for the "value risk" he runs, and by this premium the German selling price necessarily falls short of the world market price or of the price the buyer would pay if he could calculate in a stable-value means of payment.

If, however, the German seller takes the risk off the foreigner, i.e. if he does not invoice him in marks but in pounds or dollars, he must charge himself a premium for not knowing what amount of marks he will receive for the foreign money when the export goods have been produced, processed and delivered.

For the manufacturer and his workers, however, it does not make the slightest difference whether the risk premium is deducted from him by a foreigner or a national; his selling price is reduced in any case, and all the more so the more violent the fluctuations to which the German currency is exposed.

But it is not only for these fluctuations that the German manufacturer must pay. He has to accept a whole series of other premiums, because the foreign buyer not only has to live with the fluctuations in the currency, but also has to reckon with certain consequences of these fluctuations. It is a well-known phenomenon that in countries with ruined currencies, where prices change abruptly with every rise or fall in the value of money, contractual loyalty falls apart.

If prices rise sharply so that the production costs of the goods sold turn out to be considerably higher than the agreed delivery price, the seller withdraws from the contract in order not to ruin himself.

If prices fall and with them wages, it is almost certain that strikes and sabotage will prevent the completion of the goods and call into question the adherence to the delivery date.

The possibility of unrest, even political upheaval, must also be reckoned with in every valuta-stricken country.

All these dangers entail their premiums. Of course, one should not think of them in the same way as the premiums of an insurance company, which are fixed in figures for each class of risk and can be read from tables. They do not appear concretely at all, but exist only in the minds of calculating merchants, who reduce their willingness to pay by as much as corresponds to the dangers to which they believe themselves to be exposed, without exact justification, mostly purely emotionally.

So you see, my dear James, a country with a ruined monetary system does not "dump" voluntarily, but compulsorily. And if you think a little, you will see that what happens in the case of export is necessarily repeated in the case of import, only in the opposite sense.

The premium that has to be paid for the foreign exchange risk here also takes the form of a price surcharge on import, which the German import trader has to put up with, because his foreign counterpart has to take into account in his calculation all the possibilities to which one is exposed in dealings with a country that is ill with foreign exchange, i.e. a country that is shaken by fever.

In a nutshell: Today Germany has to pay too much for her imports and give away her exports too cheaply.

It is in the position of a merchant whose credit is shaken and who must therefore accept all the conditions dictated to him by his customers and suppliers.

But what does that mean?

It means that in Germany all raw materials are too expensive and all finished products too cheap. This is because domestic prices cannot emancipate themselves from foreign trade prices, but adjust to them. If foreign wheat, rice, cellulose, copper can only cross the border with a surcharge on the world price, then the German products in relation to these articles, i.e. rye, potatoes, peas, wood, zinc and the like, also rise above the world price, and if the state attempts to counteract this increase with the help of a policy of force (maximum prices, confiscation, etc.), it kills the producer's desire to work and diminishes his income and diminishes the economy's yield.

Conversely, German products are all under pressure from their low export price.

The smaller the tension between the high prices of raw materials and the low prices of manufactured goods, the smaller is the compensation with which the man who transforms raw materials into manufactured goods must be content. The reason why German wages today are so low below the standard wage considered "fair" in European terms is that the gap between the prices of raw materials and manufactured goods leaves no room for better salaries.

Especially since the German entrepreneur also draws his benefit from this gap and strives to increase this benefit in a way that corresponds to the countless dangers to which he is exposed in the money-sick country.

If one compares the benefit of the German entrepreneur with the real wage of the worker, it does indeed appear to be quite significant, even excessive.

But if one converts it into gold marks, or determines its purchasing power abroad, it turns out to be considerably lower than it corresponds to the pre-war benefit and the real capital fixed in the enterprises.

Hence the yield, which appears so high in percentage terms but is in reality extremely low, that all German joint-stock companies are yielding today.

Hence also the endeavour of large circles of working life to transfer their activity from the field of nerve-shattering production, built more on gambling than calculation, to the field of trade, which is also highly speculative, but can be conducted with less real capital and can be more easily adapted to the coincidences of a business cycle that slavishly follows all jumps in the value of money. The consequence of this is that the enterprise has to share the much too small margin between the price of raw materials and the proceeds from the factory with trade more than ever before, and this too to the disadvantage of the worker.

Thus, in Germany today, no part of the productive labour force receives the full remuneration for its work; neither the entrepreneur, whose capital and income are constantly diminishing despite their swelling in paper marks, nor the worker, whose nominal wage appears high, but for its recipient does not remotely represent the real income of the pre-war period.

Where a real increase in wealth and income can be ascertained, it is either the result of purely speculative activity and thus a stroke of luck, such as can always and everywhere occur, even in the primitive and poorest countries, or else - and this is the rule - the result of quite definite and very interesting shifts within the economy, with which we shall deal next time. Because this letter, as I see with horror, has already far exceeded the normal size of a lesson.

Talk to you soon!

Your old dad.

Third Letter

The bankruptcy of the savings idea.
The great reallocation.

Berlin, February 10th 1923

Every nation, my dear James, which has broken away from good money and has committed itself to the devil of paper money, subjects itself to a process of impoverishment by paying to all foreign countries a kind of tax or risk premium for all the dangers which business dealings with such a nation entail for every third party, because its promise of money is not granite but deceitful quicksand.

Hammer this economic truth into your head once and for all, my boy!

And do not let yourself be distracted by the fact that the process of impoverishment is paralleled by certain other processes which disguise it by producing symptoms in individual parts of the economy which seem to indicate enrichment.

For even where this enrichment of certain classes of the people is not a delusion but a reality, one must never see in it the mark of an increase in national prosperity, but always only the result of a shift in the distribution of wealth which runs alongside the process of general impoverishment.
It is this "shift" that I want to discuss in more detail today.

But first I have a few additional words to say on the subject of "'impoverishment'".

The risk premium I have been talking about is by no means the only cause of the decline in wealth in the money-sick countries. A whole series of other factors also contribute to impairing the productivity of production and thus the regeneration and accumulation of national wealth.

It is unnecessary for me to dwell at length on all these moments. For the fact that the absence of a fixed monetary value brings a general uncertainty into the economy, makes every fixed calculation impossible, thereby eliminates the "ratio" of gainful employment, makes wages and profits the plaything of arbitrariness or chance, all these and many other disturbances of the production process are sufficiently known to you. And you also know that these disturbances, and above all the disproportion between the enormous price increase, in which every fall in the currency expresses itself, and the increase in incomes, produce a general bitterness in the country, which leads to aversion to work, wage struggles and volcanic outbreaks of popular passion.

Worse than all this, however, is the phenomenon which is briefly called the "bankruptcy of the savings thought," and as it is recognised in all its gravity by only a few, I must dwell on it a little.

The decay of the monetary system inevitably sets every country back in its development by a few stages, but most of all those countries which to a great extent economise with credit.

For here not only the acts of exchange and payment are deprived of their fixed basis of calculation, but moreover all debt relations and claims of a pecuniary nature, from the three-month bill of exchange to the hundred-year bond, from the current account credit to the industrial participation.

Since all these contractual agreements are denominated in legal money, they lose all meaning the moment this money becomes the plaything of speculation.

What is one to imagine by a claim, a partnership and a hereditary claim denominated in 1 million marks or 1 million roubles?

They mean a great deal or nothing at all, depending on the concept of value one associates with the term "mark" or "rouble".

The holder of a claim of 1 million roubles embodied in mortgages or bonds was a rich man a few years ago. Today he is a beggar, for no other reason than because the rouble in nihilist land is no longer identical with a certain quantum of gold, but represents only the unspeakably small part of a million-fold increase in the circulation of money, and thus a "nihil," a nothing.

The ruin of money has also become its ruin and the ruin of all those who possess a creditor's right expressed in money.

The natural consequence is that in all money-sick countries hardly anyone is willing to convert part of his wealth or income into creditor's rights, i.e. to give credit in any form.

Those who are forced to give credit because they have collected a sum of money for which they do not yet know a suitable use on the day of receipt, choose the form of a bank deposit which can be called in at any time, because they hope that the value of the money will not deteriorate too much further in the few days until the amount is withdrawn again and utilised; but many a person resists becoming a creditor for even a few days and prefers to spend the money collected again immediately.

This has an effect which in normal times would be considered very pleasing:

The money circulates extraordinarily fast. But the circumstances under which money changes hands in the currency-sick country give this process a most unpleasant, even pernicious, scope.
For money does not circulate, as is usually the case, in the service of the production process, but in the service of a "catastrophic consumption".

The money is withheld from the producers to whom it would otherwise reach by way of credit, because no one wants to run the risk of one day receiving back from the producer his claim on him in inferior or completely worthless money, and it is instead consumed.

Either it is used for the acquisition of all kinds of goods which are valued because of their relative stability of value ("flight into real values"), in which case it causes a quite unmotivated scarcity in these areas which are in any case only inadequately supplied by production.

The price increase, which until then had only been the expression of the devaluation of money, is exacerbated by this scarcity.

Or else the money is spent under the motto "saving makes no sense" for the purposes of a lavish standard of living, i.e. it is eaten up, so to speak.

Then the additional inflation is transferred to the market of foodstuffs and commodities, depriving the people who are particularly hard hit by the devaluation of money of the most basic necessities and creating that repugnant picture

so characteristic of all money-sick countries:
Hunger on the one hand, gluttony and luxury on the other. I leave it to your imagination to imagine how provocative the carefree, almost insolent consumption of the able-bodied classes, who are completely unaccustomed to saving, must be on the mood, the morals and the attitude of the state of the hungry. If your imagination fails you, you need only go out into the streets and open your eyes and ears.

Expressed in economic terms, this process is an increased depletion of national stocks, which are actually intended to serve as raw materials or auxiliary materials for production; in other words, it is a diminution of the national wealth as the possibility of replenishment diminishes.

By changing from good money to bad money, which is useless as a measure of value and as a store of value, Germany has put herself in the position of a man who feeds on capital.

The process of the year 1000 A.D. is repeated, when all of Europe was seized by the frenzy of indulgence, because in view of the supposedly imminent end of the world, people believed that saving and collecting had lost all meaning.

Now, too, saving seems to have become foolish to the broadest strata of the population, but not for elementary but for monetary reasons.

Nevertheless, dear James, we see that certain circles of the population have managed, in the midst of the national impoverishment process, to multiply their wealth, well understood, their real wealth consisting of material assets or measurable in material assets; and not only relatively, i.e. in relation to the declining wealth of the great masses, but also absolutely.

Here again we come across the great works of our industrialists, which stretch and stretch, the many new commercial enterprises, the numerous banks which have sprung up in recent years, and realise that in most cases this growth is no mirage, no self-deception.

Even if we must not forget that since we have been measuring with a monetary unit that has become almost worthless, we see all values, as it were, through a microscope and therefore in a thousandfold magnification, it is nevertheless an established fact that the substance of many fortunes has increased quite extraordinarily and must awaken the idea of economic well-being in all those who generalise from these fortunes to the national wealth.

I assume that after all I have said about the reduction of the German national wealth, you do not share this idea.

If my explanations have become halfway clear to you, you will easily understand that there is a special reason for the increase in wealth of certain circles.

You will probably tell yourself that it is not a question here of a new creation, but only of a rearrangement:

That the wealth accumulated in one place is identical with a part of the wealth that has been lost in another place.

You will assume that somehow a great reallocation, a migration of wealth within the German national body has taken place.

But you will probably not be able to form a proper idea of the forces that have brought about this regrouping, of the dynamics of the process, and I will therefore try to explain the matter briefly to you.

In part, and to a lesser extent, we are dealing here with what the businessman calls a "business cycle". Those circles have profited from the conjuncture of the falling value of money. Inflation, which is the origin of all currency decline, has had the effect that the value of the money in which the whole nation thinks, calculates and pays has continued to decline from month to month, from year to year; occasional increases in value, which have taken place in reaction to a particularly rapid devaluation, have always been replaced by a new setback.

This has meant for every merchant and every factory owner a source of additional profit over and above normal business use.

Everything that the merchant ordered from the manufacturer had become more expensive on the day that the goods were delivered to him, in accordance with the devaluation of money that had taken place in the meantime. He could therefore sell at a high price, but in turn only had to pay the low price of the day of the order.

He held himself without any liability for any safety surcharges that the manufacturer charged him (you know the famous clause "subject to change") by paying the corresponding overprices.

He was able to do this because the whole nation was seized by the psychosis "don't save, but consume", i.e. goods were always in short supply.

He only had to be careful not to pay his suppliers before he received payment in turn, in order to enrich himself further.

The manufacturer was in an equally favourable position.

He produced his goods at relatively low national prices and wages, and a few months later he received a higher price in accordance with the advanced devaluation of money.

But even if this benefit eluded him because his customer, the trader, adopted the tactic just described and paid him in devalued money, he profited from the process that I would like to call the "staccato" of demonetization.

His main expenditure, that is, the expenditure for wages, freight, trading expenses, etc., did not follow the price increase of the commodity at the same pace, but increased only haltingly, from month to month or from week to week, so that intervals always arose during which the expenses were not yet at the full level of the income. During these intervals, which lay between one wage increase and the next, the factory owner paid sums that were tailored to a stage of lower monetary depreciation that had already been overcome, i.e. were relatively low, and collected sums that corresponded to the present stage of a more advanced monetary depreciation, i.e. were relatively high.

Each interval thus meant a special benefit for him, which was added to the usual production profit, and since the intervals followed each other almost continuously, i.e. wages, freight and expenses always lagged behind the increase in the price of goods, a chain of profits resulted for him, which in the course of a year added up to quite enormous net profits.

But I have already told you, my dear, that these cyclical profits constituted only one source of the increase in wealth of the big business circles, and not even the most important source.

The main origin of the enrichment of certain strata of the people lies not in the short-term exploitation of the demonetization tempo by a clever business policy, but in the systematic overreaching of the creditor by the debtor, i.e. in a blatant abuse of credit.

The procedure is as simple as it is interesting and proceeds as follows:

A merchant borrows a large sum on July 1, say ten million marks, for half a year, i.e. on December 31.

On July 1st he receives a sum which, according to the present state of monetary depreciation, amounts to 50,000 dollars, and uses it for the manufacture or purchase of goods which have an equivalent value.

Now the due date of the debt is approaching, namely 31 December. By this date, the devaluation of money has made such progress that those ten million marks are no longer equivalent to 50,000 dollars, but only to 10,000 dollars.

He has to pay back this amount plus the agreed interest. With about 11,000 or 12,000 dollars he gets rid of his debt.

But since the goods he has produced or bought have not been affected by the devaluation of money, but still represent 50,000 dollars, he has earned 33,000 or 39,000 dollars outright, merely by the fact that he is paying back his creditor an inferior sum of money instead of the high-value money he asked him for half a year ago.

Now imagine, dear James, that this procedure is followed on the very largest scale, and not once, but continually. Suppose that the merchant does not repay his debt on the day of payment out of his own capital, but by means of a new loan which he takes out somewhere, so that the ten millions of other people's money with which he works do not actually come to repayment after half a year, but rather after three, four or even more years.

And then visualise to what value - or unvalue - the mark has melted down in the last four years.

You will then easily recognise that the merchant, instead of the ten million he borrowed at the beginning of 1919, will have to repay less than the thousandth part, i.e. a sum with the purchasing power of hardly ten thousand marks, at the beginning of 1923, although he has to pay ten million in numerical terms.

He is enriched by 999/1,000 of the amount borrowed in his time.

Here, dear friend, you have before you the most important origin of the fortunes that have arisen in recent years, and also the explanation for the fact that in impoverished Germany today one sees enormous works and great commercial enterprises that did not exist before.

For hardly any merchant, and certainly no large merchant or industrialist, has in recent years renounced the old customary right of the German entrepreneur to work with other people's money. If private individuals have become increasingly reluctant to grant credit over time, the banks and the Reichsbank have been all the more generous.

The billions in bonds that our industry has thrown on the market to expand its factories must also be taken into account here, and strictly speaking, the enormous masses of new shares that have been issued also fall under the concept of "credit" in the sense discussed above.

With the help of foreign money, German entrepreneurship has enriched itself in a few years in a way that far surpasses anything ever seen before.

But what is this process, which is in its way world-historical, all about?

If you want to put it bluntly, it is robbery: the big borrowers have stolen from millions of creditors, partly directly, partly in a roundabout way via banks and state institutions, even if the "transfer of ownership" has taken place in strictly legal forms, with the approval of the laws and the judges.
I have described the process more mildly as "redistribution". But however it may be called, the fact remains that the great army of creditors has been impoverished by as much as the wealth of the great borrowers has increased.

It is therefore not at all a question of an increase in national wealth, but only of a transfer into new hands of the capitals which were formerly the property of millions of savers and pensioners.

One can see the new industrial centres that have been created or enlarged in this way, but one must not forget at the sight of them that they are rising on the ruins of destroyed workplaces and shattered livelihoods.

The motto under which this gigantic process of restructuring has taken place is "mark equals mark". Law and tradition allow a debt incurred in gold marks to be discharged in worthless paper marks. They do not permit this out of ill will or folly, but simply because in a sensibly governed country the national monetary unit is the measure of value of all things, and because the imagination of no legislator could have dreamed that ignorance and recklessness could ever turn this fixed measure of value into such a soap bubble as has actually happened.

It does not speak well for the state of our economic knowledge that not a single man in the countries afflicted by inflation and monetary misery has stood up and shouted to the governments: "Beware inflation is theft! A country without money of stable value is a country without law, and an inflationary state is a robber state!"

But it seems downright humorous that the sworn enemies of capitalism, the nihilists and communists, regard the means of inflation and demonetisation as their strongest weapon and believe that they can smash the rule of capital with it!

In their naivety, these people, in Russia as in Germany, have confused the terms "capital" and creditors.

They believed that they could expropriate the capitalist exploiter in favour of the masses by means of the banknote press, and instead, in all countries, they expropriated the acquiring and saving people in favour of capital.

Do you think that they have now become wise through experience?

I do not.

With love

Your old pessimistic dad.

Fourth Letter

The just price.
The struggle against inflation.

Berlin, February 15th 1923

The large box of cigars, dear James, which I sent you yesterday, represents something like an extra festive gift.
I had the provisional accounts of my bank presented to me, and they evoked two thoughts in me.

First thought:
No outsider should know these figures, otherwise they would think I had been profiteering in the past year.
Second thought: In view of such a result, I have the duty to make my boy happy.

And I hope I have succeeded with the thousand cigars.

But if you now ask me about the price of the cigars, as you usually do indelicately, you put me in great embarrassment. They have no price at all.

When I asked my purveyor for the bill, he stroked his patriarchal beard thoughtfully and said: "In Amsterdam, this cigar costs 30 cents, which is 4000 marks a piece in today's German money.

In Hamburg, the same cigar, made with cheap German labour, should only cost 2500 marks, despite the customs duty.

In reality, however, you can have it in Hamburg for about 800 marks, as there are still large batches of old goods in storage there that were made at a time when wages and the tobacco value were still low.

I myself bought the cigar half a year ago on the price basis of 150 marks.

Should I now charge you 4000 or 2500 or 800 or 150 marks?

I don't know for the life of me. Pay what you want for it."

I didn't pay the man any money at all, but gave him a few fine shares, ten bottles of cognac and a brand album.

So I have returned to the "barter economy". For I am of the opinion that in a country suffering from currency fraud one is infallibly deceiving or is deceived oneself as soon as one pays in so-called "money" of which no one knows what it will be worth tomorrow.

At the same time, however, I have decided to put the question to you as to which of the four prices that the man has mentioned to me you would consider to be the appropriate one.

And since I know very well that you would answer the question either with an evasive phrase or wrongly, I will send you the answer at once.

For my cigar purchase and the its circumstances surrounding it form an instructive example of the disorganised economic system in a money-bankrupt country.

As long as there has been economics, scholars have been racking their brains over the question of the "fair price".

Some construct it from the elements of "labour wages", "interest on capital" and "reasonable profit", others derive it not from the costs of production but from those of replacement, others again let supply and demand decide on it under the rule of free competition.

But whichever theory one may accept:

For our case and thus at the same time for all cases of present-day traffic life, none of them fits.

It is simply impossible to determine in marks, that is to say in a money without a fixed value, the price which is "just", that is to say, which secures to every participant the appropriate remuneration for his performance and harms no one.

For the simple reason that the price expressed in marks is a perpetual motion machine whose actual purchasing power changes every moment.

Let us return to my cigar dealer.

If he had asked me for the price that applies on the Amsterdam market, he would undoubtedly have enriched himself to my detriment. For the same cigar that I would have paid him 4,000 marks for, I could, as he himself said, have had made for me in Hamburg for 2,500 marks.

So one would think that this latter price would have been reasonable.

But that can't be true, because for some reason the same cigar was on the market in Hamburg for 800 marks and could be bought in any quantity. The man would have taken from me more than three times the amount for which he could "stock up" again.

Would 800 marks - plus a percentage mark-up for the dealer's profit - have been the appropriate price?

Subjectively, from my supplier's point of view, yes. But objectively? No.

For if I had gone to Hamburg on a whim and bought up the entire stock of cigars there at 800 marks each, the trading centre called the "Hamburg market" would have sold me goods for 800 marks, which it could only procure for itself at the price of 2500 marks, and which would even have cost it 4000 marks plus expenses, if the need was so urgent that the necessary production time could not be waited for and the goods would therefore have had to be bought in the Amsterdam wholesale market.

From the point of view of the general economy, 800 marks would not have been an appropriate price; any group of workers, regardless of which one, would necessarily have been harmed.

And what is true of a price of 800 marks is of course even more true of the last and lowest of the four prices, 150 marks.

So the question is rather complicated. And it becomes even more complicated if we decide to consult the practice, as I once did for fun.

At the time, it was a matter of a few bottles of a well-known perfume that I wanted to buy.

The first shop I went into asked for 8,000 marks.
That seemed too expensive, so I went to the second shop. Price 15,000 marks. I asked "why so much?" Answer: "Because I bought the bottles only yesterday and paid 12,000

marks myself. Here is the invoice. Please convince yourself."

I convinced myself and entered a third shop. Price 1,500 marks. Because the man had already had the perfume in stock for several months and had bought it according to the value date.

In a fourth shop, the owner shouted at me angrily when I asked. "I won't sell that stuff ever again! I won't sell anything at all! Every time you sell it, you get cheated! Yesterday I gave away the last bottle for 390 marks. That was my purchase price plus 30 per cent profit; that's how I calculate as long as my business exists. And do you know what the factory is charging me today for a new bottle? 12,000 marks, sir, 12,000 marks in purchasing! And so it is with all my articles. I have sold myself poor! Look at my shelves: everything empty, everything given away, so to speak, for the twentieth part of what I would have to pay for the new purchase. I have to close my shop because I have no more money to buy goods!"

What this man shouted bitterly at me, you can hear a thousand times over, dear James, in all towns and in all trades.

People have sold themselves poor, all and all, have squandered their "substance" because they acted according to the sound business principles inherited from father and grandfather and calculated honestly. They ruined themselves because they remained honest in a time of money swindling.

But if one or the other of them made an attempt to save himself from impoverishment by calculating his prices not according to the cost of purchase but according to the cost of replacement, the price-checking agencies and the usury courts intervened and punished him.

For, as you know, my son, the empire and the municipality pay innumerable officials to see to it that every merchant is impoverished according to the times. For a long time they succeeded, thanks to the money fraud in which the tradesmen were almost invariably involved. Every shopkeeper rejoiced when he "cashed up" in the evening and counted his stock of coloured paper money.

Only gradually did the realisation dawn on people that they were becoming impoverished to the extent that they were turning their stock of goods into money because they could not maintain their stock of goods for sale at anywhere near its original level for the supposedly large sums they were taking in.

I believe that a survey in Germany would show that the composure of all traders today is incapable of acquiring for their total assets even the fourth part of the stock of goods that they could have acquired for it immediately after the end of the war.

Of course, no one burns alive without eventually noticing it. And so the merchants too are now realising, much too late, what the devaluation of money means for them. No price control office and no usury court can prevent them today from setting their prices as necessary if they want to do business sensibly and maintain their existence.

And parallel to this realisation, the courts are also becoming concerned about the practice they have followed up to now, also much too late. The Imperial Court, which has to abide by the letter of laws that were written for money-honouring times, dances a tightrope walk between formal law and its own better insight, without, however, making an appeal to the legislator: "Abolish your laws that have become senseless, or return to a money that gives the laws back their meaning!"

And in between, the cry of the street resounds ever louder: "Fight usury! Hang the price gougers who deliver the people to misery!"

Shop windows are smashed, the goods on display are robbed, the merchants are beaten and the whole merchant class is threatened with bloody retribution. And the state, seeing the tide of indignation rising ever more dangerously, applies means of appeasement such as have been tried and tested with children, whom one cannot convince, but who are quietened down by small concessions:

He picks out a few malefactors who have "marked up" their prices too conspicuously, closes their warehouses, confiscates their goods and sells them at prices which popular feeling considers "reasonable".

In this way, the authorities, often against their better judgement, submit to the ignorance of the gaffes. They pursue violent "realpolitik", which is admittedly much easier than informing the people about the interrelationships, and above all much less dangerous. For enlightenment would make the people aware that the real culprit in the revolution of prices is not the trader who raises his demands, but the state which forces him to raise them if he does not want to become destitute.

"So there is no usury?" You will probably interject here, my boy. Of course there is.

Usury is practised, for example, by every cartelised industry which, by binding commission decision, raises its prices to a level which is fully adjusted to the devaluation of money, although at the same time the wages, salaries and other expenses do not remotely correspond to the devaluation level.

Usury is practised by every national community which extorts services from individual defenceless groups of the population without adequately compensating them for these services, as is done, for example, with regard to urban property, which is given little worthless money for much valuable living space. Usury is practised above all by the state, which has its services - the maintenance of order, of law, of traffic, etc. - paid for many times over what these services are worth; which, with the money taken directly or indirectly from the population (through the printing press), indulges in superfluous luxury by maintaining huge armies of officials, who could be dispensed with if it did not itself, with its foolish money economy, cause disturbances in every nook and cranny of traffic life, which it believes it can eliminate with its armies.

But what the masses generally consider usury, what often seems usurious to you yourself when you walk through the streets and study the prices in the shop windows, is very seldom usury, but the justifiable self-defence of the earning classes to protect themselves against the decline of the purchasing power embodied in money.

It is often downright a struggle of despair against the sinister powers that want to throw the merchant down by force into the proletariat.

No law and no police, no popular protest and no street struggle can prevent prices from rising to the level at which the products flowing into consumption can be produced again.

If one tries by force to push prices below this, their natural level, the inevitable result is that production, which has become unremunerative, comes to a standstill, the supply of the people comes to a standstill and prices finally - as a result of the disproportion between supply and demand - rise considerably higher than before.

The state with its means of power cannot make this law ineffective, for example by taking production into its own hands. For even then it must submit to the law which raises prices to that level at which demand adjusts itself to supply; and if it increases demand by pumping new money into circulation again and again, it itself forces supply to oppose demand at an increased price level, because otherwise the correspondence between demand and the possibility of its satisfaction would be lost.

What, then, is the proper price of the cigars I have sent you?

It is that price which leaves the importer of the tobacco, the cigar manufacturer and the middleman sufficient benefit to induce them to maintain production, to supply the market evenly and to replenish the stocks.

But if you now ask me to give you a concrete figure, i.e. to tell you whether a price of 4,000 or 2,500 marks is "reasonable" in this sense, then I can only answer you if you tell me the conditions that cigar manufacture will have to reckon with during the next production period; if you tell me how expensive the tobacco will be and how high the wages, salaries and other expenses will be.

But you cannot give me these figures, for they depend on the movement of the value of money.

**And so we come to the result:
Where there is no fixed monetary value, there is necessarily also no concept of a "reasonable price".**

Fluctuating monetary value means speculation in all areas. It makes the price the plaything of the subjective discretion of the economic circles.

Since these circles are anxious to protect themselves from harm and not to become victims of bad money, the price will tend to rise above the level justified by the current degree of monetary decline.

But since the general purchasing power, which depends on the value of money, is not able to follow the price to this level, and consumption therefore declines, the competition of producers and traders who want to sell their goods will ensure that the price returns to the level which is justified according to the state of affairs.

However, this level cannot be determined exactly in the land of monetary decline.

    With love

        Your old dad.

Fifth Letter

"Housing shortage."
Highest rents laws equal destruction of capital.
Mortgage robbery.

Berlin, February 21st 1923

Do you remember, dear James, the bitterly evil time when war and blockade forced the entire German people to take on hardships such as were previously considered simply unbearable?

The memory of hardship and misery fades quickly. The adversity of those days did not weigh as heavily on us as it did on other classes of people.

Nevertheless, every time I put on my frock coat with the yellow ribbon, I have to think of the year 1917, when the skirt around me shivered like an old sack because, despite all the privileges that a full purse enjoyed, my potbelly folded and only filled two-thirds of its shell.

What happened to you and me and all of us back then is what is happening to the entire German economy today. I don't mean in terms of physical need, of course.

With the exception of the unfortunates who have been expropriated by the process of monetary devaluation and who have not found a livelihood in working life, everyone can now eat their fill to some extent.

But in cultural terms, Germany today is a man around whose limbs the old skirt, tailored to other, better conditions, is shivering pathetically.

Just look at our railways:
The lines on which a train used to run every quarter of an hour are now used barely half as often and at a considerably reduced speed.

Take a look at the streets of our cities: they are a melancholy grey, poorly lit or not lit at all in the evening. Car traffic has dwindled, trams run at long intervals, numerous lines have gone out of business.

Glance at our newspapers:
I will not speak of their intellectual content. But how they have changed physically!
Half the old volume, a quarter of the old circulation; thousands have died of general physical weakness.

Look into the houses of your acquaintances and friends, most of whom belong to the wealthy classes: Full heating and lighting of all rooms, which used to be a matter of normality, has become a luxury, the daily bath has shamefully given way to a weekly bath.
And the same picture presents itself in numerous other areas of economic and cultural development.

The present does not know what to do with the stolen remains of the past and lets them decay like the Coliseum in Rome and the Acropolis in Athens. The old skirt has become too much for us.

Lost war? Social revolution? War reparations? Nonsense! The fourth part of the privations Germany is taking on today would be enough to more than make up for all the consequences of these political misfortunes.

It is a well-known fact that after bloody wars the number of male births tends to rise sharply and compensate for the human losses.

It is exactly the same in the economic field: the vital energy of the peoples doubles after wars and revolutions and closes the wounds suffered so quickly that one stands open-mouthed before the 'blossoming', the 'rise', the 'boom' that follows these national tragedies, indeed that some economists see in war in particular the most powerful cultural stimulus.

Even the listlessness of the working masses, which manifests itself in the eight-hour day and in reduced daily output, cannot paralyse the vital energy of an intelligent people; the inventor and the technician overcome that listlessness, and the worker, who insists on his right to inertia, sees himself displaced by the machine.

Decay almost never comes from without, but almost always from within. Those clearly perceptible signs of economic decline are only illustrations of the effects of monetary deterioration which I have described to you in my letters. When a country recklessly debases its money, thereby imposing on itself an immense tax in favour of foreign countries, killing the saving instinct and rewarding squandering, undermining its credit in the world and burdening itself with a crushing abundance of uneconomic labour (I shall return to this point later), it is inevitable that grass will grow between fine railway tracks and its cultural institutions will decay.

There must of necessity be a cutting contrast between the following building which the past has erected for a healthy economy and the inability of a sick present to help the building to use and maintain itself. The old skirt must inevitably become much too wide.

But how strange, dear James! While at every turn we have to state that the pre-war facilities are too great for our weakened economy, and that we are unable to make full use of the means of transport and light installations, nor of the places of culture and the warehouses and stores - which are scarcely half filled with goods - we see in one area that the poor present cannot manage with the legacy of the rich past; that what was sufficient for us in the pre-war days is no longer sufficient today. This area is housing.

I don't need to tell you the details of the evil that calls itself "housing shortage". It has been the talk of the town for years that countless thousands in Germany do not have a roof over their heads, which in the northern climate is one of the basic human needs.

You know that my two villas, which I own outside Berlin, were confiscated from me in order to provide a few poor families with a temporary home; that the owners of large flats are forced to take in the homeless with great severity, which is admittedly somewhat alleviated by bribery; and that nevertheless no hard father can oppose the happiness of two lovers in the way that the housing shortage does, which denies countless young couples their own oven and thus makes marriage impossible.

In the field of housing, then, the old skirt is not too wide for us, but on the contrary much too narrow.

How is that, my boy?

I know your answer even before you have written it down:

There has been little building in Germany for years. The natural increase in population therefore does not correspond to an increase in housing. The large return flow of "foreign Germans" to their homeland increases the demand for housing. And you will use a whole series of other common arguments to prove to me that there is nothing more self-evident than the disproportion between demand and supply of housing.

And yet here, as with so many apparent "self-evident facts", there is a gross error. The "housing shortage" is no more natural than it would be natural if our railway systems, our sources of light, our newspaper system, etc., did not meet today's demand and had to be significantly expanded. If our economy is not even capable of maintaining the last-mentioned indispensable cultural achievements to the same extent as before, it can certainly not be capable of paying interest on, amortising or even increasing the enormous capital in our urban property in the way it has done up to now.

For unlike transport, which is a mainstay of the economy and as such would have to be kept intact even at a loss, housing can, without harm to the economy as a whole, at least temporarily, be the subject of far-reaching retrenchment.

This is particularly the case in Germany, where until recently people lived in considerably more spacious and luxurious accommodation than in any other country in Europe, England excepted.

There are areas of the elementary necessities of life in which a restriction is extraordinarily difficult for man.

For example, the area of food and necessary clothing. It is also very difficult for cultural people to give up some habits they have grown fond of, such as the contact with the environment provided by the newspaper.

But spacious living space is not one of these necessities of the first order.

Man may like to live comfortably and conveniently, but when he is faced with the bitter choice of giving up a meal a day, his Sunday dress, his newspaper, or one of his two or three rooms, he will decide without hesitation in favour of the latter, i.e. in favour of a reduction in living space. And rightly so.

One can also be happy in a single room, if necessary even in a kitchen, but not with an insufficiently filled stomach, in proletarian clothes and in ignorance of what everyone else knows. Nevertheless, we see in Germany today that countless people only eat half their fill, go about without clothing befitting their status and even no longer keep the beloved newspaper, but still live in their old flat of two, three, even often five and six rooms.

Anyone who knows these people and the scale of their needs must definitely say to themselves:

Hello, something is wrong here!

And something is indeed wrong here. Whereas in all other areas of life every single one of us comes up against the insurmountable barrier of his income ("I can't afford this luxury", he tends to say), the state has removed this barrier in the area of housing.

Today, every German can afford any flat, because housing is the only thing in Germany that is given as a gift, so to speak.

Before the war, the limit to the urge to expand was that a flat, consisting of a room and kitchen, cost one-fifth of the average worker's wage.

Since the worker could not sacrifice a second fifth of his wage for living space if he wanted to feed his family poorly, he had to do without a second room.

All the other professions were in the same situation, except that here it was not a choice between one or two rooms, but between three or five, between four or seven.

The limited income forced all professions to make do with limited living space.

But today?

While the fat alone, which a family of five needs, absorbs about a fifth of the average income of a worker and a daily newspaper devours at least a twentieth of this income, the above-mentioned room and kitchen costs about one two-hundredth of the same, until recently even only one five-hundredth.

In other words, people in Germany live for a few percent of the rent they used to have to pay, which is necessary if the capital in the houses is to earn interest and be amortised properly and if the housing stock itself is to be saved from decay.

This is the cause of the so-called "housing shortage". The German population, which is forced to do without in all areas because its real income has fallen sharply, and which cannot even maintain its most important cultural assets in their old state of usability, is being called upon by the state in all forms to make itself as broad as possible with regard to housing.

While it would be right, in view of the general political and economic conditions, to force the population to move together into a smaller living space by means of high rents and thus create space for the "foreign Germans" and the growing offspring, while it would also be right to promote house building by guaranteeing them an adequate pension, the opposite is being done:

By means of "maximum rents", every German is entitled to occupy a whole flight of rooms for the price of half a pound of butter per month, thus preventing the necessary spatial restriction, killing building activity and in this way artificially creating a shortage of living space which in reality does not exist.

Of course, in this, as in all economic policy measures, one is guided by highly benevolent considerations:

One does not want to make the people too aware of the state of impoverishment into which they have fallen.

Just as farmers were forced for a long time to hand over bread grain below its value, so that the population felt the effects of the printing press as little as possible on its most sensitive organ, the stomach.

And in terms of realpolitik, this is perhaps not at all wrong, because the more clearly the people recognise the devastating consequences of a bad monetary policy, the more unrestrained will be the outbreak of bitterness, unwillingness to work, theft, destructiveness and rebellion, these inevitable companions of every monetary deterioration.

But morally the procedure is just as reprehensible as all other attempts at deception and acts of violence with which one tries to cover up the effects of monetary misery, because these effects cannot be eliminated from the world, but can only be passed on from one section of the people to other sections of the people.

If, in order to deceive the broad mass of the urban population as to the real extent of the inflation - i.e. of the decline of the currency - the price of bread is lowered below the natural price corresponding to the purchasing power of money, the farmer is taxed if this is done within moderate limits, and he is robbed if the price pressure is excessive.

And if, for the same reasons, the rent is reduced to one fiftieth or one hundredth of its natural level, the owner of the house is made a poor man.

But let us not dwell long on the moral side of the matter, my son, for it is easy to touch upon the ridiculous when one speaks of morals and ethics in a money-sick country in which, by its very nature, one section of the people always enriches itself at the expense of the other.
Let us rather briefly consider the economic effects.

But as I dip my pen into the inkwell, I am confronted with such an overwhelming abundance of economic perversities that I hardly know where to begin and where to end.

I will therefore confine myself to a small selection for today.

First, an economic moment with a humorous twist.

Imagine that in an industrial area with 500,000 workers, the eight-hour working day is proclaimed instead of the usual ten-hour working day.
This means that 125,000 more workers are needed to cope with the old workload.

If these are now brought in from other areas, housing must be created for them in the precinct.

This normally happens automatically:
The demand for housing increases the rents and forces the established population to move a little closer together; instead of one worker, two then live in one room, many families give up an expendable room, storerooms are converted into flats, in short, the thing regulates itself as it regulates itself in trading cities at the time of the fair or in capitals at the time of a congress.
But since German housing policy prevents rent increases, it prevents this automatic supply of housing.

The state, province or municipality must therefore build, even though - here is where the humorous moment comes in - in the areas from which the workers have been brought, just as much housing has become empty as is being newly built in the coalfields.

But since the costs of the new buildings can neither pay interest nor be amortised by the low rent, the general public has to pay for these costs.

So the whole nation is taxed for a strictly speaking superfluous building programme with all its large apparatus, only as a result of the maximum rent policy. But this economic nonsense is going on today all over Germany on the largest scale, and we all, including you and me, are involuntarily contributing to the costs of this nonsense.

We have to pay a "housing tax", out of the proceeds of which those superfluous dwellings are built - insofar as the "apparatus" created to build them leaves anything for them.

Far more serious, my dear James, is the following consideration: Under the old natural system of self-regulation of rent, the one-fifth of the urban national income which had to be raised for rents found an eminently rational use.

Insofar as it did not pay interest on savings capital (mortgages), it served in the hands of the house owners to keep the national housing stock, which is one of the largest assets of the national economy, in good condition, to protect it from decay, to prolong its life by decades and to accumulate a fund from which replacement buildings could later be financed.

In this way, Germany's real estate assets remained intact.

But what is the situation today?

Since the house owner does not even receive as much rent as the management costs require, the houses are falling into disrepair. (People are finally beginning to realise this and have recently started obliging tenants to contribute to the costs of maintenance, but this misses the point because the owner's interest in his own house has been killed off; the most powerful driving force of economic efficiency is egoism).

What now becomes of the billions which formerly served to maintain the national capital substance?
Do they perform useful services elsewhere in the economy?

No, my boy, they do not. They are, after all, fragmented in the form of a "rent discount", of which, however, no one is clearly aware, in the hands of millions of people who regard the money, which according to the laws of reason is destined to maintain and renew the substance, as a part of their income and as such spend it for purely consumptive purposes.

Money, therefore, does not convert itself into capital, but is absorbed into consumption. The tendency to eliminate the savings instinct and to increase hedonism, this characteristic of every catastrophic economy, is extraordinarily increased by the demagogic housing policy, which, incidentally, is pursued not only in Germany but also in other countries with deteriorated money. This has such a devastating effect on national prosperity that the so-called housing shortage loses all significance beside it.

By the way, to return briefly to the moral side of the matter:

The state derives the right to take away the rent due to the house owner from the consideration that the house owner, for his part, is satisfying the mortgagee, who lent him gold marks in his time, with worthless paper money, thus virtually stealing from him.

This is factually correct: with regard to mortgages, the house owner does not belong to the robbed, but to the robbing part of the population. (I have already told you that in every country that has become money-dishonest, the whole people necessarily disintegrates into robbers and robbed). But the conclusion which the state draws from this assertion - if I do not impute to it considerations of justice which it does not in reality have - this conclusion is false.

Insofar as the house-owner enriches himself at the expense of his creditor, the state is faced with the alternative of whether to protect the threatened creditor, that is, to force the house-owner to pay a surcharge corresponding to the depreciation of money, or whether to confiscate his profit or robbery.

But this is difficult to the point of impracticability, since what would be right for the mortgagee would be cheap for all other creditors, but the network of claims and debts is so immense and so complex in all shades of contractual will that the letter of a law of purpose would only create new injustice and new acts of violence here.
A state with broken money cannot be just, no matter how hard it tries.

So there remains only the second way, that of confiscation, which does not prevent or cure robbery, but at least makes it useful to the general public.

In conversations with high state officials, I have been advocating for years that the huge sums (today more than 50 billion gold marks) by which the army of German mortgage creditors has been damaged be transferred to the treasury.

By the way, the entire reparations could have been paid off from this source in one fell swoop. But it was preferred to throw the "profit" of the house owners (and much more than this profit) in the form of rent reductions to the urban population living for rent and thus scatter it to the winds.

How long this letter has become again!

If you want to conclude from this the greatness of the economic mischief that the letter castigates, I have nothing against it.

Your old dad.

Sixth Letter

The state and the symptoms.
"Usury"
The state apparatus.
Waste of strength.

Berlin, February 26th 1923.

How devastating the economic, social and moral effects of the decline of money are, my dear James, you should have halfway understood after reading my last letters.

I write "halfway" advisedly. For the whole scope of this process which is destroying peoples can only be understood by those who tirelessly study the shocks which continue in waves into the remotest corners of the economy, the administration, the jurisprudence, the social policy, even the family life and the mental constitution of each individual, and examine them for their coherence.

The expropriation of whole classes, malnutrition, the decline of morals, the transfer of national possessions into foreign hands, economic and political dependence, the conversion of working life to gambling and arbitrariness, corruption, the return to the law of the jungle, impoverishment and decay, the physical decline of the race - in these and in many, many other processes a national destiny of such staggering tragedy is expressed that he who does not carefully trace all the symptoms back to the last source of disease will necessarily say to himself:

Such a sum of misfortune cannot possibly be due to a single element; many strokes of fate must have worked together here to plunge a whole people so abruptly from the highest level of culture into the depths of anarchy.

And yet the root of all this evil lies solely in money, and anyone who smiles incredulously when he is told that an occasional mishandling of this instrument of commerce can and must produce such disastrous effects has not understood what money is.

But do you know, my son, what is even worse than all those sinister phenomena which the decline of money brings about? Worse than hunger and homelessness, theft and usury, expropriation and alienation?

Let me tell you, because you will hardly find the right answer.

Worse than all the symptoms of national decline is the struggle of the state against these symptoms.

Every economic process has certain economic consequences. These consequences cannot be eliminated by any law or administrative act. One can only change their outward manifestation. If, for example, a bad harvest causes the food stock of a country closed to foreign countries to fall by half and the price of bread, meat, etc., to rise so high that the poorer part of the population is condemned to starvation, the state can confiscate the stocks and distribute them among the population according to some formula.

In this way it prevents the destruction of large sections of the people, and thus takes a sensible action. But has it eliminated the crop failure or its consequences?

No, on the contrary, he has exacerbated the crop failure and its consequences. For the confiscation of stocks and the suppression of natural pricing do not produce a single grain of corn, but they paralyse the farmers' enthusiasm for production and the important activity of the stockholding trade, and cause the next harvest to turn out worse and to be used more irrationally than the meteorological conditions and the means of production justify.

The consequences of the bad harvest have taken on a very different feeling, but they have not become smaller, they have become larger. Nevertheless, one will agree with the state when, even at the price of an absolute aggravation of the evil, it prevents it from striking individual cripples with deadly force; just as one agrees with the doctor who injects antidotes into a poisoned body, thereby increasing the quantity of poison but weakening its acute effect.

But such violent cures have two preconditions: first, that they are really useful, and secondly, that it is not a matter of an ailment which the doctor himself causes in the first place.

Neither of these preconditions apply to the state's fight against the effects of monetary degradation.

The violent cure to which the economy is subjected remains without the slightest success, and the suffering against whose radiations the cure is directed has been produced by the state with its monetary policy and would disappear of its own accord if the state changed its policy. The cure, therefore, is bungling, and its effects consist merely in aggravating the evil which it seeks to combat.

I am not asking you, my boy, to take my word for it, but I am asking you to look a little more closely at the practical measures which the state is taking against the effects of monetary decay.

In the foreground is the fight against "usury". (I have already dealt with this phenomenon in an earlier letter). Every government pursues the fight against "usury" with particular zeal, whether out of a sense of duty or out of fear of the weapon of the ballot in the hands of a population that does not know the context.

In Germany, a whole army of price inspection agencies and usury courts has been sent into this fight, and the counter-army of the so-called "racketeers" has come under severe pressure. Many thousands of traders have been sentenced to heavy fines and imprisonment, enormous stocks of goods have been confiscated, numerous traders have had their trading licences revoked.

In all the years that the struggle has been going on, have you ever noticed even the slightest success? Have prices in even one area been prevented from rising to exactly the level that corresponded to the respective degree of monetary deterioration?

Perhaps you will interject here that a certain success can be stated insofar as the price increase in many areas has obviously taken place much more slowly than the decline in money. By preventing traders and shopkeepers from "marking up" their prices with each new fall of the mark, and instead forcing them to sell their goods at the purchase price plus profit percentages, the population was enabled to cover their needs very cheaply in many cases, say at a thousand times the pre-war price at a time when the value of the goods would have justified a price three thousand times higher.

True. But what has been achieved by this? Not the slightest thing.

First of all, in the most important area, i.e. fast food, the price reduction could not be implemented at all, because in a country dependent on imports from abroad, the world market price is decisive for all foodstuffs exposed to spoilage.

And since the prices of related goods influence each other, the world market price has also asserted itself on the market for other consumer goods. (With the exception of bread, of course, since here the state provided billions in aid, i.e. took part of the price for itself).

In other areas, however, it was possible to inflict losses on wholesalers and retailers by forcing them to sell their goods, which they had paid for with 100 marks in purchasing power, for 125 or 150 devalued marks, i.e. for a price that allowed them to procure a quantity of goods that was only half as large or even much smaller.

What did this mean?

First of all, it meant that the trading circles concerned gradually gave up most of their "substance".

In every larger city you can find out by asking the commercial associations; hundreds, in Berlin even thousands, of shops that had to be closed because the owners could not even buy a small stock with the proceeds of their old, large stock.
They have "sold themselves poor", and I fear that my cigar supplier, of whom I wrote to you in an earlier letter, will not fare any better if he does not soon realise that he is deceiving and ruining himself by giving away his cigars at the purchase price plus profit percentages.

On the other hand, however, the violent pressure of prices means that everyone receives the articles kept under pressure below their value, that is, that he can buy 3 cigars, 3 glasses of liqueur or 3 magazines, although the relation between his present income and the present production price of those things actually only allows him the enjoyment of a cigar or a glass of liqueur and the reading of a magazine.

But this means nothing else than: Everybody consumes more than corresponds to the production possibilities; the demand exceeds the supply, which is constantly decreasing as a result of the shrinking stocks of the traders who have "sold themselves poor".

According to an economic law which even the laws of blood of the state cannot overrule, a great demand for goods in the face of a small supply results in rising prices.

And if the state nevertheless tries to prevent price increases in certain areas, production and consumption flow to other areas which can more easily evade the police, or there is a general disregard for state regulations and a completely anarchic traffic which often takes the form of a barter trade -commodity for commodity.

The state price policy has then made itself ridiculous and nothing remains of the campaign against "usury", which has been undertaken with great effort - I will come back to this effort later - but the economic nonsense that a people in need is virtually forced to consume much and produce little, i.e. to do the opposite of what is right.

A small interjection: as you can see, I always speak of "usury" only in inverted commas, because what is commonly regarded as usury is nothing other than the endeavour of the business world not to "sell itself poor".

I explained this to you the other day.

After all, the quotation marks might lead you to suppose that I was denying the existence of real usury, which would of course be paradoxical.

Usury does exist, and in times of monetary decline more than ever. Only it takes quite different forms than one usually thinks, and is never to be found where the police and usury office look for it.

A small, obvious example:
At the beginning of January this year, the mark had fallen to about 1/1,700 of its former monetary value, and at the end of January to about 1/12,000.

Now, on 3rd of January, two merchants bought one and the same commodity at a price of 1,000 Marks, A against cash payment, B against "four weeks target". A sells his goods on 1 February at the price of 5,000 marks, because he has calculated that he will have to pay about 4,000 marks himself as a result of the market crash if he orders replacement goods from the manufacturer. B, on the other hand, sells his goods at the price of 2,500 marks, i.e. for exactly half.

Which of the two is now usurious?

Public opinion, the police and the courts believe that A is the usurer.

In reality, however, it is B. For A only earns the difference between 4,000 marks (the replacement price) and 5,000 marks (the selling price), i.e. 25 percent of the first amount.

B, on the other hand, who does not pay his supplier until January 1st and uses 1,000 marks of the 2,500 marks he receives at the sale for payment, keeps 1,500 marks as profit, i.e. 150 per cent. The moment of "replacement" does not apply to him, since he has not made the transaction described with his own money, but with the money of his supplier; the depreciation of money that has occurred, which justifies a price surcharge of 4,000 marks for A, because otherwise his stock of goods, his substance, would melt down, does not affect B at all, but his supplier, and a price in excess of the customary profit is therefore usury here.

You can see from this example, which I have taken at random from everyday life, what the term "usury" means in times of fluctuating monetary values, and now you also know the reason why I always write this word in inverted commas only.

I would have to fill volumes, my boy, if I wanted to explain to you exactly why what applies to state price policy also applies to all other coercive measures with which the public authorities try to make the effects of monetary decay ineffective.

I have already spoken of housing policy in my previous letter:

It amounts to creating a "housing shortage" through pressure on rents at the very time when the national loss of wealth, which forces the German people, with few exceptions, to restrict themselves, should result in an abundance of housing.

Private building activity is stopped by making it loss-making and replaced by public building activity, the results of which would make one laugh if the matter were not so exceedingly serious. Finally, the fund derived from the "natural" rent, from which the capital in the buildings should be kept intact, is scattered to the winds and wealth is dissolved into daily consumption.

Just as disastrous is the effect of the compulsory economy in the field of food, where every artificial price pressure inhibits production and increases consumption. (A well-known peasant saying: "Before I let myself be forced to give away half my butter, I'll spread it on my own bread as thick as my finger!").

In whatever area the state attempts to prevent the natural effects of monetary decay by force may extend, everywhere they lead to consequences that are economically more disastrous than the evil they are supposed to combat.

But this is far from exhausting the scope of the policy of force with which a state combats the consequences of its own pernicious monetary economy. I will not speak of the psychological and moral effects in this context; after all, appearances show where it leads when one half of the population is raped and the other half is systematically accustomed to sneaking around the foolish laws on smuggler's paths.

But I must at least say a few words about the organism that the state creates for itself in order to be able to carry out its policy of violence with sufficient vigour.
For as disastrous as this policy is, the most disastrous thing is the "apparatus" it uses.

Let us return to the policy of compulsory rents.

Whole armies of civil servants are employed here to settle the disputes that must naturally break out between each and every one of the raped landlords and each and every tenant to whom the state grants the permanently impossible right to live for one hundredth of the natural rent.

These disputes give rise to a plethora of work of which one cannot even imagine in countries with normal conditions. The same phenomenon is found in the related field of housing welfare and public settlement policy:

In order to provide only one tenth of the housing that is in order to provide only a tenth of the housing that is created elsewhere all by itself, because in the free economy every need satisfies itself, an army of offices and organisations is at work here, whose costs bear no relation to their usefulness.

And it is exactly the same in all other areas of state economic policy:

Down to the last village, an amount of labour is expended which would have an eminently people-enriching effect if it were applied to useful things, but which today drains the whole of the people of a vast sum of its best strength, because it creates no values but only disturbances.

The enormous masses of civil servants which the state employs in its enterprises (railways, post office, state workshops, etc.) beyond their actual needs also fall under the concept of "apparatus". It would seem that this is a purely socio-political question, determined by party egoism.

But from above, from an economic bird's-eye view, it is easy to see that here again we are dealing with the struggle against the effects of monetary decay: the labour market, where business insecurity combined with the impoverishment of large sections of the people results in a strong oversupply of labour power (e.g. women's work!), is relieved by the fact that part of the labour on offer is absorbed by the public enterprises. But this in turn amounts to a conversion of economically valuable labour power into barren activity.

In this way, the German economy is now idling on a large scale. The resulting reduction in national income is matched by an enormous increase in expenditure.

In order to cover this expenditure, attempts are being made to put the thumbscrews on the German people fiscally; again by creating an "apparatus" with economically worthless functions.

But all in vain:

The direct and indirect costs of the struggle against the effects of the currency collapse far exceed the tax power, which is already supposed to yield more for other purposes (e.g. reparations) than the gagged economy can produce.

So, of necessity, one resorts again to the printing press and gives the process of currency devaluation a new impetus.

A bizarre statecraft:
One recognises the pernicious effects of monetary misery and wants to fight them.

But instead of putting an end to the monetary misery itself, which requires nothing more than an honest financial policy, huge armies of civil servants are deployed to fight the thousand symptoms of this misery, which achieves nothing but accelerating the pace of monetary decay and generating new symptoms of misery, which must then be fought again - naturally with the same economically negative and value-destroying results.

Thus, Germany is today wasting its best energy on administrative measures, each of which seems reasonable, but which in their entirety represent an unprecedented donquichotry.

With love

Your old dad.

Seventh Letter

Passive trade balance?
The foreigner in Germany.
The export of capital assets.

Berlin, March 2nd 1923.

There are people, dear James, who, blind to the thousand-fold symptoms of decline, claim that the German economy is getting richer by the day.

However, the assertion that Germany's

prosperity continues to increase under the rule of currency decline, is couched in paraphrased words.

For the claim sounds too unbelievable to be made as clearly and firmly as I am doing here. It is customary to express oneself differently, in a version that has exactly the same meaning, but disguises the meaning in such a way that the listeners can think of the words as something quite different from what they actually say.

This version reads:
Germany has a passive trade balance month after month and year after year and an equally passive balance of payments.
I would like to bet that you yourself have made this assertion several times every week without being clear about its meaning.
What you meant to say is this: Germany, which produces less raw materials and food than its population needs, is forced to import far more goods than it can export.

As a result, there is always a liability balance that has to be paid, and these continued payments make Germany more and more impoverished.

But what are you saying in reality?

You say: Germany receives more than it gives. It pays for the more it receives not with gold or other stable means of payment, but with note money. (For if it were to pay with goods, exports would be correspondingly higher, and the balance of trade would not be passive).

However, Germany produces note money in arbitrary quantities without assuming an obligation to redeem it in metal.

Ergo: Germany does not need to pay for its import surplus -or at most with the little that it costs to produce the note money-, and everything that it imports more than it exports means an improvement in its income or its assets.

You did not mean to say that, did you?

But you did say it, and every single person who claims today that Germany has a passive trade balance says it.

The statistics also say it, and they try to prove this passivity month after month in figures. The more a country imports in excess of its exports, the more prosperous it becomes; there is hardly a more reliable index of a country's increase in prosperity than the degree of passivity of its balance of trade.

England, Germany and France, before the war the three largest European creditor countries, have always had passive trade balances, because their fortunes increased year after year by the interest of their capitals working all over the world. And if Germany today really imports more goods than it exports, its prosperity will increase.

Unless, of course, it obtains the entire import surplus on credit. But that is obviously not the case. The inclination to grant credit to Germany is very low in the whole world today.

So if it were true that the German trade balance is passive, this would conclusively refute our assumption that a process of impoverishment is taking place in Germany.

Even more: it would document an unprecedented economic power. For our export is not the export of a normal trading state, but of a state that is forced by enormous payment obligations to increase its export far beyond the usual level.

We have to pay and have actually paid enormous sums to foreign countries for the so-called "reparations" and for the "compensation payments", i.e. for covering pre-war debts.

For this we needed foreign currency, and we could not and cannot procure it other than through a corresponding increase in our exports.

Those who claim, nevertheless, that German imports are always considerably greater than these forcibly increased exports, are stating a net enrichment of Germany even beyond the reparation and compensation payments.

Since, unfortunately, the exact opposite is the case, the common assumption that Germany's trade is strongly passive cannot be based on truth. There must be an optical-statistical deception here. And this is indeed the case. The error stems firstly from the fact that foreign trade statistics only cover goods, but not property transactions, which signify the transfer of ownership of the most important goods, and secondly from the fact that the cross-border movement of goods, but not of persons, is recorded from the point of view of the balance of trade.

To begin with the latter miscalculation:

How high do you estimate the number of foreigners who stayed in Germany last year? Let's assume that it averaged half a million; I think this figure is much too low.

It is difficult to estimate how much these foreigners have spent on their livelihoods in Germany and what sums they have spent on purchases.

But if we assume that each foreigner spends 1,000 gold marks a month on living expenses and the same amount on purchases, this would amount to 1 billion gold marks a month or 12 billion a year. We have to add these 12 billion gold marks to our export figure.

For whether Mr. Vanderstraaten and Mr. White have the purchased foodstuffs and commodities sent to Amsterdam and New York for consumption there, or whether they consume them in Germany, is factually quite irrelevant.

According to this, our exports in 1922 would not have amounted to 4 billion gold marks, as stated by the Statistical Office of the Reich, but to 16 billion, and our balance of trade would not close with an additional import of 2.2 billion, but with an additional export of almost 10 billion gold marks - merely because of this one error correction.

In reality, we have exported quite different amounts of value. We have delivered to foreign countries countless houses, even entire streets, which were transferred from German to foreign ownership on the basis of notarial deeds of sale, and which constitute an export, although the new owners have left the purchased objects, which are difficult to transport, in their old location.

We have exported numerous German plants, factories and commercial warehouses, mostly not as a whole but in parts, by transferring shares, bonds and other titles of ownership or debt to foreign countries.

If we add all these values to our exports, we arrive at figures that make our blood curdle with horror. For we then realise that in a few years we have exported a high percentage of our labouring national wealth, and that our balance of trade is as "active" as even a rapidly impoverishing state has hardly ever experienced.

And above all: we have not sold the valuable German capital substance, but we have squandered it. German tenements that were worth 100,000 dollars before the war were sold for a few million paper marks, that is, for 1,000 to 2,000 dollars.

And abroad it has been repeatedly calculated that by buying shares on the Berlin stock exchange, German industrial enterprises could be bought for the scrap value of their machines and boilers.

Almost in all foreign countries there are now cannibalisation companies (officially they are called "Markverwertungs-Gesellschaften") which want to take advantage of this sell-out of Germany at bankruptcy prices. And people who reached the maturity for the quinta three or four decades ago speak of an increase in imports, of a "passive balance of trade", as if Germany had entered a period of enrichment!

I can literally hear your interjection:
"And the balance of payments?"

Talking about it in this context does not serve much purpose. For if a country overpays for everything it imports by the value-added risk premium and on the other hand gives away half or even nine-tenths of everything it exports, what is called the "balance of payments", i.e. the relationship between the credit available at a given moment and the debts immediately due, must naturally be passive.

It then requires enormous quantities of exports to multiply the ridiculously small proceeds of the individual exported items in such a way that the expensive imports and, in addition, all other debt obligations can be paid from them.

The natural passivity, however, is intensified by the fact that the proceeds of centrifugal exports are never fully used to balance the balance of payments in countries with currency problems, but are often used by the exporting circles to accumulate foreign means of payment.

In Germany, enormous sums of dollars, guilders, pounds and francs have accumulated in this way, which have been withdrawn from their purpose of balancing the balance of payments.

These sums do not relieve the balance of payments, but burden it, because their owners stockpile them just like copper or cotton, i.e. make an import article out of them, which in turn must now be paid for again.

For the purpose of payment, new quantities of goods are then squandered, but without a corresponding useful effect; for the proceeds from these goods are taken into stock as "import articles".

The passive balance of payments is the natural concomitant of every currency decline, and we will have it in Germany until the day when we have made our money honest and stable again.

The greatest aid to the squandering of German capital assets, apart from the state housing policy - which has driven down the price of a house to the price of a carpet through its maximum rents - has been the stock market. However, involuntarily.
For if it kept the price of all German shares so low for a long time that the whole of German industry operating in share form could have been bought up for one or two billion gold marks, it had its good reasons for doing so, and it would have been reckless if it had driven the prices higher.

For the value of a company is not determined by the capital one has put into it, but by the annuity it yields.

And according to calculations that have been made, the shares of the German coal mines, at their price at the end of 1922, yielded only 1.1 per mille, i.e. barely one fiftieth of the normal yield of a good industrial paper.

After that, the price would have been unjustifiably high.

But it was assumed that the real result would have been considerably higher than 1.1 per mille and would have been largely hidden by all means of accounting techniques. This assumption was undoubtedly correct insofar as all companies endeavoured to distribute few dividends and to use the main part of the profit to strengthen their substance.

But whether the profit thus accumulated really means an increase in commercial power can only be seen after a year and a day.

It is possible that the earnings will then make it possible to pay adequate interest on the real capital working in industry; but it is also possible that the decline of money and its economic consequences will never allow the annuity to reach such a level.

The stock market has drawn a cross-section between these possibilities, and prices rose sharply in the previous January.

Nevertheless, few shares are paid more than a quarter of their old gold-mark value, and any American can buy German shares for which he had to pay $300 before the war for $50 or $75.

If it turns out later that the advertising power of the companies has only sunk temporarily and will rise again to justify the old price of 300 dollars, we will have given away three quarters of the shares that have flowed abroad in masses.

But if it turns out that the shares are really worth only 50 or 75 dollars and remain worth that, then the decline of our currency has cost us three quarters of our entire industrial capital.

Impoverishment will therefore result in any case, whatever the course of development may be.

I would have liked to end this letter on a less pessimistic note. But if things turn out to be so dark, it is because of things and not because of

>your old dad.

Eight Letter

The dynamics of monetary decay.
The four acts of inflation.
The process of impoverishment.
Money decay equals wealth decay.

Berlin, March 6th 1923

Monetary decay means impoverishment, dear James, and we see the symptoms of the impoverishment process before us wherever we look.

The effects of bad money appear in a hundredfold disguise: here as pauperisation of the broad mass of the people, there as "usury", elsewhere as lack of essentials such as bread and housing, then again as waste of strength and human resources, as careless consumption of the national substance, as squandering of national wealth - always as inefficiency and decline, never as stimulant and welfare promoter.

We see the symptoms and we understand them.

We know why this or that class of people is in a bad way, why a certain price movement degenerates into "usury", why valuable parts of wealth flow abroad for a mockery of money, why the will to consume is stronger than the will to produce, and why, finally, all concepts of law and morality undergo a transformation. But we see and understand all these processes so far only if we look at them individually. The causal bond that encloses them all and stamps them as effects of one and the same cause, namely, the decay of money, is not yet clearly visible to our eye. We lack the synthesis that groups all these individual elements in such a way that they appear as necessary expressions of a single moving force. And yet we would so much like to understand our economic experience in context. We would like, in short, to know the dynamics of monetary decay.

I believe, my son, that there is no better way of recognising the original connection between money and the totality of all those economic phenomena than by looking at things historically, so to speak, and following the processes chronologically, that is, by forming a chain that reaches from the beginnings of the decay of money to its final effects. I cannot promise you that I will be able to do this completely within the framework of a letter. But I will try.

Imagine, then, the beginning of a monetary decline. It is always triggered by the fact that the state does not, as hitherto, draw the means of payment it needs for some purpose out of the economy by taxation and borrowing, but procures them by producing additional monetary tokens. The intention guiding it in this is to appropriate a purchasing power without withdrawing a corresponding purchasing power from the economy. And he can realise this intention without further ado. The new money tokens he has produced are endowed with exactly the same purchasing power as the old "legal tender" in circulation, and enable him or the economic factor for whom the money is intended to acquire any goods or services.

The second act follows: with the help of the newly created means of payment, the state has brought into its possession large quantities of goods, say railway material, and many services, say the services of a large army of civil servants.

The necessary consequence: a rise in the prices of all those articles which are either railway material or can easily be converted into such; and at the same time a rise in wages and salaries in those parts of the labour market from which the new armies of officials have been drawn.

The rise in the price of materials brings a corresponding profit to the entrepreneurs who have stocks and induces them to replenish their stocks.

They thus -third act- place orders with the iron producers which would not have been placed under normal conditions, and thereby transfer the price increase to a new area, from which, little by little, corresponding to the subcontracting of orders to the auxiliary industries and raw material suppliers, the price increase spreads further and further until -fourth act- it has seized all areas of acquisition.

But this does not restore the balance in the economy. For at the moment when the fourth act of price equalisation takes place at an increased level, the first act of a new drama already begins at the starting point of the movement, at the state, provided that the issuing of slips continues:

A new wave of price increase pours over individual areas and reaches the periphery of the economy only when it has already been replaced in the centre by a third, a fourth wave.

The price increase, also called "inflation", therefore does not affect the whole working life evenly, but one area quickly, the other slowly, one with full strength, the other to a lesser extent.

Where the new purchasing power reaches first or where it raises prices the most, enrichment occurs because those working in this segment of the economy can still buy cheaply in the other segments, but themselves achieve excess prices. Conversely, where the new purchasing power reaches last or only to a lesser extent, impoverishment occurs because those working here are still paid low wages at a time when everything around them has become more expensive. This is the "restructuring" that we encounter in every money-sick country, the expropriation of certain classes of people in favour of other, privileged classes.

It is a process which takes on particularly blatant forms in countries where the economy is conducted on a large scale with other people's money, because the rights of debtors are an article which is not at all affected by the rise in prices, and whose owners (creditors) are therefore most thoroughly expropriated, while their counterparts (debtors) enrich themselves most extensively.

Up to this point we have only come to know the effect of the arbitrary creation of money as a shift in the economy, since the impoverishment of individual strata is counterbalanced by the enrichment of other strata.

We have not noticed anything of a general impoverishment. Why not?
Only because we have not yet looked sharply enough, my dearest!

We have still not grasped the material significance of the apparently purely abstract process of "money creation". So we have no choice but to start all over again and proceed strictly systematically.

First act: The state produces means of payment in order to increase its purchasing power. Does this have any effect? Apparently not.
As long as no use is made of the purchasing power that has been created by printing slips of paper, as long as the slips

of paper lie idle at some central office, not the slightest thing changes.

Second act: Purchasing power enters the market, in that the state buys goods and services with it. We have already seen that this has the effect of bringing about a price increase, which triggers certain reflex effects in the third and fourth acts.

But is that all?

Don't concrete consequences of a material nature occur in addition to the immaterial, calculative effect? Apparently so:

The state consumes goods and services that, if it had not artificially put itself in possession of a previously non-existent purchasing power, would have been consumed by the private economy. What the state has bought with the new money is missing elsewhere.

And now we also realise the significance of the price increase, of which we have hitherto only known the effect:

It is the expression of the diminution of the supply of goods and services by an unjustified consumption; it is the self-defence which the limited supply of goods puts up against the incursion of a purchasing power coming from outside.

This resistance would be successful and actually thwart the unjustified excess of consumption if it applied itself evenly along the whole line of the economy threatened with collapse.

But we have seen that this is not the case: while the area initially threatened by the state's claim to consumption entrenches itself behind the rampart of price increase - incidentally in vain, for the printing press very soon floods the rampart with a rising tide of notes - consumption in the other areas, undeterred by any price resistance, continues for the time being in undiminished quantity.

Thus, the increased consumption of the state is not offset by any restriction of private consumption. And when the wave of inflation has finally seized all economic areas and subjected consumption to a restriction, the state has long since entered a new stage of increased surplus consumption.

This alone results in a certain melting down of the national substance, since the state, which takes recourse to the printing press, never consumes "reproductively", i.e. does not replace the economy with the stocks it consumes.

But the unevenness with which the price increase affects the individual economic areas has other and more serious consequences.

We are all familiar with the so-called "flight into material assets", which consists in throwing away money, which is continually devaluing, and acquiring "substance" for it.
This process means nothing other than taking advantage of the temporal and gradual gap in which price increases penetrate the various economic areas. One looks for "left-behind" material assets, i.e. material assets that one can still buy cheaper than the devaluation of money would allow.

This search for opportunities is the bridge that inflation uses to gradually penetrate all economic areas. But before this stage of approximate price equalisation is reached within the economy as a whole, quite considerable parts of the mobile national wealth have fallen victim to completely uneconomic consumption.

But where do the individual economists get the necessary purchasing power? How do they finance their will to consume?

Here again we encounter the moment of flight from money. Just as the individual turns his purchasing power to things whose acquisition still seems possible to him at relatively favourable conditions, so he turns away from those areas where acquisition seems to him to be loss-making.

And no field seems to him more dangerous than that of rights of claim, of credit, of savings. To engage in this means to accumulate money, and money is the only article that depreciates when the prices of all other articles rise. It is therefore savings capital that provides the means for the overconsumption to which the population indulges in times of monetary degradation. The accumulation of capital and the reproduction of goods slow down while consumption increases.

But can an economy continue to produce consumer goods if its stock of goods is not renewed accordingly? It can do so just like the individual private citizen and in the same way: by "turning assets into money". And it can do this in a roundabout way via foreign countries, which buy German houses, factories, art treasures and the like and give grain, meat, cigars and other consumer goods in exchange.

Again, we find here the unevenness with which the price rise asserts itself according to degree and tempo in the individual fields, as the Ariadne's thread by which the economy - here the world economy - orients itself:

Foreign countries buy in the areas that are lagging behind in price and sell the items that have risen fastest in return.

And since, for the reasons I have just mentioned, the values serving the investment of wealth belong to the "cheap", the consumer goods to the "expensive" objects, the traffic of a money-sick country with foreign countries always amounts to an exchange of wealth for articles of use and enjoyment.

In other words, the foreign country enables the money-sick country to gradually consume its capital. And the government of the money-sick country again helps foreign countries in this by seeking to mitigate the social effects of the decline of money by measures which depress the value of capital goods and play them even more cheaply into the hands of foreign countries than would otherwise be the case.

But the process of impoverishment enters its fatal stage when the flight from national money takes the form of a mass purchase of foreign means of payment. For as soon as the foreign means of payment become the area on which the purchasing power emanating from the new money first and most wildly rushes, their price rises above that of all domestic goods and to an objectively unjustified lover's price. But since everything that the country obtains from abroad must be paid for with this overpriced means of payment, the aforementioned import is correspondingly overpaid, while the export, which in any case already comes from the areas "lagging behind" in price, is given away under value in the same proportion. In this way, many domestic goods continue to be given away for few foreign goods, and every passing over and over of capital and consumer goods across the border means a loss of national wealth.

Hence it is, dear James, that not only the dispossessed portion of the population, but also the apparently enriched portion, sees its wealth substance melt away.

Although the business-savvy manufacturers and traders are constantly taking advantage of the difference between the prices rushing ahead and those lagging behind, i.e. producing or buying cheaply and selling expensively, they must from time to time state with horror that their capital, measured in terms of goods of stable value, has diminished.

The national impoverishment, which must somehow find expression in the individuals, appears here as a loss of substance, the origin of which the individual cannot account for, but which, very briefly, can be explained as follows:

The benefit which the business world derives from the aforementioned price difference, although it appears to be great, nevertheless falls short of the damage which results from the further decline of the currency, i.e. the progressive inflation, because the reproduction costs of the sold commodity are regularly higher than the last-preceding selling price. Each individual and thus the entire economy sells too cheaply and buys or reproduces too expensively, so that an impoverishment occurs, which is further increased because it is concealed by the inflation of all prices, which tempts the apparently enriched to over-consume, i.e. to further consume their sub-tance.

Money decay means wealth decay, my son.

But to this bitter truth I can fortunately attach a word of consolation: the decline of wealth is not a final one in a labouring country; it carries within it the elements of a new increase in wealth. For by shrinking both the capital and the current yield of the economy, it forces the population to work harder.

As long as the decline in money continues, labour remains barren. In part it consists of spoken Sisyphean labour, with which one tries in vain to combat the bad effects of the decline of money; in part it is deprived by these effects of a large part of its natural yield.

But one day reason will finally return in every country and with it good money of stable value. Then all those dead costs with which the economy was dis hitherto burdened fall away, the machine runs smoothly and economically again, and the extra work to which the people were educated during the period of impoverishment leads to extra yields which gradually cause the national prosperity to rise again.

If only it were only so far in our poor Germany!

    With love

        Your old dad

Biography of Alfred Lansburgh

By Prof. Dr. Jan Greitens

1872–1907

James Alfred Neander Lansburgh was born in London on March 27, 1872 and was of Jewish origin.
Alfred's father was W. Neander Lansburgh and his mother was Jenny Lansburgh, nee Jacobsohn.
The family moved from London to Berlin between 1872 and 1875. The father traded in wine and continued to live part of the time in London. He died on November 7, 1875, which meant that Alfred was half-orphan from the age of three.

Alfred attended the French Gymnasium, a school popular among diplomats and businesspersons, where almost half of the students at that time were of Jewish origin. However, Alfred did not graduate from the school, and, as assumed by his son, the later journalistic and scientific activities of the "prevented professor" were compensation for this.

When Jenny Lansburgh died in 1886, Alfred became an orphan at the age of 14 and was taken in by relatives. In 1907, he married Frida Neuberg, who was born in Sarstedt-Hannover, on January 31, 1880. Her father ran the Max Neuberg & Co Mechanische Weberei in Hannover-Linden employing four hundred weavers.

Subsequently, on February 2, 1908, the first daughter, Gerda, was born, followed by the son, Werner Neander on June 29, 1912. Together with the baptism of their children, Alfred and Frida converted to Christianity.

Werner characterized Alfred as a "maverick" who remained a loner, outsider and lateral thinker all his life.
Alfred was an employee of Berliner Handels-Gesellschaft (BHG), which, at the time, was headed by Carl Fürstenberg.

Lansburgh worked in the issuing department around 1895. During this phase, he read many economic texts in his spare time and continued his auto didactic education.

He remained with BHG until 1903, and during that year transferred to "Ratgeber auf dem Kapitalmarkt" (advisor at the capital market) as an editor. The newspaper was founded in early 1903 by the banker Siegmund Friedberg. The journal covered all financial and stock market topics of importance to an investor. The editorial office was located in the same building as Friedberg`s bank.

This arrangement led to massive criticism regarding the independence of the newspaper. Eugen Schmalenbach, too, saw the problem since the newspaper had to be subsidized by sales of securities by the Friedberg Bank.

But: "On the whole, the ‚Ratgeber' is an excellent publication (…). Instead of ignoring it we should emphatically endorse it."

During his role as banker, Lansburgh was elected at the General Meeting of the Lederfabrik Aachen Actien-Gesellschaft on August 28, 1904, together with Friedberg, to an audit commission, as a result of voting by "Banquier Friedberg (Ratgeber auf dem Kapitalmarkt)." At the 1905 General Meeting, he gave a critical report as "auditor." Hence, the separation of editorial office and bank can be seen to be rather doubtful.

In early February 1908, Friedberg was insolvent. On Saturday, February 8, he withdrew cash from the Deutsche Bank and fled to the United States via London. The damage amounted to 2.5 million marks, mainly to private investors who had entrusted their savings to Friedberg, who was also strongly advertising beyond the "Ratgeber".

During the subsequent court proceedings it became known that "Friedberg had spent approximately 1,150,000 marks in cash on behalf of the 'Ratgeber' in the period from February 1903 to

September 1908, but had received only approximately 220,000 marks in advertisements and subscriptions, so he had sacrificed approximately 900,000 marks of "Ratgeber's funds," all at the expense of the savers and investors, who had been foolish enough to get involved with him."

On February 11, 1908, in the "Ratgeber", and a few days later in the second issue of "Die Bank", an open letter appeared from Lansburgh on the "Friedberg case."
Although Lansburgh had left the "Ratgeber" in the fall of 1907 to found his own publishing house, he was determined to defend his and his colleagues' work.
Lansburgh admitted that there were conflicts of interest: "To assume otherwise would be naive." In the "Ratgeber", "the appearance (...) had convinced me (...) that the theoretically unthinkable—separation of the business interest from the content of the paper—was possible in practice."

In the issue of April 25, 1908, it was announced that Alfred Lansburgh and his Bank-Verlag "have acquired the journal of 'Der Ratgeber auf dem Kapitalmarkt-Gesellschaft mit beschränkter Haftung' and will continue it under the same name and with the participation of some of the best of his current and former employees in as little changed a manner as possible."

However, the takeover was unsuccessful for Lansburgh in the long term. Advertising for subscribers continued to increase, and in 1912 the newspaper was restructured and reduced in size. 1914 the journal was sold to Hermann Zickert.

1908–1934

In 1907, Lansburgh had left the "Ratgeber" and used his wife's dowry to found the Bank-Verlag publishing house. This was primarily to publish the journal, "Die Bank," which appeared monthly from 1908 to 1929, and weekly from 1930. With the weekly publication the size of the journal and the number of employees increased. "Die Bank's" circulation was 2,500 copies in 1926.

On April 7, 1924, Lansburgh started a liberal-conservative Monday newspaper under the title of "Die Chronik," at great financial expense. Editors for politics, economics, culture, and sports were hired. However, we can assume that there was a high percentage of articles written by Lansburgh.

The newspaper had an extensive business section and a clearly liberal positioning. There were repeated attacks against the labor movement and national tones.

The circulation was 35,000 copies, but it was an obvious failure, and so it had to be stopped after only six issues on May 12, 1924. Perhaps it was also due to the style, which was not suitable for a newspaper since Lansburgh did not want to do without footnotes and Latin and Greek quotations.

Of special interest is an article from April 22, 1924, on the front page, in which Lansburgh wrote, for once, not about banks and money, but about anti-Semitism.

The article describes "the Jew" as a guest who paid for hospitality "with the blood of their sons" during World War I. In the article, an uncultivated luxury consumption by Jews is denounced, and thus provokes envy. "Thus the Jew himself helped raise the swastika against himself."

Any radical political position is rejected: "The völkisch movement is a radical political phenomenon just like communism. Radicalism, however, is a symptom of illness in the body of the nation, and as a result, the German people are really sick."

The reasons given are the confusion that was present from 1914 onward, especially as a result of inflation and the occupation of the Ruhr. "The attempt to realize this idea of the "völkisch" would only lead the whole German nation into a new misfortune."

His son Werner, too, reports Alfred's concern that the Jews who "make themselves mousy" (meaning the all too visible, especially prominent, rich or communist Jews) would make an ideal scapegoat for the bitterness and aggressiveness.

Alfred Lansburgh identifies himself with this description. He saw himself as an outsider who had to fight for his position in society. He also saw himself politically as a democratic liberal.

In addition to "Die Bank's" success, recognition grew at other levels as well. For example, Lansburgh became a close interlocutor with the President of the Reichsbank, Hans Luther. Lansburgh wrote only positive things about Luther at "Die Bank" and even called him "Hercules-Luther." The latter wrote a foreword for the 25th anniversary of "Die Bank", read in detail Lansburgh's statements and articles during his time as Reichsbank President, and invited him to the 1931 meeting of the Friedrich List-Gesellschaft.

For the Friedrich List-Gesellschaft conference, held in September 1931 on the possibilities and consequences of credit expansion, the "Lautenbach Plan" was an initiative, which came from Hans Luther, who was on the board of the society. Luther saw the discussion on credit expansion in the prevailing crisis as an obligation, which needed to be undertaken by a Reichsbank president, but was critical of the risks involved with this policy.

All invitations went out with only four days' notice, but there was only one cancellation. Although Lansburgh was not a member of the society, he received an invitation, and perhaps Luther wanted to have him support his skeptical position.

Lansburgh was then critical in the debate: "Why is this called a crisis? Why is this time of rest, as I want to call it, necessarily called a crisis? Why is it bad if the businessperson works four hours a day instead of eight hours or closes his store two days a week?"

The "time of rest" is only impossible because companies and households have insufficient reserves and depend on credit. "But these economies with credit, on which not only our German economy, but also foreign economies, are based, cause the time of rest to be deemed a time of crisis."

Lansburgh, therefore, cautiously argues in favor of bridging loans to maintain employment: "It is more important that those enterprises that can keep themselves afloat in times of need, perhaps healthy enterprises that would go under if this were strictly executed, should be kept afloat and be able to continue to employ their workers, than bringing them to the brink of ruin."

His approval of the Lautenbach Plan is ultimately only politically justified: "We live in a state governed by parliament, so we must consider the mass psychosis, which is now such that if one expects a reduction in wages, that the people are happy to hear some activity, some plan." For him, expansionary economic policy is only a concession to the voters, not an ideal economic solution.

Alfred Lansburgh supported the policies of Luther and Reich Chancellor Heinrich Brüning. Werner Lansburgh later speculated on his father's self-reproaches because his "orthodox economic ideas, in the spirit of the Manchester School," may have involuntarily contributed to the National Socialism's success in the crisis.

1935–1943

Ludwig Mellinger, born in 1900, joined "Die Bank" in 1930 and became its editor the year after. Due to the Schriftleitergesetz (Law on Editors) of October 4, 1933, according to which a chief editor had to be "Aryan" (§6), Lansburgh could no longer be the editor and Mellinger became managing director of the Bank-Verlag and chief editor of "Die Bank" in June 1934.

The articles of association for the foundation of the "Bank-Verlag GmbH" as a continuation of the "Bank-Verlag Alfred Lansburgh" were concluded on June 8, 1934 in the offices of the

Centralverband der Deutschen Bank- und Bankiersgewerbes in Berlin.

The purchase price was paid by a "bank consortium for the safeguarding of the journal 'Die Bank'" and the GmbH was not burdened with debts because of the price. 95% was held by Ludwig Mellinger, and 5% by Hans Koch.

Walter Hofmann wrote the following to Mellinger in 1960: "It was soon after the beginning of the era of the '1000-Year Reich' that you, in a very serious conversation (I was one of the closest collaborators of the then President of the German banking industry, Otto Christian Fischer) told me your great concern about the future of the journal you were editing, which you had to consider endangered because of the threat to the Jewish publisher and editor, Alfred Lansburgh.

Thanks to the initiative of Otto Christian Fischer, a way was found at that time which did equal justice to your human obligations to Alfred Lansburgh and the professional interests in the preservation of the journal, and which enabled the transfer of the editorial function into your hands." Fischer was the most important bank functionary in the "Third Reich" and one of the few directors of banks that had publicly supported the NSDAP before 1933.

Melllinger requested proximity to Fischer, as follows: even before 1934, he repeatedly mentioned him positively in essays, and from 1934 he regularly offered him space at "Die Bank." On the occasion of the 30th anniversary of the publishing house in December 1937, Fischer wrote the introductory congratulations and wished the journal "to be a widely respected representative for the most valuable forces in the development of the National Socialist economy."

The National Socialists watched "Die Bank" and, even after the takeover by Mellinger, criticized that Lansburgh could continue to advocate his "orthodox gold currency theory."

They passed comment that "from the intellectual narrow-mindedness of a blood-foreign writer and theorist who does not understand the world of today, he demands that the facts be subordinated to his theories."

"Die Bank", they wrote, could still be enjoyed "only with great caution. After all, it is not in the spirit of the Law on Editors that a discharged editor should continue to be active as the main writer of the same journal.

"Therefore, after the "Aryanization" of Lansburgh in 1934, only six essays and five "Briefe" were published, and in 1935, only two essays.

In accordance with the order of the Reich Press Chamber of April 5, 1936, the "Bank-Verlag GmbH" was converted into the partnership "Bank-Verlag Dr. Ludwig Mellinger" by a shareholder resolution on March 31, 1937. Under this arrangement, Mellinger bought the 5% GmbH shares from Hans Koch for 1,000 marks. The conversion and sale of the 5% share, in 1937, was carried out by the notaries Karl Bennecke and Karl Meidinger, who had run a joint law firm with Hans Koch.

From the connections mentioned, we can assume that Fischer wanted to maintain the journal and therefore organized the financing of the "Aryanization" of the publishing house by Ludwig Mellinger with the banks of the Centralverband. Lansburgh received the purchase price of 49,000 marks, and, through a straw man, held a 5% share in the publishing house until 1937.

In 1950, the widow, Frida Lansburgh, initiated a compensation procedure with the aim of obtaining "compensation for the loss in the forced sale of the Bank-Verlag Berlin (…), allegedly worth 175,000 RM, with proceeds of 25,000 RM."
She was informed that the publishing house no longer existed and that claims could only be made against Ludwig Mellinger personally.

Thereupon Frida decided that she did not want to make a claim against Ludwig Mellinger and subsequently withdrew the claim.

The company value of the publishing house, in the summer of 1934, can only be estimated. Unfortunately, there is only one balance sheet, from 31.12.1936. The turnover, in 1936, was 142,047 marks and the net profit was 15,156 marks. The profit carried forward from 1934 and 1935 was 29,680 marks, therefore the development could be considered relatively stable. Consequently a valuation of 175,000 marks is not unrealistic.

After Lansburgh had been banned from writing in 1935, he could only earn money by selling articles to foreign newspapers. Alfred considered himself too old to learn a new language in which to write, and there was not enough money for a pensioner's life abroad. Alfred Lansburgh committed suicide on September 11, 1937.

Acknowledgments

Our most heartfelt thanks go out to Prof. Dr. Jan Greitens, who has made this publication possible.

He has taken upon him the hard work of digitalising and partially transcribing the original texts, used as basis for this translation.

Furthermore he hosts a wealth of additional letters and information on the works of Lansburgh/Argentarius on his website:

https://www.lansburgh.de/

Printed in Great Britain
by Amazon